THE

FOOLISH GUIDE

TO PICKING

STOCKS

The
Motley Fool's
Rule Breakers,
Rule Makers

 **David &
Tom Gardner**

Simon & Schuster

SIMON & SCHUSTER
Rockefeller Center
1230 Avenue of the Americas
New York, NY 10020

Designed by Meryl Sussman Levavi / digitext, inc.

Manufactured in the United States of America

10   9   8   7   6   5   4   3   2

Library of Congress Cataloging-in-Publication Data is available.

ISBN 0-684-84400-1

This book is dedicated to everyone who calls him or herself a

F O O L

now or in the future,
on this planet or any other.

And in particular, we dedicate this book
to all those who have already tapped into
the Motley Fool
and helped answer someone else's question
on our message boards.

Every one of those answers strikes a blow for freedom.

Finally, we wish to acknowledge our grandparents,
who throughout our childhood taught us about
Rules,
how they are made and when they should be broken.

Contents

A Note
from the Gardners

This book closes out a trilogy of investment works that begins with *You Have More Than You Think* and then progresses to *The Motley Fool Investment Guide*. So if you're new to investing, you should put this book down and start with *You Have More Than You Think*, then read *The Motley Fool Investment Guide*. And only after that, pick up this book again!

As the closing book in our trilogy, *The Motley Fool's Rule Breakers, Rule Makers* is the most "advanced" work of the three, which isn't to say that it's harder to read or any more complicated than the others. That *is* to say, however, that its contents are intended for more experienced investors, people willing to take greater-than-average risk to own the most dynamic growth stocks, and knowledgeable enough to evaluate that risk. It is also for serious business thinkers.

Indeed, this book is as much a "business book" as it is an investing book. Increasingly, we believe that the most successful investing strategy simply involves locating winning long-term businesses.

To become involved in the search (or just watch from the sidelines), we invite *all* readers to visit our Web site at http://www.fool.com.

We both spend many of our waking hours contributing to our site, which offers scads of articles and features about individual stocks and investing in general, as well as an interactive discussion specifically about this book. The Motley Fool can help you track your portfolio, buy a mortgage, and get answers to tax questions—the latter for free, via our Foolish CPAs. You can also follow our own investment strategies: David runs the site's Rule Breaker Portfolio, while Tom runs the Rule Maker Portfolio. Both are real-money portfolios, for which we provide daily recaps and updated outlook and investment lessons. Each portfolio's returns are displayed, too, and compared to the market averages on daily, monthly, annual, and historical bases. (And yes, both are kicking the market's @$$.)

Finally, if you would like to send e-mail pertaining either to this book or to getting online with The Motley Fool, just shoot us a line to

RuleBook@fool.com

Or, you may write. Send snail mail to The Motley Fool, c/o Rule-Book, 123 North Pitt Street, Alexandria, VA 22314. (Consider visiting Fool HQ if you're passing through town!)

Foreword: O, for a Muse of Fire

In the character of King Henry V, William Shakespeare gave to world literature one of its brightest military heroes. Henry is the young king who charges across the English Channel, wins a shocking upset at Agincourt, and becomes heir to the French throne. He achieves these things by his eloquence, his guts, and his love of his men, all of which Shakespeare renders evocatively and, as always, quotably.

If you went back a couple of plays, however, you'd see another side of Henry. *Henry IV, Part I* introduces us to Prince Hal, a dissolute youth who whiled away his days hanging out with scapegraces and ne'er-do-wells at an Eastcheap tavern. Pranking with common thieves, carousing with bar wenches, cracking jokes past midnight in a seedy neighborhood . . . this was a prince most unprincelike. But from this acorn one could nevertheless envision the tall oak that would one day sprout: Prince Hal's love of fun, for instance, would come back as Henry's battlefield daring, and the low company he kept provided him with the common touch that he expertly applied as he led his men into the open ground between two woods that was Agincourt. On that day, October 25, 1415, largely by dint of French ineptitude combined with the deadliness of the English longbow, Henry's forces slew almost seven thousand Frenchmen while sustaining losses of only a few hundred of their own. Henry's leadership and victory remain among the bravest in military history.

Even though the young Prince Hal takes an unorthodox approach to his princeship, he nevertheless knows what he was about, as he states in *Henry IV, Part 1:*

> *I know you all, and will a while uphold*
> *The unyok'd humor of your idleness:*
> *Yet herein will I imitate the sun*
> *Who doth permit the base contagious clouds*
> *To smother up his beauty from the world,*

That when he please again to be himself
Being wanted, he may be more wond'red at. (I, ii)

By the end of the play, Hal is indeed pleased again to be himself; he emerges, in fact, as a hero through his defense of his father's kingdom from rebellion at the Battle of Shrewsbury and by slaying his audacious rival Hotspur. In so doing, Prince Hal reasserts himself as the true heir—in both blood and temperament—to the English throne. He is the Rule Breaker ascendant. The comic irresponsibility that was so much a part of his charm early on has been replaced by an equally charming graciousness and generosity, demonstrated by his willingness to allow his Foolish old friend Falstaff to claim the credit for vanquishing Hotspur.

By *Henry V,* Henry the Rule Breaker has become Henry the Rule Maker. He leads his men through his eloquence and his example, each by turns tender and brutal. Shortly after refusing to stop the execution of one of his old drinking buddies (Bardolph, who'd robbed a church), Henry dons a cloak to disguise himself so that he can mingle among his troops the eve of battle and discuss with them the morality of war. Similarly, after victory, he woos Catherine of Valois with words of great beauty but then also at another point in the play orders his French prisoners killed. These are the actions of a Rule Maker, and a very good one.
As the historian Rafael Holinshed (Shakespeare's source) wrote,

> This Henry was a king, of life without spot, a prince whom all men loved, and of none disdained, a captain against whom fortune never frowned, nor mischance once spurned, whose people him so severe a justicer both loved and obeyed (and so humane withal) that he left no offence unpunished, nor friendship unrewarded; a terror to rebels, and suppressor of sedition, his virtues notable, his qualities most praiseworthy.

The Bard didn't always remain true to his sources, but he did here. Shakespeare's Henry is the best metaphor we could find for the precepts set forth in the book before you, because he begins as a Rule Breaker—Prince Hal—and becomes a Rule Maker—King Henry V. And that transformation, in a different context, is what this book is about.

Alexandria, Virginia
St. Crispin's Day, October 25, 1998

Introduction

Breaking, and Then Making, Rules

Many things, having full reference
To one consent, may work contrariously;
As many arrows, loosed several ways,
Fly to one mark; as many ways meet in one town,
As many fresh streams meet in one salt sea;
As many lines close in the dial's center;
So may a thousand actions, once afoot,
End in one purpose, and be all well borne
Without defeat.

—WILLIAM SHAKESPEARE, *HENRY V* (I,ii)

This is a book about rules—how they are made and how they are broken.

In the business world, every industry has its rules, which are determined by the industry leaders. In order for a new business to come into existence and gain significance, it must consciously break those rules or be doomed to follow them, ever the pawn on someone else's chessboard. To survive and prosper, entrepreneurs therefore invent new rules or change the game altogether, and out of those efforts come competition, capitalism, innovation, and improvements in the standard of living. All great businesses begin by being Rule Breakers.

After a company has broken the rules, it enters into a middle stage, becoming what we term a "Tweener." Tweeners ultimately face one of two mutually exclusive destinies: The best achieve sufficient speed, size, efficiency, and scope to usurp the throne and make the rules in their industry. These are the Rule Makers, which, like kings, are legalized monopolies. They maintain high valuations, wield outlandish power in their industries, and exert great influence over the business world at large. These companies make *great* long-term investments and are of tremendous benefit to society in that they provide important goods and services at unparalleled combinations of high quality and low price. However, sadly, the vast majority of Tweeners do not manage to make the rules. For them, failure may come quickly, or it may come after many years of falling just short of becoming Rule Makers. When it becomes apparent that they will never be Rule Makers, the treatment they then receive from the stock market is rough, if not deadly, as they fall hard from high expectations and high valuations. We call this the "Tweener death rattle," which is akin to the treatment given by kings to failed usurpers. In most cases, fallen Tweeners never rise in any significant, sustained way again.

The aspiration of thousands of corporations to the throne is what fuels capitalism and, by extension, the general improvement in the standard of living. Without those aspirations, our world would be a far poorer place. Today, for example, many people living below the poverty line own a telephone and a television set, powerful devices completely unavailable—not to mention unknown—to even the richest potentates of the premodern world. These technologies exist because somebody had a dream that turned into a design that itself in turn became a reality—because somebody broke the rules. And these products then became affordable, were improved, and were distributed across the planet because of the companies that made the rules. Again, these are the fruits of capitalism and competition.

Investors can reap raging returns by investing in Rule Breakers, young companies that hold out the possibility of copious moneymaking as they drop down onto the chessboard and suddenly, outrageously, put the king in check. In so doing, these upstarts also place themselves in danger of being quickly eliminated, which means that investors in Rule Breakers take on extreme risk—but extreme risk can bring extreme reward. Investing in Rule Breakers—in great companies at their infancy—is the subject of the first half of this book, written by David Gardner.

Investors can also reap royal returns by investing in Rule Makers, playing the kings for profit as regularly and lucratively as medieval kings used to tax their own people. Investing in Rule Makers involves substantially lower risk, and lays the foundation for a lifetime of investing. Rule Makers make money at market-beating rates for years and years, like a tollbooth or the tax man. Investing in them—which should always be undertaken before and then in addition to investing in Rule Breakers—is discussed by Tom Gardner in the second half of this book.

Both Rule Breakers and Rule Makers can pay off handsomely by themselves, but the best investments of all involve buying a Rule Breaker and holding it all the way through to its becoming a Rule Maker and beyond. It only takes one of these in a lifetime to make an investor rich.

A lesson to all investors: Business is as simple as changing the rules at the beginning and then making the rules at the end. This is a book about rules. On the face of it, it may look like an investing book, but it's also a business book, too. And maybe something more.

Rule Breakers: David Gardner

The Rule Breakers section of this book started out as an attempt to answer one of the more frequently asked questions on www.fool.com: "Why did you guys buy America Online and Amazon.com? They don't seem to fit *any* of your parameters!"

First we should explain that when our interrogators said "buy," they were referring to transactions in our Fool Portfolio (now renamed the Rule Breaker Portfolio), the real-money online account whose holdings and results we publish every day for all the world to see at http://www.fool.com/rulebreaker. (The Rule Breaker Portfolio is up 645 percent since its inception in August 1994, versus gains by the benchmark S&P 500 of 160 percent during the same period.) It was to this portfolio that we would occasionally add a new growth stock that did not fit our traditional parameters, which we laid out in *The Motley Fool Investment Guide*. There, we almost went so far as to make them our set of rules for finding good growth stocks. Among other things to look for, the list included strong sales and earnings growth, meaningful insider holdings, and a cap on daily trading volume. When our latest addition to the Fool Portfolio seemed to break some of the guidelines we'd outlined, many people who had learned to evaluate stocks using our parameters tended to get bemused or frustrated. *Rule Breakers, Rule Makers* is, in part, meant to address their concerns and explain these very situations. (And I'm writing the section because this is the form of investing I most love.)

The results of this effort constitute the first half of this book. All Rule Breakers, I found, share six attributes, and I have dedicated a chapter to each. These characteristics can be tested for, applied like litmus paper to a given growth company, and only those companies that display all six may be considered Rule Breakers.

While not every Rule Breaker will beat the market, most (in my experience) do, and they often do so magnificently. Look at the early stock performance of these classic Rule Breakers (all of which we'll be learning more about) and you'll see what I mean: America Online, Amazon.com, Amgen, Apple Computer, Cisco Systems, Iomega, McAfee, Microsoft, Nucor, Starbucks, Wal-Mart, Whole Foods Market, and Yahoo! Ten-baggers all (these are stocks that have risen in value at least ten times), and some of them—the ones that have gone on to become Rule Makers—have made more than several hundred times one's initial investment.

To close, it's not surprising that the stocks we bought *despite* their breaking our previously published dicta have wound up being our best ones. That's really the way it *should* be. If you're going to break your own rules, you had better be justified in doing so! We thought then, and know now, that we were. But it's been very valuable to reexamine these various companies and identify the key attributes that they all share, attributes that have contributed directly to their success on the public markets and the riches that they have created for their shareholders. I hope that in conceiving of this model, I have helped readers think in original and rewarding ways, and contributed something new to investment literature.

In that order.

So let's spend a few hours together learning exactly why this has happened, and how in the future we can profit off of the narrow, though neverending stream of true Rule Breakers.

Rule Makers: Tom Gardner

The Rule Makers section of this book began with another question frequently asked on our Web site: "What am I to do if I don't want to risk my savings on upstart companies? Even if I did want to, I haven't the time to research and track them. I don't want to buy mediocre mutual funds, but I don't have a lot of time each month to follow my investments."

That call for an investment approach focusing on stabler yet still-flourishing businesses provided the impetus for the online Cash-King Portfolio (now the Rule Maker Portfolio) created to profit from corporations that systematically lay down the laws in their markets. These are the heavyweights with broad smiles, wooden forearms, and their competitors' lunch money; they're the companies that you know darn well will be around in ten years, probably inking masterpiece earnings reports while boxing the ears of any who would impede their growth.

As natural monopolies today, they will never deliver the awesome returns of the greatest Rule Breakers. Accelerated growth is for the first half of their life cycles and the first half of this book. In visual terms, the Makers more resemble a turn-of-the-century freight train grinding west across the Mississippi than they do the multistage, liquid-propellant rocket of a Breaker. They are portraits of patience and steady dominance, kings in untarnished crowns. And while they're unlikely to triple in size next year, they can still be expected to provide market-beating investment returns year after year—sometimes even for a lifetime. In fact, at the core of the Rule Maker thesis is the belief that an investor can build a portfolio around these stalwarts and hold it for a decade—without once waking his or her spouse in the small of the night. The Rule Maker model is designed to be convenient and superior.

It's also designed to be accessible. Investing in Rule Makers provides every single American—regardless of age, race, gender, or income—with an entry into the public markets. Through online discount brokers, an investor with anywhere from $1000 to $100 million can build a portfolio of ten Rule Makers, to be held for ten years, for about $50—a fee substantially below the ten-year fees you'd pay for mutual funds.

And quite unlike (as well as far more lucrative than) owning a mutual fund, investing in Rule Makers gives you a direct stake in corporate America, helping you fulfill Alexis de Tocqueville's Foolish ideal of self-sufficient participation, of economic independence as a necessary condition for intellectual independence. Tocqueville, a French political scientist, traveled throughout the United States in the 1830s and from what he observed concluded that democracy was working because America could be a land of property holders—a general public of owners. As individual stakeholders, the citizens not only had the right to influence the prevailing political system, they had a reason to do so—it affected them directly. Today, stock ownership of the world's leading public companies extends those same claims and interests to you.

After *that* jabbering, you may suspect that the second half of our book is going to be a preachy and stuffy evaluation of overlarge businesses, more apt to sedate than inspire. Let's hope not. As evidence to the contrary, I offer this: In 1995, www.fool.com published an unsophisticated, easily understood review of ten emerging monopolies. There wasn't anything magical about my selections—nearly anyone could have made them; they included businesses such as Microsoft, Dell Computer, the Gap, Cisco Systems, and Intel. Then I suggested that these ten stocks could be purchased and profitably held for a decade—pure heresy to the movers and shakers on Wall Street. Three years later, the collection has taken on the confused appearance of some bizarre transport vehicle: half freight train, half liquid-propelled rocket. As a group, they've beaten everything in sight, generating returns of 440 percent versus S&P 500 gains of 100 percent. Regarded as past their prime by many investors, these locomotives were pushing forward, creating manufacturing efficiencies, and chugging into international markets, all the while broadly expanding profits for their owners.

How those corporations were selected, and how you can find your own collection of Rule Makers, is the subject of the second half of *Rule Breakers, Rule Makers*. Our focus will be on the real rewards deriving from long-term compounded growth, because while a $10,000 investment that doubles in two years is a thrill, the public market can provide so much more. The doubling of that double, and then the doubling of that doubled double, and then the tripling of that doubled doubled double is how stock-market wealth is accumulated over generations.

Wall Street will not inform you of this. With its market strategists, its brokers selling on commission, and its underperforming mutual funds loaded up with fees, the Street long ago stopped preaching the benefits of simply buying and holding stock in exceptional businesses. The Street's fee structure cannot tolerate patience and compounding. Accordingly, The Motley Fool stands in direct opposition to this present incarnation of Wall Street. We believe that, in time, democracy, the Internet, and an educated public will view the corner of Broad and Wall in lower Manhattan as nothing more than a quaint historical reminder of shortsighted commercial greed. The citizen's market lies ahead. Our aim here is to beat its average return.

And so, now to the business of rule breaking, where we will focus on companies that break their industries' existing rules, to their shareholders' wild happiness.

 **PART I**

Rule Breakers

Once more unto the breach, dear friends, once more.

—WILLIAM SHAKESPEARE,
HENRY V, PART 1 (III, i)

Chapter 1

Rule Breakers Introduction: Evolution

I say the earth did shake when I was born.

—WILLIAM SHAKESPEARE, *HENRY IV, PART 1* (III, i)

As Charles Darwin did before him, the celebrated Harvard paleontologist Stephen Jay Gould has made much ado—has filled whole books, actually—about one of our society's common misconceptions regarding evolutionary theory. Namely, that many of us fallaciously view evolution as a process of continual improvement, as if our species—all species, in fact—were following a constant upward progression from less complex to more complex, from less intelligent to more intelligent, from weaker to stronger.

We tend to think this way because we all tend to place our own species (not without some cause, mind you) at the height of the "evolutionary pyramid." It is *we*, after all, who have developed self-consciousness, who are capable of creating tools to build everything from fast cars to junk cereals, who have thought things through enough to touch the moon. And we're the latest thing, as species go, the most recent arrival to the party. (Humanity has only been on the planet for the last 45,000 years, meaning that our character's first appearance comes in the latest chapter, 100,000, of our planet's long-running drama.) Given all this, one can easily see how some might conclude that evolution must involve constant improvement: the most creative species of all has been the most recent development on planet Earth. Everything must have been a prelude to the Coming of Man.

Gould counters this fallacy by explaining that evolution doesn't necessarily entail something getting better and better, only that it is continuing *to adapt successfully to changing environments*. He would argue, for instance, that if global environmental conditions suddenly made it advantageous to be stupid, only the stupid among us would survive and eventually propagate—that's just natural selection, the principle at the heart of the theory of evolution, at work. Of course, that's a silly example, but it's useful in distinguishing what is "true evolution" from what isn't. Natural selection simply causes species to evolve in a way that best suits their given environment; it does *not* by definition result in species that are inherently and progressively "smarter," faster, stronger.

If you're wondering just what the heck this has to do with a business-and-investing book, wonder no more. Consider this: Natural selection, the crucial driving force of organic evolution, is the cleanest metaphor I can think of for what drives success in business—and success is of utmost interest to business managers and long-term investors alike.

In the context of this book, the things being naturally selected are not advantageous genetic traits, but, rather, the advantageous characteristics of a business model or strategic plan, as well as those of a particular workforce capable of dreaming up such plans and executing them. The agents of natural selection in business are not, of course, environmental conditions, but customers and their needs. It is customers who naturally select businesses, and thereby cause industries and economies to evolve over time. Some companies will win and some will lose, and what separates the one group from the other will be its ability to adapt to the needs of customers in changing consumer and marketplace environments. If you understand this, you're already well on the way toward understanding what a Rule Breaker is.

Before progressing, let's make this really clear:

> organic evolution = business evolution
> competing species = competing businesses
> natural environment = marketplace environment
> natural selection = customer selection

OK, with that said, know that the evolution of the business world has fixed a number of rules that have become so ingrained as part of the status quo that many of us take them for granted. Do these examples feel like rules to you? They do to me:

- **Typewriters will never come back to displace computers.**

- **By virtue of their sheer global dominance, Coca-Cola and PepsiCo cannot be dislodged as the number-one and number-two market leaders in soft drinks.**

- **What worked yesterday in fashion will be flouted today but could emerge tomorrow as the Next Big Thing.**

- **Home-cooked meals are yielding to eating out, takeout, and delivery.**

- **With its superior technology and near monopoly, Intel cannot be dislodged as the market leader in microprocessors.**

These truisms and many others form the "rules" of our time; they define the way our world works, the way things *are*—the way that business has evolved. Most businesses did not have a part in creating this status quo, but they probably still benefit from it, as in some cases they work to supply the beneficiaries (the Rule Makers), or, in most cases, at least buy from them.

But the only constant, as we've heard again and again, is change. And thus the changing needs of customers change the business environment and create opportunity. Indeed, it is when established industries fail to evolve that opportunities arise for the Rule Breakers.

So let's make like Scrooge and spend some time gazing back at the rules of Business World Past. Do these sound familiar?

- **Ma Bell telephony provides consumers with the cheapest, most efficient way to exchange information when not face-to-face.**

- **World markets are best understood by matching them with their political alignments; economies are NATO-aligned, Soviet-aligned, or other.**

🐯 **Superstores are the natural, most profitable, and emphatic endpoint to retail, the final stop in a progression that ran from mom-and-pop to boutique and on through mall.**

🐯 **The bubonic plague is incurable.**

At one or another point in history, each of these was a rule every bit as unwavering as our previous set of examples. Yet now, they are all in tatters. This list could go on and on, too: the horse-and-buggy—hello, Ford . . . the candle—hello, Edison . . . the iceman came, then—hello, refrigerators!—the iceman went!

How does this happen? Remember the fallacy that Stephen Jay Gould points out in our ideas about evolution: most of these companies or industries are guilty of it. Once-successful companies that ultimately became unsuccessful believed in and focused on constantly improving, rather than adapting. Their research and development money went to upgrade their existing products and their marketing money was spent on promoting these products; they were always looking to cut costs, and their competitive research was confined to the study of industry players who were playing the same game by the same set of rules. Companies like this are doing all the right things, but it may be the beginning of the end.

For in such circumstances, the original business solution that brought a company into being in the first place may suddenly be lost. But whether due to myopia, arrogance, fear, or sheer inertia—or a combination of these—the company's in too deep and can't turn back. Time for some competitor, some naughty entrepreneur, to come in and kick down the doors, and the one thing you can say for sure about capitalism is that this is exactly what will happen: someone's going to start breaking all the rules.

As an investor, you want your money riding on that entrepreneur. As a businessman, you should aspire to *be* that entrepreneur. (And as citizens and customers, we will all benefit hugely due to that entrepreneur.)

This part of the book attempts to define, locate, and illustrate what sets these Rule Breakers apart. Each of the following half-dozen chapters will introduce and examine one of the Rule Breaker's attributes, *all six of which* must be present in any true Rule Breaker.

Why Rule Breakers? Why bother reading on? Two reasons:

First, Rule Breakers provide investors with the most dynamically high returns achievable on the public markets—period. Inspiration enough? OK, if not, consider this (we're thinkin' T-shirt here): Rule breaking investors have more fun. (It's true!)

Second, Rule Breakers provide inspiration and guidance to all business people, be they managers, planners, or executors. Rule-breaking is capitalism's special sauce, its tastiest and most necessary condiment. So, let's spend some time together eating like gourmands and studying like chefs.

Then, *be* the sauce.

Chapter 2

First to a New World

Our hands are full of business, let's away,
Advantage feeds him fat while men delay.

—WILLIAM SHAKESPEARE,
HENRY IV, PART 1 (III,ii)

Even though he was known more as a master navigator and mariner than as an entrepreneur, if you study the life of Christopher Columbus, you'll recognize a fellow who had as much affinity for business as he had for sea charts and caravels. Indeed, the Admiral of the Ocean Sea possessed the entrepreneur's sine qua non: persistence. After his adopted Portugal rejected his proposed expedition in search of the fabled western passage, Columbus packed up his duds in 1485 and scooted over to Portugal's Iberian rival: Spain. Spain too turned him down, once and then a second time. And maybe many more times— we're not sure. But it wasn't until *at least* a third pitch session, in April 1492, that Columbus received his thumbs-up from Queen Isabel.

If you picture Columbus as one of history's better-known entrepreneurs, you must cast the Spanish crown in the role of successful venture capitalist. The united kingdoms of Aragon and Castile risked 2,500 ducats on a business plan with a killer objective: to find a direct sea route westward to India and the rich continent of Cathay (modern-day China). Today, we tend to picture King Ferdinand and Queen Isabel as powerful monarchs condescendingly loosing the purse strings to give

Columbus a tiny fraction of their vast fortune, but the situation couldn't have been more different. Spain, in fact, was virtually broke, bankrupted by years of military campaigns against Moorish domination. So while the Moors were gone—vanquished for good in the siege of Granada in 1492—Ferdinand and Isabel needed Columbus to succeed because they needed the money!

With that in mind, picture the two of them surrounded by their bankers and advisors late one night as they sweat out the decision. They'd been presented a classic Rule Breaker, a man who, in the words of historian Lisa Jardine, proposed to undertake "a daring and improbable attempt to forge an entirely new set of trading routes westwards and thereby . . . sustain the same vigorous trade *without recourse to the existing network* of Christian, Jewish and Islamic agents, merchants and middlemen." (Italics added.)

But their present debt wasn't the only thing troubling the Spanish sovereigns. Spain was, quite literally, falling behind other European nations, and if it continued to do so, it would never replenish its treasury. Portugal, following the vision of Prince Henry the Navigator, had for more than sixty years been systematically exploring and charting the west coast of Africa, planting its stone pillars *(padrões)* on African soil to mark each voyage farther south. Then, in 1488, Bartholomeu Dias rounded Africa's southernmost extremity and named it the Cape of Good Hope. "Hope," though, was no longer necessary; Dias's journey made it perfectly clear that India could be reached by sailing east around Africa, which Vasco da Gama eventually did in 1497. Ferdinand and Isabel saw John II, their Portuguese counterpart, getting ready to reap the riches of the Orient—while they were doing nothing.

Being outshone by its powerful neighbor and nearly out of currency, Spain was in the unenviable position of needing to gamble but not having much to gamble with. Enter Columbus and his vision: "I should not go by land to the eastward, by which way it was the custom to go, but by way of the west, by which down to this day we do not know certainly that anyone has passed." He had made his work familiar to the king and queen over the previous five years, executing commercial projects in their service while he pitched them on the side. To bolster his case, he invoked ancient geographers and astronomers like the Greek masters Ptolemy and Marinus of Tyre, whose work had convinced him that Japan lay about where the Virgin Islands are. (That's what comes of ancient geography—best to stick with ancient *philosophy.*) Columbus, for his part, convinced the Spanish throne. In April 1492, Ferdinand and Isabel chose to back him, hoping to circumvent the elaborate networks of agents and import-export middlemen who dominated the overland and sea routes east, slowing trade and sapping profits.

In October of that year, Columbus made his famous landfall in the West Indies and cruised along the coast of Cuba before heading home. Then, over the next half century, the Spaniards established a huge empire in America and made their first settlements in East Asia. By 1550, Spain had become the undisputed foremost power of the world. Before the sixteenth century ended, Spain would own Portugal.

We may not find many better examples of true rule breaking than Columbus's first voyage to the New World. What were the previous rules? How had things "always been done"? You already know: Europe followed the trail of Marco Polo, conducting its trade overland, to the east. *Nobody* had *ever* done things differently (you can just hear all the naysayers going on about this)—done things differently and survived, anyway.

No better analogy comes to mind for the first attribute we find in our corporate Rule Breakers, which we shall now introduce:

Top dog and first-mover in an important, emerging industry

Let's now spend the rest of this chapter breaking up that phrase into its constituent parts.

Top Dog

"Top dog" should be one of the simpler concepts to understand in this already-simple book. It simply denotes "market leader," "largest player," or what have you. To determine top dog, we typically evaluate public companies based on their market capitalizations and private companies on their revenues.

The reason for gravitating to top dogs is simple: Top dogs, as a result of their positioning, possess natural advantages over all other competitors. Top-dog advantages include any or all of the following: pricing power (due to market share), rapid deployment of new products (using established distribution networks), "automatic marketing hype" (gained from constant mentions in the press—and even by competitors), safety margin (a benefit of sheer size—top dogs can get away with making some horrible errors that would cripple a smaller canine), and numerous others.

These, however, are only the obvious ones. Perhaps more important for investors are the less-apparent, and perhaps less-tangible, assets of top dogs. Remember, top dogs don't generally reach their alpha status by luck: The brains and vision that got the company there in the first place are its real advantages, and must be recognized as the assets that they are. Was Columbus lucky? In some ways, *absolutely*—the man died still thinking that he had landed in Asia. But your authors nevertheless come down on the side of those who believe that you create your own luck, that, as Branch Rickey used to say, "Luck is the residue of design." Columbus was a good investment on his own merits.

Was Microsoft lucky? Sure. Microsoft was lucky to have such a talented and flawed competitor in Apple. Microsoft was lucky, first of all, that Apple was so talented, because Microsoft learned a great deal from Apple . . . but then Microsoft was lucky as well that Apple's business approach shunned cloning and therefore limited outside software development and, ultimately, ubiquity. We should all be so lucky to have competitors like that. But yet, while acknowledging this good fortune, we shouldn't miss the main point. Microsoft's destiny was only helped by luck, not predicated on it. Microsoft, like so many successful enterprises and people, mostly created its own luck through its own talent and effort.

So let the Foolish word on luck be writ right here: In this world, you mostly create your own. And the bigger you are, the more you can create. That's another reason to favor top dogs.

You may wonder about the point of the following list, because, after all, *of course* the top dog is going to be bigger than number two! The list shows the differences in market valuations, but neglects to display these companies' respective sales. Yet despite hugely better valuations, many of these top dogs have sales levels quite comparable to those of their second fiddles. So, to see what really sets the top dogs apart, note the distinctions between these companies' price-to-sales ratios, which compare market capitalization to revenue. These simply show us the "price tag" that the market has put on each company, the overall value of each as a multiple of their sales:

Market Caps*

Industry	Top Dog Market Cap	Number Two Market Cap
Soft Drinks	Coca-Cola: $173 billion	PepsiCo: $53 billion
PC Manufacturing	Dell Computer: $74 billion	Compaq: $49 billion
Fast Food	McDonald's: $44 billion	Tricon Global (KFC, Pizza Hut, Taco Bell): $7 billion
Leisure Footwear	Nike: $11.5 billion	Reebok: $0.9 billion
Internet Search Engines	Yahoo!: $11.4 billion	Excite: $1.7 billion
Electronic Commerce	Amazon.com: $5.8 billion	Barnes & Noble: $2.0 billion

*Market caps are as of October 1998.

These numbers bear out the claim: the stock market clearly prefers top dogs. When you think of the price-to-sales ratio as a price tag that

Price-to-Sales Ratios

Top Dog	Number Two
Coca-Cola: 9.1	PepsiCo: 2.5
Dell Computer: 4.9	Compaq: 1.7
McDonald's: 3.7	Tricon Global: 0.8
Nike: 1.3	Reebok: 0.3
Yahoo!: 72.1	Excite: 11.8
Amazon.com: 17.6	Barnes & Noble: 0.7

the market puts on a stock, you can clearly see in the table above how much more expensive (and therefore valued) the top dogs are when compared to their next-largest competitor. Typical is the situation in PCs: Dell is worth *$25 billion more* than Compaq, yet its revenues ($15.2 billion) are about *$12 billion less* than Compaq's ($27.6 billion). Similarly, Coke's sales are right about even with PepsiCo's, but not so the market valuation multiples. And so with the rest.

Now, did we handpick these industries, selecting examples that would prove our point? No. These were literally the first six industries that came to mind when composing this chapter. Make your own list of six other industries and run the numbers: while the comparisons may not be this much of a blowout in every instance, we expect that you'll discover the same thing we did. This is not happenstance, but rather the way that the world and the stock market work.

The top-dog advantage causes some stocks to be priced like Mercedes Benzes while others are priced like Kias. As we're aiming here to locate young companies that will eventually sport the Mercedes price tag, we *demand* that our Rule Breakers be the top dog in their industries.

All that said, we should explain that we selected the admittedly cliché phrase "top dog" over its many equally clichéd variants ("big cheese," "number one banana," and the like) for a good reason. Top dogs are active, fast-moving bundles of canine particles, as opposed to inert fruits and dairy products. And that metaphor of aggressiveness and activity leads very elegantly into the next component of Rule Breaker attribute number one.

First-Mover

When you break the rules, you better be the first one to do it.

It's the cookie jar rule: The first hand in the cookie jar always wins. Take the top off, shoot your fingers in, grab the cookie, and eat it quick.

OK, you got away with it this time—but we saw what you did. If you or *anyone else* tries that again, you are BUSTED.

(It's much harder to break the rules a second time.)

It works like that in business, too. Let's go back to something we talked about a short while back: "It is when established industries fail to evolve that opportunities arrive for the Rule Breakers." This eternally true and constant dynamic presents our so-called first-movers with their greatest advantage: the time necessary to put distance between themselves and their competition—the time to emerge as top dogs.

Of course, no first-mover advantage can be sustained forever. But still, the edge gained by being a first-mover is incomparable. By way of example, look back to Columbus—he provided Spain with one of the great first-mover advantages of all time. That initial "me first" momentum push into the New World gave Spain an economic edge over her rivals that lasted for decades and decades.

Whole Foods Market (Nasdaq: WFMI) was a first-mover. Founded in 1980 as a single store in Austin, Texas, it was the brainchild of three businessmen who wanted to create a horse of a different color—or, in this case, a supermarket of a different flavor. The men themselves—John Mackey (still the CEO almost twenty years later), Craig Weller, and Mark Skiles—all had owned and operated local natural-food stores, and believed that they'd hit upon a ready-for-prime-time concept: natural foods sold in a supermarket format. At the time, there were less than half a dozen natural-food supermarkets in the United States, and the sight of organic food in Kroger and Safeway and Giant was rare indeed. Whole Foods was thus sailing into uncharted territory, competing either against nobody (one way of looking at it), or against grocery stores (which as an industry did $436 billion in sales in 1997, to give you some sense of scale).

Today, Whole Foods owns and operates the nation's largest chain of natural-food supermarkets; at the close of fiscal 1997 it was doing $1 billion in sales via seventy-five stores. The company continues to enjoy the benefits of visionary management, which used its first-mover advantage to practically create its own niche industry. And in an industry whose net profit margins historically hover around 1 percent, Whole Foods's margins were last seen trending up to 3.5 percent. That's not much compared to Coca-Cola, but compared to industry peers, it's pretty cotton-pickin' good. As of late summer 1998, WFMI stock, up 330 percent since its debut at the start of 1992, had more than doubled the S&P 500 (up 160 percent) in the same period.

Whole Foods's success is impressive, but one simply cannot write about first-movers and not analyze Amazon.com (Nasdaq: AMZN), the pioneering Internet bookseller. Amazon had no meaningful competition when it did its first sales in 1995, and, amazingly, when you consider the potential of the Internet and the hype surrounding it, enjoyed a *two-year* head start on major competition. Barnes & Noble was the first to challenge Amazon.com in its online book sales, but at the close of 1997, Amazon recorded $66 million in sales for the fourth quarter, while the much much larger Barnes & Noble tallied just $6 million. And how did the largest "real-world" book store competitor, Borders, do for that same quarter? Nada. Borders didn't get its online store up until the second quarter of 1998.

Billionaire Jeff Bezos founded Amazon.com after leaving Wall Street to research what products would sell best on the Internet and latching on to the notion of selling books. "You can build an online bookstore that cannot exist any other way because there is no way to have 2.5 billion titles in a bookstore in the physical world," Bezos told *Advertising Age* in July 1997. Then, while competitors were researching ways to duplicate his electronic-commerce model (steep discounts, convenience, prompt delivery), Bezos busied himself with what most good first-movers will do—forging ahead into new territory. For Bezos and Amazon, that meant initiating an "associates program," which essentially created a global sales force. Participants in the program—and virtually anyone on the Internet can take part—build Amazon "mini-storefronts" into their Web pages and are awarded 15 percent commissions on sales of all books sold through these outlets. The associates program was invented by Bezos, and it has gone on to be copied by numerous other electronic retailers. But Amazon invented, so Amazon moved first.

Indeed, in moving first, Amazon created such business momentum that its customer list ballooned far past all competitors' lists. In October 1998, the company announced that it had served more than four million customers, 64 percent of whom were repeat purchasers. Indeed, when it came time to expand its business into CD-music sales, Amazon already had an active clientele that dwarfed those of any other Internet retailers trying to specialize in music CDs. CDNow, whose public offering had benefited from the bullishness about electronic commerce that was partly the result of Amazon's efforts, suddenly found itself competing with Amazon yet armed with but one-quarter the customer base of its counterpart.

As Amazon went on to buy out the Internet Movie Database, shareholders and other, more disinterested observers began to recognize that Amazon had parlayed its first-mover advantage gained through online bookselling into a position as the best-known electronic-commerce company just as the Internet's popularity exploded. Indeed, the company was dubbed "Amazon," not "Books.com" or something like that, to match its ambition to generate a stream of retail sales that might rival the mighty river itself. And you can do that—*if* you're a first-mover.

We could fill a book with other examples of first-mover advantages, but we'll hope that the point is now evident. We can move on to the final component of the Rule Breaker's first attribute.

Important, Emerging Industry

In the quest for true Rule Breakers, we must next consider the actual industry in which a given company operates. You already know that we are looking for companies in "important, emerging industries." But what does that mean, exactly?

Well, I'm tempted to suggest some sort of numerical parameter to make this determination brainless, but the ones I come up with are so hypothetical that they undercut the intended convenience of working with numbers in the first place! For instance, one could project the industry's sales over the next ten years, hazard a guess at a given company's hypothetical market share at that point, and then estimate the company's market cap at three times those sales (a mature industry leader's typical multiple). This formula might sound plausible, but to see its weakness, let's just make something up for Amazon.com, calling its industry Electronic Commerce for Entertainment Products (books, music, movies, and the like):

Electronic Commerce for Entertainment Products: 2009 A.D.

Industry Sales: $20 billion

Amazon market share: 30 percent

Amazon sales: $6.0 billion

Amazon market cap: $18 billion

From the late-1998 price, this projected $18 billion market cap would represent a ten-year annualized rate of return of 12 percent on Amazon's present $5.8 billion market cap.

However, this is mostly, if not completely, ridiculous. Projecting most industries' business models forward much past three years is difficult; projecting *anything* having to do with the Internet forward ten years is impossible. We can't even know whether Amazon will be that narrowly restricted in its product offerings then. If I had to guess, I'd offer a definite N-O. Plus, Amazon today sells objects—what happens when these products become electronic, become digital, so that our computers are routinely playing back movies, music, and even books that today we are buying in tangible form? I'd guess that Amazon has as good a chance of pioneering that shift in commerce as anyone, but how do I factor that in? Can't, usefully. Heck, there's always the chance that Amazon won't even be around in ten years. It could implode, explode, or whatever's in between by then. (By then, for all we know, there may *be* something in between!)

In emerging growth situations, specifically numerical parameters involve so much speculation that I don't find them very helpful. (The scenario described in this exercise *may* be helpful in some situations and is, I suspect, as scientific as "professional" money managers get with stocks like Amazon.com.) Rather than use numbers, try common sense. Let's ask ourselves this simple question: What if the industry of the company I'm looking at vanished from the face of the earth tomorrow? Would everyone notice? Would anyone?

Well, sure, somebody somewhere would notice. But would *everyone?* Let's revisit our two most recent examples. First, would everyone notice if electronic commerce disappeared? *Yes.* Even though only a small percentage of the population has actually bought anything via the Internet so far, the disappearance of this industry would be such a big story that everyone else would hear about it. What about natural-foods supermarkets? That's a less important industry, and, admittedly, many people would not notice its disappearance. Grocery stores *are* an important industry, of course, because most people buy their food from one each week, but natural-foods supermarkets are still enough of a niche business that the sudden disappearance of them overnight would not create a nationwide stir. That said, though, due to their growth and the strong trends in place behind their growth (namely, that people are willing to pay up for fresher food these days), I would still consider natural-foods supermarkets fairly important in the grander scheme—and definitely emerging.

That's the other side of this coin. The true Rule Breaker is operating in an *emerging* industry, and that's certainly true of both natural-foods supermarkets and electronic commerce. So, in evaluating industries, you must equally balance "important" and "emerging," never having one without the other (though you can allow the scales to tilt one way without excluding a given candidate). Electronic commerce is a classic balance: it is both important and emerging. Natural-foods supermarkets, on the other hand, are definitely emerging, but they're only somewhat important. With them, the scale tips, but because both items are present on the scale, we give Whole Foods Market the nod here as well.

Before proceeding to the embarrassing example I'd like to use to further prove my point about the dual significance of an industry being important and emerging, we should address what you do when you can't really figure out what industry your company is in. This, believe it or not, is often the best situation of all! When some of the Internet's first great brands popped up and went public, one would typically find them lumped together into an industry classification called something like "Internet." There, one would find America Online (a service provider), Yahoo! (a search engine), Netscape (software), and Amazon.com (books), and all manner of others. Was Amazon.com a bookseller (peers: Barnes & Noble, Borders Group) or an Internet-commerce company (peers: CDNow, Cyberian Outpost)? How confounding! When you have a hard time figuring out where to place a company, that inability frequently indicates that a company is *creating its own industry*, one of the most powerful Rule Breaker situations of all. Smile at such opportunities.

Such opportunities, though, are always gambles, and because this book is all about locating businesses and stocks that will provide handsome returns to their shareholders, it's as helpful to be aware of the pitfalls in that search as it is to focus on the objects of our quest. So, in this chapter as in others we're going to identify pretender companies that may appear to some to have been Rule Breakers or Rule Makers, but were instead Faker Breakers or Faker Makers. And that leads to a somewhat "embarrassing" look at some of my own past investments.

Each of these companies had the feel of a Rule Breaker to me at a time well before I had even thought of businesses or stocks in such terms. They were emerging growth companies in the late 1980s or early '90s and represent some of my first forays as a young investor. All were on the Nasdaq or American Stock Exchange at the time, and none were penny stocks:

Styles on Video (SOV)
New Image Industries (NIIS)
TCBY (TBY)
Media Logic (TST)
International Colin Energy (KCN)
DigiTran Systems (DGTS)
The Stephan Company (TSC)

Today, TCBY and Stephan are the only ones you can even still locate as you casually flip through the stock pages in a newspaper. All of the others are either defunct or pathetic-looking low-volume penny stocks.

Yet, interestingly enough, I more than doubled my initial investment on every one of these. (But that's not really the point; I had others I lost money on, too!)

Back then, these seven were my high-fliers, my stars. Styles on Video was selling digital-simulation photography that showed women what their new hairstyle would look like *before* they got in the stylist's chair. New Image Industries put a camera in your mouth during dental check-ups so that you'd have visual proof and agree with your dentist that you needed that dental surgery. TCBY was going to market the "new ice cream," frozen yogurt, billed as a healthier substitute. Media Logic, geez, I can't even remember what exactly they were going to do . . . something about floppy-disk duplication equipment for the overseas markets. International Colin Energy was my ace small-cap oil driller in Alberta (I remember making the frequent long-distance call to discuss operations with the CFO), while DigiTran Systems was selling software simulations to instruct and provide practice for crane operators. And for millions of average people everywhere, "The Stephan Company" would be synonymous with the phrase "hair tonic."

Big plans all, and some top dogs and first-movers there, too. But I hope you can see that in each of these instances, the company in question was not operating in an important *and* emerging industry. The only possible exception is TCBY, which was my first great stock and did succeed in creating a nationwide franchise (albeit at low—or later no—margins). These businesses were not important, and the companies that worked them are completely unmemorable.

These were Faker Breakers, dear reader. Let my early-career misadventures with short-term, high-risk investing serve as a good lesson. Even though these actually wound up being good investments for me, had I instead invested in true Rule Breakers, I would have made a lot more money. I'd probably still own a few today, a dozen years later, and I'd be staring down Uncle Sam's gullet as I considered how to deal with some potentially heavy capital-gains tax situations. Instead, I have no such decisions to make because those smaller piles of money were long ago rolled into other investments. I am poorer for having taken that approach, but not quite so poor as if I had stuck it out in those Faker Breakers!

You now have an appreciation for each component of our first attribute of the Rule Breaker: "Top dog and first-mover in an important, emerging industry." Note that the true Rule Breaker *must* conform to this principle, just as it must also to the five introduced in the chapters that follow. So far as naming names, we've already introduced two Rule Breakers in this chapter: Amazon.com and Whole Foods Market. We'll continue to look at these companies, as well as others, as we, like the master mariner of yore, sail deeper into uncharted waters.

Chapter 3

Anatomy of Melancholy

Advantage is a better soldier than rashness.

—WILLIAM SHAKESPEARE,
HENRY V (III,vi)

'Sblood, I am as melancholy as a gib cat or a lugged bear.

—WILLIAM SHAKESPEARE,
HENRY IV, PART 1 (I,ii)

Learned, loose prose of seventeenth-century England may be no better exemplified than by Robert Burton's *Anatomy of Melancholy*, which first appeared in 1621. Burton's literary style, a forerunner to our own informality, directly contrasted with the rigid formality of essayists from a generation before. Writing from Oxford, where he spent his entire adult life, Burton published his amusing, digressive, and citation-filled work pseudonymously—as Democritus Junior, in tribute to the Laughing Philosopher of ancient Greece. According to Burton, Democritus late in life "lived at last in a garden in the suburbs wholly betaking himself to his studies and a private life, 'saving that sometimes he would walk down to the haven [the town of Abdera] and laugh heartily at such variety of ridiculous objects which there he saw.' "

My beat-up old green copy of *Seventeenth-Century Prose and Poetry*, still kicking around from college, mentions in its introduction to the work "the oft-cited story of [Burton] going to the bridge at Oxford to amuse himself by listening to the bargemen swear," an activity "overtly an imitation of his Greek forebear laughing at human folly at the port of Abdera."

We can all relate to this: from time to time, we are all Democritus and Burton, inclined toward the enjoyment of others' folly. That's OK—it's mostly harmless pleasure. But it's also just a short stop away from this pleasure's wicked stepmother: enjoyment not just at others' folly, but at their *demise*. A great word for that comes from German and has been incorporated into English: "schadenfreude." It's one of those simple German compound nouns that are never simple to read or pronounce. In German, *Schaden* just means "damage," while *Freude* means "joy." Thus, "joy at others' damage."

We must watch ourselves, because the very act of anatomizing melancholy can give way to fits of hellaciously addictive schadenfreude. Nevertheless, anatomizing melancholy is what we're about to do. So guard yourself, dear reader, as we cut our path toward the second attribute of Rule Breakers via a short disgression to look at a Faker Breaker: Boston Chicken.

How Not to Run a Business: Boston Chicken

At the stock market's closing bell on November 11, 1993, market watchers were utterly shocked. Boston Chicken (Nasdaq: BOST), the "meal-replacement" take-out diner specializing in chicken, had just completed one of the great IPOs of all time. Expected to open at $20, the Chicken laid a golden egg and started over $40. It peaked over $46 that day before closing at $42, up 110 percent over the IPO price. Boston Chicken became one of the hottest stories of the year.

The company was a franchise restaurateur that would locate "area developers," lend them money with which to open bunches of stores in specific regional areas, and then take a slice of store revenues in addition to collecting interest on its loans. The successful IPO spurred the Chicken's already-aggressive expansion, as it generated significant funds to loan to franchisees old and new, growing the business and giving it a national presence. Despite its aggressive expansion, however, Boston Chicken stock had dropped to $14 just a year after the big IPO. That's not as bad as it sounds—in fact, it'd be downright misleading if I didn't point out that in September 1994 BOST underwent a two-for-one share split. Nevertheless, compared to the split-adjusted first-day close of $21, the stock had still lost 30 percent. But then 1995 saw the stock market follow up 1994's poor performance with a gain of over 20 percent, and Chickenmania got contagious. Indeed, the stock almost doubled in 1995, reaching a high of 35\frac{7}{8}$ (or 71\frac{3}{4}$ unsplit), before closing out at 32\frac{1}{8}$. That was a gain of 84 percent.

The stock reached further new heights in 1996, surging to an all-time, never-again-equaled peak of 41\frac{1}{2}$ in early December. This performance was fueled by numerous bullish announcements throughout the year, two of which were considered particularly significant. The first told of Boston Chicken becoming a major shareholder in Einstein/Noah Bagel Corp. (Nasdaq: ENBX), itself an expanding high-flier that had earned a valuation in excess of three times that of three larger competitors *combined*. Then, in August, Boston Chicken revealed plans to triple to 2,700 the number of Boston Markets (the outlets' name had by then changed) that it intended to open in the following five to seven years. Considering that the company had 900 restaurants at that point—having had only 83 stores open three years before!—these brash plans vaulted BOST even higher. And these gains were certainly helped along by the strong rumors that Boston Chicken would be expanding abroad, as well as putting its food (which now included hamburgers, meat loaf, and turkey in addition to chicken) in supermarkets.

And, of course, it never hurts to have Merrill Lynch behind you, bestowing a strong "buy" rating for both the near term and the long term.

The stock market flew this coop in 1997, though. Boston Chicken's shares fell from a January opening $36 to a December closing 6\frac{7}{16}$, down more than 80 percent.

What happened?!

Well, for starters, the CEO resigned on May 29, 1997, after management declared itself unsatisfied with the results from its aggressive lunch discounting and announced plans to restructure. The Chicken was also sitting on notes receivable totaling $850 million—these were the debt repayments due headquarters from area developers and franchisees. Then, while denying that it needed to hoard any additional cash as reserves against some of these loans going bad, the Chicken announced that it was not only restructuring but offering another 4.5 million shares for sale. On top of that, the company that week also introduced a new line of kids' meals with the requisite toy premium: a dog named Digs—leading wags to ask whether Boston Chicken could dig itself out of its mess.

Meanwhile, Boston Chicken's interest in Einstein/Noah Bagel Corp. wasn't faring too well either, having lost almost two-thirds of *its* value over the previous six months. The Motley Fool's food-industry analyst Rick Munarriz had put out a near-perfect "short" call on the stock the previous October 30, noting that its $1 billion market cap at that time was severely distended, particularly when one noted that Quality Dining had bought out the nation's *largest* bagel chain, Bruegger's, for just $120 million. Sure, Einstein/Noah was extremely profitable and growing faster than Bruegger's, but not *that* much faster . . . and how long could it continue to grow, now that Dunkin' Donuts, among others, was beginning to offer bagels?

Of course, one needs to note that Einstein/Noah also had strong backing from Montgomery Securities, which had brought the company public and published aggressive long-term earnings estimates of 50 percent annualized growth. Unfortunately, this analysis, like so much of Wall Street's analyses, may have been affected—I'm tempted to write "tainted"—by Montgomery's financing relationship with Einstein/Noah. Indeed, resident Fool wit and writer Louis Corrigan pointed out, "Public filings show that Noah himself has been selling shares, perhaps to put money into his ark before the stock gets too far underwater." Einstein/Noah, already having fallen from $36 to $13, would drop to $4 before the middle of 1998.

As of the middle of 1997, Boston Chicken itself still looked relatively healthy, at least on paper. Trailing twelve-month sales were $334 million while net income was $73 million, putting the net profit margin at an impressive 21.8 percent. The stock was capped at $1 billion, which translated into a nice price-to-sales ratio of 3.1. Yet despite these rosy numbers, the area developers had lost $157 million in 1996, causing observers to wonder whether the simple operations of a Boston Market could ever be made profitable enough that debts might be repaid. An ambitious plan of three thousand stores by the year 2000 might *sound* good, but if each individual unit were losing money and racking up debts, how much would a manager want to push this business model? Three thousand stores was two thousand more than the Chicken had in 1997, leading Fool analyst Munarriz to quip, "Why did Boston Chicken cross the road? To get leveled by a streetcar named reality."

August brought advisories from the company that third-quarter earnings might possibly *decline*, due to soft same-store sales. With that, even Merrill Lynch tempered its short-term rating from "buy" to *(ahem)* "intermediate-term accumulate," though it did leave the long-term buy rating in place. BOST at this point stood at $12. Then, on February 26, 1998, Merrill went from "long-term buy" to "long-term accumulate," for those who are still scoring at home. As 1998 wound down, the stock dropped below $1. And on October 5, Boston Chicken declared bankruptcy.

This story could go on and on, but it only gets more depressing and it's pretty darned depressing right now. So let's cut to the chase. Boston Chicken has been selected as only one particularly good example from a large number of companies that fail to meet our second attribute shared by all true Rule Breakers.

Sustainable advantage gained through business momentum, patent protection, visionary leadership, or inept competitors

Boston Chicken, in other words, was a Faker Breaker.

Let's examine the components of this second attribute one by one, through chicken-stained lenses. (Yuck.) The operative question: Did Boston Chicken have a sustainable advantage? We are defining "sustainable" here as two to three years.

So, first, did Boston Chicken have business momentum? In other words, did the company's strong growth create its own sustainable momentum such that BOST could beat back competition through sheer force of growth? No. Now that we're students of its business model, we know that the more momentum Boston Chicken had behind it, the quicker it would reach the edge of the precipice. Why *did* the Chicken cross the road? Because it was stapled to its area developers. And they had to dot the landscape with as many Boston Markets as possible, to feed those one-time payments from headquarters into "earnings per share" as fast as possible, to satisfy Merrill Lynch. The more momentum behind this effort, the harder for any one Boston Market to gain a foothold in a neighborhood and make money. Business momentum doesn't count as real momentum when the business model is so flawed that one cannot foresee a company making money through achievement of ubiquity. Another way of saying this is that income statements whose revenues are dominated by one-time purchases do not indicate sustainable advantage.

Next, did Boston Chicken have patent protection or any such equivalent? We use "patent protection" here as a figure of speech for some sort of mandated or near-mandated defense against competition. And the answer is, again, no. The closest thing might have been its brand name, but then the company changed that, too!

Third, did Boston Chicken enjoy a sustainable advantage through the vision of its founders? Quite the opposite. The man behind the Boston Chicken concept, George Naddaf, sold the company before it went public. The new owners were a syndicate (not a great sign) headed by two former Blockbuster Entertainment executives who had very little knowledge of the restaurant business (an even worse sign). As Jerry Ackerman wrote in the *Boston Globe*, "The new owners changed the concept that [Naddaf] had nurtured for the company—the concept that had attracted them to Boston Chicken in the first place. Renaming the stores Boston Market, abandoning a simple menu built around chicken, spending extra money for dining space in what was meant to be a takeout business—it all broke the mold." And Naddaf himself is quoted as saying, "What did they know? They weren't food guys. They were video guys. They got bad advice from the managers they brought in." Needless to say, none of this smacks of visionaries creating sustainable advantage.

Fourth and final, did Boston Chicken have inept competitors? No sirree. Boston Chicken wound up *playing* chicken with companies whose managers were smarter and more experienced hands at this game. Competitors like Kentucky Fried Chicken not only have an intimate familiarity with the business, but they have also already blanketed the world with far more stores and enjoy incredible name-brand recognition. And lookee there—KFC began heavily promoting its own "rotisserie chicken" not long after Boston Chicken popularized the idea.

Competitors who are able to duplicate your primary concept and instantly spread it to more customers are not inept. Just ask CDNow (Nasdaq: CDNW), which once aspired to be the premiere retailer of music CDs on the Internet. That all seemed OK to the market, which bid CDNow's shares up from an IPO of $22 to $37. But the shares promptly fell back when Amazon.com announced that it would begin to sell CDs—through its far more trafficked site to its far larger lists of customers. Within a month and a half of its high, CDNW was in the teens. (And in its first full quarter of CD sales, Amazon.com did indeed establish itself as the sales leader. By the time of this announcement, CDNow had dropped to $8.)

We now close the book on Boston Chicken and move on to Wal-Mart, Amgen, and Microsoft, a trio of true Rule Breakers who have clearly exhibited this second attribute of Rule Breaking.

Business Momentum: Wal-Mart

Dominant and monolithic, Wal-Mart isn't a company that one would immediately call a Rule Breaker. But long ago, at the company's birth in 1962, Sam Walton founded Wal-Mart as a classic Rule Breaker. The idea was simple yet novel: *huge* stores stocked with a *huge* variety of products sold at *huge* discounts. Consider the history of American retail and you find many different precursors with their own days in the sun: the eighteenth-century specialty stores (the chandler, the weaver, the apothecary, and such) transitioning into neighborhood general stores (offering candles, fabrics, *and* cough drops), from which evolved boutique specialty stores (a larger selection of one-category items with discounts and greater selection), later to become our twentieth-century department stores (biggest yet, but you had to pay up for selection). Then came Sam Walton and the *superstore*. In many ways, this development seemed to complete the cycle: biggest of all at the biggest discounts. (Electronic commerce is the next transition, by the way, if that isn't already evident.)

The additional twist? Put all this big stuff where it's most irresistible: small towns. Talk about crushing the competition: Wal-Mart swaggered in as the fifth-grade bully picking fights with the kindergartners, never listening when they began screaming "Uncle!"

Wal-Mart went public in 1970 and saw completely amazing growth as a business and an investment during the 1970s and '80s. Before hitting a stagnant run beginning in 1993, WMT stock had returned its public shareholders almost *two thousand* times their money: $10,000 invested at the IPO became worth almost $20 million. (Insert homily about buy-and-hold investing *here*.) What fueled that growth? The same thing that usually fuels stock-price growth over long periods: tremendous sales and earnings growth. Despite the increasingly Brobdingnagian size of the enterprise, Wal-Mart frequently tallied net-income gains of 25 percent or more during the 1980s.

What creates momentum in retail is conceiving of an attractive, *profitable* model that can then be duplicated for a mass market. Once Sam

Walton had envisioned his superstore, and then recognized the advantages of bringing it to small-town America, he and his managers set the business model into motion like a big, intelligent, mobile domino hunting out any other little dominos still standing. Sales were $44 million when Wal-Mart came public in 1970, they crossed $2 billion a decade later, and another ten years after that, at the outset of the nineties, Wal-Mart had $30 billion in revenues and over $1 billion in net profits.

From an investor's point of view, it wasn't hard to detect the momentum, and one could see the numerical proof when the company came public, having gone from $0 to $44 million in sales in eight years. It was further evidenced in the company's ongoing operations, and from all of this, an investor could easily visualize how Wal-Mart's strategy had lots more room for expansion.

Indeed, this whole concept of business momentum is a terribly easy one for anyone to recognize. Companies earn credit for attribute number two, sustainable advantage, by showing escalating sales numbers accompanied by a sound business model indicating that the growth is likely to continue.

We can drop business momentum and Wal-Mart right here, because the point is clear—but I'm tempted to go on just a bit more about this amazing company. Amid all of its growth, Wal-Mart has also experienced some adversity, like the shocking misfortune that befell it in early 1996: After one hundred consecutive quarters of reporting earnings greater than those of the previous year's comparable quarter, its fourth quarter ended January would show only forty cents in earnings per share, versus the previous January quarter's forty-five cents per share. For the first time in Wal-Mart's twenty-five years as a public company, a quarterly earnings comparison was down.

One must recognize that sometimes what defines our heroes best of all is the tininess or relative insignificance of their weaknesses. Think of Achilles and his heel, Superman and kryptonite. Or the end of *Schindler's List*, when Oskar Schindler chastises himself mournfully for money he has spent idly in the past, money that he couldn't now use to save a few more Jews than the 1,100 he already had saved. Such weaknesses really only underscore the true greatness of their possessors.

And each reminds me of Wal-Mart and its one poor quarter—not anywhere near a loss, mind you—just lower earnings than the same quarter a year before. Wal-Mart's chief operating officer Don Soderquist recently stated, "The wake-up call in the fourth quarter a couple of years ago was probably the best thing that could have happened to us." That's the proper attitude, of course. Successful companies tell the truth, and then reinvent themselves when the truth hurts. Wal-Mart used that quarter to spur a key change in its business model.

What key change is Wal-Mart using to create a new business momentum, as we close out the 1990s? A move toward even bigger Wal-Marts. The traditional 90,000-square-foot store is in many cases now being replaced by a 180,000-square-foot "supercenter." From a business point of view, this initiative will shortly vault Wal-Mart past Kroger as the world's biggest grocery-store chain as measured by sales volume. From a customer's point of view, a Wal-Mart superstore offers unprecedented convenience and variety. Supercenter customers can have their eyes checked, hair done, papers copied, and photos developed. They can do their banking, get food, clothing, fishing and hunting gear, housewares, garden plants or supplies—all this while having their car's oil changed and new tires installed. All under *one* roof—in *one* store.

From the standpoint of sheer volume, the move makes sense: At twice the size, the supercenters draw more than twice the revenues (packing that food in at $65 million per store annually, versus $25 million for normal Wal-Marts). And according to Nick White, the company's executive vice president for supercenters, gross margins haven't been affected. Wal-Mart stock, having languished throughout most of the 1990s, has returned to its old ways, doubling from mid-1997 to mid-'98.

Wal-Mart's status as a true Rule Breaker is forever fixed. But we're now long past that chapter in its company history—and all the amazing returns that went with it. As retail-industry observer Isadore Barmash has written, "The company's success is so great that it throws out all the previous benchmarks and measurement criteria in retailing." You want to be a good investor, you study the best stocks. And it's pleasing to see that even as this one continues to make rules in the present day, it's still pretty good at breaking them.

Patent Protection: Amgen

When Amgen (Nasdaq: AMGN) went public in June 1983, the Thousand Oaks, California–based company had just one hundred employees and no earnings in sight. It wasn't until 1989, in fact, by which time it had grown into the world's largest biotechnology concern, that it put up any earnings at all—and at that point the stock was wandering back and forth between $3 and $4 (these numbers are all adjusted for subsequent stock splits), on earnings of 2 cents per share. But then, while it had taken six years for the company's stock to do its first double, only three years would pass before AMGN shares rocketed up an additional ten times in value. And on January 2, 1992, Amgen joined the S&P 500.

With its 20 percent market share of the entire biotechnology industry, Amgen today is the world's largest and most successful biotech company, having achieved the objective laid out in its mission statement, "To be the world leader in developing and delivering important, cost-effective therapeutics based on advances in cellular and molecular biology." (More about mission statements in chapter 6.) Amgen's 1997 sales were $2.4 billion, and its market cap as of this writing was roughly seven times that. Though the company took nine years to achieve profitability, today Amgen is exceptionally profitable: net income for 1997 was $644.3 million, making for stellar net profit margins of 27 percent.

As it strives to achieve true Rule Maker status, Amgen, ironically, operates in biotechnology, the world's ultimate Rule Breaker industry. Talk about breaking rules—biotechnology is pushing beyond merely changing the lives of millions of people; it is threatening to change the whole concept of life itself through genetic engineering. Curing previously incurable diseases, slowing or stopping the aging process, and even human cloning are treated as distinctly possible. And while many moral and ethical as well as technological issues in the field have yet to be resolved, one thing is certain: Nothing might happen any time soon, but whenever it does, as an investor, I'll want a piece of the action!

Amgen's present products are few and not earth-shaking. In fact, as we look a bit more carefully at the business model, it is amazing to consider that the company owes virtually all of its $2.5 billion in 1997 sales to just two products: Epogen ($1.2 billion) and Neupogen ($1.1 billion). (A third product, Infergen, was introduced in late 1997, its sales negligible.) Given that we're going to examine the business model in a bit more detail, let's first study up for a minute on exactly what these two billion-dollar "biopharmaceuticals" do.

According to Amgen's literature, Epogen "is a recombinant version of a human protein that stimulates the production of red blood cells and is used in the treatment of anemia associated with chronic renal failure for patients on dialysis." Let's put that in English. Your blood contains five quarts of water, which slosh through your kidneys every forty-five minutes, meaning that about 160 quarts of water move through your kidneys daily. *(Glug, glug, glug.)* The kidneys "clean" the blood by filtering out waste and impurities and eventually prepare one and a half quarts of soon-to-be-expelled urine. In addition to cleansing our blood, the kidneys regulate the production of red blood cells.

Those with kidney problems ("chronic renal failure") use machines ("dialysis") to purify their blood for them. But what about the creation of red blood cells? The machines can't do this, meaning that patients wind up with low red blood–cell counts and very little energy (red blood cells spread oxygen through the body), a condition also known as anemia. The traditional treatment for anemia has been potentially dangerous, repetitive blood transfusions. Enter Epogen: Epogen is a genetically engineered substance that stimulates red blood–cell production in the bone marrow, and it can be self-administered by injection. Voilà! You now fully understand "the treatment of anemia associated with chronic renal failure for patients on dialysis." Epogen has virtually ended these patients' need for blood transfusions, and has allowed them to enjoy safer, more productive, and higher-quality lives.

Neupogen sounds far more complicated, but it's actually just as easy to understand. Here's how Amgen describes Neupogen (are you ready?): "A recombinant human granulocyte colony-stimulating factor used to prevent infection in cancer patients undergoing certain types of chemotherapy and bone marrow transplants, to mobilize progenitor cells for collection in peripheral blood progenitor cell transplants, for treatment of severe chronic neutropenia and to support treatment of patients with acute myeloid leukemia." I kid you not. *(Who writes this stuff?)*

Here's the translation: A primary (and lethal) characteristic of cancer cells is their ability to divide rapidly. Chemotherapy is designed to attack such cells, but unfortunately for cancer patients, not all cells that divide rapidly are bad cells. Good cells that can be harmed by chemotherapy, for instance, are those infection-fighting caped crusaders of the plasma, white blood cells. White blood cells, like their red counterparts, are produced in bone marrow, which can be severely mucked up by chemotherapy. To combat this, Neupogen stimulates the production of white blood cells, thereby decreasing the risk of infection in chemotherapy patients and helping to keep them out of the hospital.

So there you have it: $2 billion in revenues built on two products that stimulate production of blood cells in the bone marrow.

Of course, you're probably aware by now that this whole song and dance about Amgen is merely prelude to the introduction of that cheekiest of phrases: "patent protection." Patents are, in fact, the raison d'être of this section; I just get carried away sometimes explaining why cool companies are successful. Anyway, let's now refocus on the topic at hand—patents.

In the United States, patent protection for inventions is provided for in Article I, section 8 of the Constitution, which authorizes Congress "to promote the Progress of Science and useful Arts, by securing for limited Times to Authors and Inventors the exclusive Right to their respective Writings and Discoveries." Following from this, under Title 35 of the U.S. Code, any person who "invents or discovers any new and useful process, machine, manufacture, or composition of matter, or any new and useful improvement thereof, may obtain a patent," subject to the various conditions and requirements of the law.

Now consider that the average new drug costs $359 million and can take as long as fifteen years to develop and bring to market. This tremendous expense of money and time imposes a corresponding burden of risk on the companies that undertake it. Hence, without patent protection, few pharmaceutical companies would exist, and medical progress would have been much slower. With patent protection, an industry titan like Amgen will willingly spend hundreds of millions of dollars in research and development ($630.8 million in 1997, to be exact . . . roughly on par with the company's net income).

A U.S. patent, which gives its owner the right to exclude others from making, using, or selling a particular invention in the United States, is today valid for twenty years from the date on which the inventor files his application. Patents issued before June 8, 1995, however, ran only for seventeen years from their date of issuance. (Until that time, the United States followed the stipulations of the General Agreement on Trades and Tariffs (GATT). On June 8, 1995, GATT was superseded by World Trade Organization regulations.) Epogen, Amgen's first drug, is one such example: The first of its several patents has seventeen-year patent protection ending in 2004. (Others run out in 2012 and 2013.) All of Neupogen's patents run out in 2006.

Patent protection represents another form of sustainable advantage, because, in effect, the law strikes a bargain with the inventor: in exchange for disclosing your invention to the world, you get to keep others from using it for two decades. A good Rule Breaker in the area of pharmaceuticals or extremely high technology will almost always have established this "moat" around its company castle. The payoff for doing so is quite easy to see, and Amgen illustrates it very well. Having spent several hundreds of millions developing its products, it now rakes in *billions* annually from their sales. Investors following the company back in its early Rule Breaking days would've noted the 1987 patent and understood the sustainable advantage it promised, two years prior to the stock's blastoff.

One final note on patents: A U.S. patent protects an inventor from only those who would make, use, or sell his invention *in the United States*. To get protection elsewhere, inventors need to file patent applications in many countries. To make this process easier, approximately 140 countries reached an agreement whereby applications filed in one country are honored in others as of the date of first filing, provided that the applications in the additional countries are made within a certain limited time. Thus, these later applications take precedence over applications of other people for the same invention filed during the "international lag" period. Not all countries grant the same level of protection as does the United States, though: pharmaceutical companies in particular have had problems with Third World governments refusing to grant patent protection for important drugs, thus permitting local companies to take advantage of patent-holders' R&D efforts.

Visionaries 2, Inept Competitors 0: Microsoft

We'll keep this last section brief, because Tom is writing about Microsoft at greater length in the Rule Maker portion of the book. But as a classic Rule Breaker early on, Microsoft elegantly combined the two as-yet-undiscussed requirements for sustainable advantages: visionary leadership and inept competition.

Truth be told, the one (visionary leadership) often *creates* the other (inept competition). Relative to the seer, everyone else can sometimes appear blind.

What's a visionary? "One whose ideas or projects are impractical; a dreamer," according to my dictionary. Yes, perhaps. However, when a visionary entrepreneur actually manages to fashion supposed "impracticalities" into a tangible business—converting what were once considered dreams into reality—he unleashes a very powerful force. The question on an investor's mind is how to recognize such visionaries and the true visionary leadership they provide that leads to sustainable advantage.

Perhaps the example of Bill Gates can shed some light on the subject.

Microsoft was incorporated in our bicentennial year of 1976, just twenty-three years ago, though the company didn't come public until 1986. Thus, people as young as teenagers who are reading this book had the opportunity to get into this stock on the ground floor. Yes sirree, that's right, you could've bought Microsoft in 1986 and held it to a gain (as of this writing) of 28,940 percent, a smooth and silky 290-bagger since inception.

A major factor enabling Microsoft to once break rules and now make them has been the leadership of the oft-maligned Bill Gates. Please ignore the envy of success that plagues too much of our society. Look past that and you'll find visionary characteristics that deserve tremendous admiration.

From the very founding of his company, Bill Gates consistently exhibited the most prominent feature of the visionary leader: He often figured out where things were going in his industry before anyone else, and acted on that knowledge. This isn't always about foreseeing technology trends; Gates, in fact, was slow in adapting to the Internet, calling it hype and maintaining that opinion until the summer of 1995. Soon enough, however, Microsoft established its own Internet division. (Back to Robert Burton again, who wrote in *The Anatomy of Melancholy*, "No rule is so general, which admits not some exception.") Rather, Gates has been consistently visionary about foreseeing the winning business models and been able to always wed what was most important to his customers with his company's efforts to earn profit and market-share gains. Figuring out where things are going in your industry is only a small part of the battle; acting on that knowledge by designing the right business model to win the game is the visionary genius of Bill Gates.

In 1975, Gates believed that every work desk and every home would in the near future have a personal computer. Sounds obvious today, but back then, that was *not* the conventional wisdom. Given his belief, though, you can see why his focus was always to create standards—programming languages (PC BASIC), operating systems (Windows), and applications (Microsoft Office suite). Building his business model around creating standards meant that he'd eventually have his products deployed across a huge percentage of *all* the world's work desks and home-office dens.

The initial problem facing Gates's vision was that in the mid-1970s, computer hardware—microcomputers and mainframes—drove the computer industry. Software had to be tailored to specific hardware, and was often incompatible across different systems. In the face of this status quo, Gates and his partner, Paul Allen, broke the rules by aiming to build their business on software alone—though I am reminded by Fool reader John Hall that early on Allen argued that Microsoft should be partly a hardware company. The decision to focus on software brought with it a radical notion and a fantastic possibility: If software could be standardized, eventually the tables could be turned, so that hardware would have to be tweaked to conform to software, rather than vice versa. The profit margins would be high, the penetration of the market very deep.

Thus, Microsoft embarked on an ultimately successful quest to make PC BASIC the standard software language for personal computers. They did this by selling it to original equipment manufacturers (OEMs) of microcomputers for a single, low flat fee. This encouraged the OEMs to put PC BASIC on every machine they sent out the door. Again, in a world dominated by mainframes, this was a visionary and Foolish tactic, as it ignored the biggest business market at the time (mainframes), and it didn't feature per-unit pricing. Microsoft signed up dozens of OEMs, effectively sealing its programming language as the standard, and its sales in 1979 were just over $1 million.

As the IBM PC debuted in 1980 (it would sell into the millions of units within just a few years), Microsoft obtained the contract to develop the operating system for that landmark product. How? For starters, IBM rushed the product to market and had to outsource the operating system. The idea was originally pitched to Digital Research, which had the most advanced and popular operating system at the time, CP/M. Digital Research, however, felt that IBM's quick time to market for the PC did not provide enough room to reconfigure and deploy CP/M, so it declined. Enter Gates: Without any time to develop something from scratch, he broke the rules again by simply buying a CP/M clone called Q-DOS and updating it to "MS-DOS." Perfectionist tinkers like Digital Research simply couldn't win the war in a rapidly developing industry like PC software; Gates saw the wisdom in just getting a product out there and tweaking it as you go. Thus, virtually no version 1.0 of any Microsoft product has ever been top-notch and bug-free. Play the game by the perfectionist's rules, and you're down six runs in the second inning. Break those rules and you may just have yourself a billion-dollar business.

When Microsoft then obtained permission to license its MS-DOS software to other manufacturers of "IBM PC–compatible" computers like Compaq, it was setting itself up one day to *become* a billion-dollar company. It wouldn't be public for another few years, but Microsoft was already fixing its second standard.

Myriad similar stories exist, and we won't retell them all, but we must mention one more here. It's Gates at perhaps his most Visi-Onary. You see, in 1982, Bill Gates went to Comdex—the computer industry's annual exposition—and saw a graphical user interface—a technology that would eventually replace DOS—on display for the first time. Then and there, he heard the death knell for his number-one product. The potential DOS killer's name was—ironically, for this chapter—Visi-On, and it came from an industry power at the time, VisiCorp, maker of the early smash-hit spreadsheet VisiCalc. Visi-On came with an elegant "integrated environment" of point-and-click software applications, and Gates was worried. A visionary himself, he recognized the future when he saw it, and it wasn't looking like his. He had to do something.

Gates's answer to this challenge, as Adrian Slywotzky writes in his fine 1998 book, *The Profit Zone*, was preemptive-strike marketing. When he showed up at the COMDEX trade show the following year, Gates didn't bring a functional competing product, but he did have an amazing marketing campaign designed to take all attention away from Visi-On (which was then due to ship) by focusing the market instead on a new thing called "Windows." Gates went all out; Slywotzky describes how "[Windows] banners at Las Vegas airport greeted conference delegates. Taxicabs were plastered with Windows ads. Cocktail napkins were printed with 'Look Through the Microsoft Windows' and offered discounts at local restaurants." The market lost interest in Visi-On as purchasers waited for Microsoft's product. A year later, in 1984, a red-ink VisiCorp would be gobbled up by Lotus for an unpretty penny.

With that look at the third component, visionary leadership, we transition to inept competition, the fourth and final component of sustainable advantage. We can begin with VisiCorp. While the company had a revolutionary product, that product primarily served only to revolutionize Microsoft's business model; Visi-On had numerous fatal flaws that indicated poor management at VisiCorp. First, it cost over $1,000 to purchase. Second, it had a steep (for the time) random-access memory (RAM) requirement of 512 kilobytes. Third, it required a hard disk—an uncommon peripheral in the early 1980s. Fourth, it wasn't preinstalled on systems or compatible with DOS. The product and the business were both designed around proprietary "closed" systems that would maximize benefit to VisiCorp—were the world not moving toward "open standards." Ay, that was the rub.

As Fool reader Craig Gordon puts it, "I think Bill's true vision came in realizing that the computer industry would not have grown like it has if Microsoft had been the only game in town. From the very beginning, he made it very easy for other developers and other companies to create programs and applications for the DOS and Windows operating systems." Gates had the right vision—open standards—and built a model to take advantage of it amid inept competitors who were trying to create proprietary products serving proprietary business models.

One of the few entities possibly more maligned than Bill Gates is Apple Computer, which we'll not dwell on here (it's all a cliché by now), other than to point out that Apple was guilty, in a grander way, of what VisiCorp was just accused of. Apple's proprietary products were part of a proprietary business model that caused it to break down and lose tons of shareholder value. The company and stock were amazing throughout the 1980s, during Apple's Rule Breaker stage (read more about this in chapter 5). But from 1991 to mid-1998—the greatest period in the stock market's twentieth-century history—Apple not only failed to create any shareholder value but it went from the mid-$60s to the mid-$20s!

Making longer-term money in the stock market is more about great business models than it is about great products.

Anyway, today Bill Gates is making substantial investments in companies like Teledesic, which will soon be offering Internet access, videoconferencing, mobile communications, and similar services, all via low-Earth-orbit satellites. Teledesic is another example of forward thinking, and the lion's share of the credit for it goes to chairman and co-CEO Craig McCaw, a visionary in his own right, who founded the company. And while Teledesic remains a private company as of this writing, making it harder to obtain much info about it, my own expectation would be that the business model behind Teledesic (reflecting Gates's input) will probably be as visionary as the "Internet-in the sky" product itself. It's coming to a computer near you, with service targeted to begin in 2003.

To close, the second necessary attribute shared by every Rule Breaker is sustainable advantage. True Rule Breakers create this sustainable advantage through business momentum (Wal-Mart), patents (Amgen), visionary leadership (Microsoft), or by outdistancing inept competition.

Only one of these is necessary to create sustainable advantage, but the more of them you have present, the greater the sustainability.

Of course, determining sustainable advantage will not always be easy. In many cases, this attribute is highly debatable. That's one of the reasons that we value discussion in The Motley Fool: observe the exchange of ideas among thousands of smart people from varying backgrounds and experiences, and you'll see their manifold opinions take on the spirit of a gentle but spirited debate. Meanwhile, your own process of consideration will more often than not turn into a process of discovery. When determining a subjective attribute like sustainable advantage, we should all be interested in discovery as well as using all the help that we can get.

That said, in many cases, identifying sustainable advantage, or lack thereof, is clear-cut. Blessings will come to those businesses that have it, while melancholy will eventually befall the Faker Breakers that do not. "What can't be cured must be endured," wrote Robert Burton. Indeed yes, especially when it comes to watching an otherwise interesting company's stock give away half or more of its shareholders' investment due to lack of sustainable advantage. That's a whole lotta melancholy goin' on.

Chapter 4

Sir Isaac and the Land of Mo

He that rides at high speed and with his pistol kills a sparrow flying.

—WILLIAM SHAKESPEARE, *HENRY IV, PART 1* (II, iv)

Out of the experimental work done by Galileo in the mid-seventeenth century emerged the three laws of motion that were first formally iterated by Sir Isaac Newton—and therefore bear his name. Newton's Laws of Motion relate the forces acting on a body to that body's motion, and one in particular—the first—informs our discussion as we examine the third attribute of the Rule Breaker.

Newton laid out these laws of motion in his most famous work, published in 1687 under the title *Philosophiae Naturalis Principia Mathematica* (even those who don't regularly read Cicero in the original can guess this one: "Mathematical Principles of Natural Philosophy"), known more commonly as the *Principia*. In addition to the laws of motion—on which classical mechanics is based—*Principia* contains Newton's theory of tides as well as his theory of gravitation—itself particularly important in working out the motions of planets. Needless to say, *Principia* has been called one of the most significant works of science ever written, and its author is high on the short list of the greatest scientists. Yet Newton was such a tirelessly energetic man that he accomplished much besides this. Just one example, near and dear to Foolish hearts: Newton served as warden, and then master, of the Royal Mint from 1696 on, and he didn't treat this duty as a mere sinecure. With typical Newtonian vigor, Sir Isaac tirelessly pursued counterfeiters, many of whom he had hung. (So if you ever do happen to pass through Hell, do take note of the occasional "I WAS CAPITALLY PUNISHED BY SIR ISAAC NEWTON" button.)

On a side note, it will interest the reader to know that Newton was an intellectual rival of Gottfried Wilhelm von Leibniz. Longtime Foolish readers, or at least those who have read *The Motley Fool Investment Guide*, know that the fantastic Leibniz Pre-Harmonic Oscillator is, to our way of thinking, still the only really useful tool for interpreting the market's future direction. Leibniz also created the calculus independently of Newton's own development of it, and at roughly the same time. The result: an intellectual controversy between the two men that included charges of plagiarism, dishonesty, and open displays of anger and hatred. Indeed, as the late professor Richard Westfall notes, virtually anything Newton wrote during the last twenty-five years of his life "is apt to be interrupted by a furious paragraph against the German philosopher, as he [Newton] honed the instruments of his fury ever more keenly. In the end, only Newton's death ended his wrath."

And now, with this book, Newton's work is carried on directly to the present day . . .

(Before we go into that, what is one to make of this fellow Leibniz, who proposes that some things called "monads" make up all living matter? "Monads"?! The idea isn't even original, given that this pompous Germanic philosopher has attempted to popularize the concept after essentially stealing it from the already misguided work of the sixteenth-century Italian Giordano Bruno. To call monadic philosophy even desperately speculative is to muster the highest praise that can possibly be accorded such irresponsible and plagiaristic work. If you desire to corrupt and destroy your enemies' offspring, I say teach those children about monads, tell them of these alleged substances that purportedly constitute the universe despite their complete lack of any spatial property. Leave it to a Teutonic intellectual pipsqueak, born, most likely, out of wedlock in a squalid back alley of outer Leipzig, to foist upon his gullible countrymen the notion that they themselves are composed of countless indestructible, dynamic, soullike entities that have both perceptions and appetites. Indeed, Baron? Allow me to try out a word on you, a concept with which you appear to be unfamiliar and with which you would do well to acquaint yourself: ATOMS?!)

. . . Yep, Newton's work provides us even more useful stock-market analysis than Leibniz's. We cite Newton's first law of motion, known as the law of inertia.

Applied to common stock, Newton's first law of motion—"Every body remains in a state of rest or in a state of uniform motion unless it is compelled to change that state by a force impressed on it"—can be understood to state that unless some outside force comes in to change its trajectory, a stock will tend to continue on a constant, unfaltering trajectory.

Planes tend to stay up in the air. Rivers will flow from source to mouth. The earth continues to rotate clockwise around our obscure star (one of two hundred billion in just our galaxy alone). Your heart beats. The Atlanta Braves win ninety games a year and go to the play-offs. The Social Security deficit rises inexorably. And great Rule Breaker stocks maintain market-beating trajectories for at least a few years or more.

But because the only constant is change, no trajectory (or body at rest) that we can think of is going to stay that way. In the stock market and in life, there are too many outside forces to contend with. The Atlanta Braves have put together one of the great decades in baseball history, but in an increasingly competitive world, athletic dynasties are hard to maintain. Unless Amgen or one of its compeers dramatically changes the nature of mortality, every heart presently beating will cease doing so at some point in the next 150 years. Meanwhile, at *some* point, *someone's* going to implement a definitive solution to the Social Security debacle. But if that doesn't happen within 5 billion years, our sun will cool and massively expand into a red giant, likely blowing our little pebble of a planet to smithereens. Orbit over . . . as well as any likelihood of seeing the money that's being suction-hosed out of young Peter's salary to pay old Paul.

In *The Motley Fool Investment Guide*, we talked about Newton's first law in the context of relative strength, one of several measures of past price performance. The relative-strength number is the percentage of all stocks that a given stock outperforms. If a stock is a 78, for instance, it has outperformed 78 percent of all other stocks over the measured period. Relative strength affords us a quick glance at just how well a stock has done. Relative strength numbers become freely accessible at our Web site, www.fool.com, in early 1999.

Put relative strength and the first law of motion together and you get our third attribute of Rule Breakers:

Strong past price appreciation equivalent to a relative-strength performance of 90 or greater

Of all the attributes so far, this is the simplest to understand, as it's pleasingly numerical and intuitively straightforward. As in *The Motley Fool Investment Guide*, what we're looking for is stocks that have already done well, on the assumption that they'll continue to do well. No guarantee, of course—outside forces, anything from a broad market decline (hurting all stocks) to suddenly shrinking profit margins, from industry weakness to a story about fraudulent company accounting in your local paper, could deflect our moving body downward from its course. Thousands of factors can drive stocks up or down, and a market watcher can go mad attempting to explain or justify short-term stock-price movements. There be dragons.

But, despite potential pitfalls, winning businesses drive winning stocks, and, often enough, the winners just keep on winning.

Another way of looking at attribute number three is to relate it to attribute number two. The last chapter found us hunting for sustainable advantage gained through business momentum—very helpful! Here, we're looking for a corresponding momentum in the stock price. Newtonian physics makes momentum out to be mass times velocity. (Done any of those calculations recently?) We're keeping things simpler in Gardnerian stock analysis: *We want dat performance number to be over da 89.*

Monster Stocks: Cisco, Yahoo!, and McAfee Associates

The growth in value of every Rule Breaker business, by definition, accelerates at a high rate. That's not surprising, given that we've already limited our pool to top players that maintain sustainable advantages in important, emerging industries.

In fact, Rule Breakers may often be spotted simply by the growth in their valuations (that is, their rising stock prices)—which sometimes look so excessive and unjustified as to be rule breaking themselves!

Thus, it's a pleasure to be able to spend some space in this chapter simply gawking at the beauty exemplified by the performance of what we'll occasionally refer to as "monster stocks."

CISCO SYSTEMS

"Cisco Systems is one of America's great corporate success stories." That line is lifted verbatim from Cisco's Web site, but don't just take their word for it. Take a look at the numbers.

Cisco shipped its first product in 1986 and went public in 1990. That year, its sales totaled $69 million. It closed fiscal 1998 with sales of about $8.5 *billion*, which means that over the course of just eight years, it has multiplied its top line by 125 times. Net-profit margins ain't too shabby either, recently tipping the scales at 22 percent. That's 22 percent *net*. Of course, an achievement like that comes easier when you're the world's foremost networking products company and pretty much all of your products rank number one by market share in their respective categories.

Cisco's stock has risen from a split-adjusted $3/8 (you read it right—no whole number there) in 1990 to $100 as of this writing—more than 250 times an initial investor's money. We'll take a little bit o' dat—on an off-day, anyway. It's pretty much your basic 99 relative strength all the way up.

The stock's move has been almost consistently outrageous. From its low point in 1990, Cisco's value increased by a factor of ten by the start of 1992. Even now, you can hear the market gooroos talking about how due for a correction this stock was, following such a move—but then it doubled once more by the end of that year. In 1993, the stock took it easy, recording a comparatively disappointing gain of 64 percent. So, by this point, Cisco had risen about thirty times from its 1990 IPO. However, a weak summer for technology stocks in 1994 was compounded by a negative announcement from Cisco that May, and this Wall Street darling got cut nearly in half. It rebounded somewhat, and by the end of the year Cisco clambered back to report a 1994 gain of 9 percent. Since then, the stock has never looked back. In 1995 it posted a gain of 112 percent, and in 1996 and 1997 its growth was 71 percent and 33 percent respectively. And as of November 1998, Cisco had already rung up year-to-date gains of 69 percent. Just look at that again:

1995: 112%
1996:   71%
1997:   33%
1998:   69% (as of this writing)

In the time that it has been publicly traded, Cisco has maintained a relative strength of at least 90 with more consistency than virtually any other stock in the United States. The stock has only taken three meaningful swoons, the already-mentioned drop of 40 percent in 1994, another 40 percent drop in the spring of 1997 when uncertainty about how the networking industry would consolidate shook out a lot of short-term institutional investors, and yet *another* 40 percent drop in the fall of '98 after Wall Street and the analysts following Cisco got spooked by world economic conditions. Aside from these isolated incidents, though, you're looking at a stock that has perennially and emphatically fulfilled Rule Breaker attribute number three.

Of course, Cisco's stock performance isn't the only thing that made the company a Rule Breaker: It had to fulfill the five additional requirements as well. Cisco nailed our first two Rules; it was indeed top dog and first-mover in an important, emerging industry, one that revolutionized the business world as it hooked together computers and enabled them to share information and resources among disparate machines across disparate networks and platforms. Cisco achieved (and continues to maintain) sustainable advantage by capitalizing on business momentum, patents, visionary leadership, *and* inept competition. And it has had other forms of sustainable advantage in play for some time now, including a focus on creating "end-to-end solutions," which essentially means they can now provide you a Cisco router, switch, or thingummy for any point along the network line. Many companies, when designing their own networks, prefer to deal with just one family of products from one provider wherever possible. Cisco has made that total-solutions approach part of its business model, and it has prevented encroachment from competition for a decade now. You'll be able to see how well Cisco satisfies our three remaining Rule Breaker attributes when we introduce them over the next few chapters.

Of course, read the second half of this book and you'll find soon enough that we have no hesitation about liking Cisco's stock even now. In fact, Tom only added Cisco to his online Rule Maker portfolio *after* the stock had already gone up a couple hundred times. As a Rule Breaker investor, I would like to claim that I scooped my brother by several annums on this stock, but I have never owned any Cisco, largely because back in the day, I had not yet devised the Rule Breaker parameters. And, in hindsight, anyone who knows these parameters will see that Cisco was a screaming Rule Breaker, screaming like a banshee, yelling like a kamikaze, howling like a Baskerville hound loud enough to curdle the blood. Cisco was such a raging Rule Breaker that even if you too have never owned the shares, give yourself the benefit of the doubt and say that if you'd read this book at the time, you definitely would have made at least fifty times your money by now. There, don't you feel rich now? I certainly do.

Curdled the blood, I tell you.

Rule Maker that it now is, Cisco continues to break rules even still. At the time of this writing, www.cisco.com remains the answer to the trivia question: "Whose Web site is the single most profitable Internet e-commerce address?" They don't much play it up over at Cisco global headquarters in San Jose, California, but right now they're doing some $11 million in sales every single day off their Web site (quick math puts that at $4 billion annually, about half the company's business). And it's certainly the most profitable e-commerce going on anywhere, too.

YAHOO!

Yahoo! is another bloodcurdler, especially so in light of it being another great stock that I haven't owned. Run it through the rings again. Top dog? Sure, it was the number-one Internet search engine on the day it went public. First-mover? Yes. Important, emerging industry? I'd say the Internet qualifies. Sustainable advantage? This is a more subjective call, but Yahoo! has always fit the bill for me in terms of its business momentum (it's remained at the top in Internet advertising revenues and has multiplied those at an impressive rate) as well as its having visionary leadership (I'm an admirer of "Chief Yahoo" Jerry Yang).

The stock rose from its April '96 initial public offering to become a ten-bagger in just over two years, and we Rule Breaker Portfolio managers watched it all the way. At one point, when the thing had fallen to a split-adjusted 9\frac{1}{2}$, I said to portfolio co-manager Jeff Fischer, "If it hits 8\frac{1}{4}$, we're adding it to the Rule Breaker Portfolio." (This was our reasoning at the time, based on some idiotic valuation concern.) Next stop was $131 . . . where it stands as of this writing.

(We don't kick ourselves too hard over this. Our portfolio's ownership of America Online (NYSE:AOL)—and, later, Amazon.com—created some redundancy with the industry overlap. Still, straight up on its own merits, Yahoo! was a classic Rule Breaker that should have been bought.)

Even at a valuation of seventy times sales in a stock market that may be overheated in its affection for Internet stocks, Yahoo! probably remains a good buy for anyone with the proper long-term approach (ten years plus). It's been one of those Rule Breakers that can make a serious run at becoming a Rule Maker, and it is priced accordingly. Moreover, it's already been a monster stock, and one shouldn't forget Newton's first law . . .

MCAFEE ASSOCIATES

McAfee Associates (Nasdaq: MCAF), a developer of PC software designed to provide protection against computer viruses, went public in 1992. The company's flagship product line at the time, VirusScan, was a set of programs designed to detect, identify, and eradicate viruses, and, breaking all the rules, McAfee distributed that software mostly for free over the Internet (70 percent of its business was done online). For free?! How could the company make money?

Well, shareware can work—just ask the developers of Doom, the smash-hit shoot-'em-up multiplayer computer game that debuted as Internet shareware. In McAfee's case, many people who downloaded VirusScan would then purchase updates and other software via McAfee's Web site. Why? Well, the company offered constant updates to eradicate the stream of new computer viruses while at the same time making it inconvenient for home users to download all of these upgrades for free. McAfee also parlayed its popularity and brand awareness into a major share of the business and government software markets. McAfee's CEO Bill Larson is a visionary leader who recognized a good product, and a great business model for distributing it cheaply and broadly.

McAfee was one of those stocks that conformed beautifully to the principles laid out in *The Motley Fool Investment Guide* for selecting strong small-cap growth stocks. For one thing, it sported high—often triple-digit—quarterly gains in sales and earnings, which spurred revenue growth from $32.9 million in 1994 to $350 million in 1997. That translates into annualized gains of 120 percent. Also, through this period of growth, McAfee achieved and maintained net-profit margins of 26 to 27 percent, not only because it was a software company but also because of the way its software was being distributed. Furthermore, McAfee had no debt, and its stock price initially stayed low enough that it was easy for individuals to buy in, but much harder for institutions to do so.

In its first three years of being traded publicly, McAfee puttered around, flirting with a split-adjusted high of $6 per share. But as that revenue growth took hold and the profits emerged, McAfee began its amazing ascent and hit the Fool's radar screen. (We never bought the stock—argh!—despite my using it to win a family stock-picking contest. MCAF was worth only a good bottle of wine to me.) In 1995, the stock rocketed virtually straight up from $4¹/₂ in January to $23¹/₂ at year end as McAfee carried away $23.2 million in net income from its $90 million top line. Then, in 1996, after a stumble following its first three-for-two stock split, McAfee recovered from a low of $14 in January to once again ascend straight up throughout the year. It closed at $53. In this saga, note that here again we have a Rule Breaker that suffered a quick and hard-hitting 40 percent decline in its stock, only to come back even stronger. Yet more proof that patience with these stocks is rewarded.

McAfee's upward momentum continued into 1997. The company scored net profits of approximately $100 million for the year, and anticipation of that drove the shares to a midyear high of $78¹/₂. That peak represented a gain of over 1,600 percent from the low of two years earlier. It didn't last, however. Over the second half of the year, MCAF stock declined and eventually settled at $45 in December. This represented a second 40 percent drop, and the negative sentiment surrounding growth stocks in the fall certainly had something to do with it. That October, of course, marked the tenth anniversary of Black Monday, and we watched as every media outfit in America made sure to point out. That, combined with the beginning of the Asian crisis, produced the worst day for stocks in the 1990s (up to that point), as the S&P 500 dropped 7 percent on October 27. Additionally, a bizarre lawsuit hung over McAfee stock; lagging competitor Symantec accused McAfee of copyright infringement concerning one of its products.

This suit originated with a story claiming that a close inspection of VirusScan's software code had revealed striking similarities to—perhaps duplications of—a Symantec product. A McAfee press release on August 21 refuted these charges, claiming that the code in question (.01 percent of the program—one one-hundredth of one percent) was there to support a particular model of Japanese computer, and had been available in the public domain. So saying, McAfee leveled a $1 billion defamation suit against Symantec a day later. A week after that, Symantec issued a formal apology to McAfee, admitting to "lying" about the pending litigation in that it had issued press releases saying that it had already won the case in Japan when in fact no judgment had been made. McAfee "honorably" dropped its lawsuit in Japan. Numerous injunctions of both sides were dismissed as time went on, while Symantec won a minor victory when the court indicated that "Symantec had demonstrated a likelihood of success on the merits of certain copyright claims" and issued a preliminary injunction regarding the 1997 version of McAfee's PC Medic. Back and forth it went. McAfee eventually dropped its $1 billion suit, but some elements of this silly fiasco remain unresolved as of this writing. However, despite it all, neither company nor its stock has done particularly poorly since. To get back to our Shakespearean roots quickly, "Sound and fury signifying nothing."

Anyway, at the end of 1997, McAfee purchased Network General, the network-management company, and renamed itself Network Associates. (It trades today on the Nasdaq as NETA.) By late 1998, the stock had since risen 20 percent from its December 1997 opening price. Meanwhile, Network née McAfee has arguably left the Rule Breaker stage (we'll talk about that in chapter 9 on Tweeners), and will probably have Microsoft to contend with in order to become a Rule Maker. Or maybe not—we shall see. The company now offers the industry's most comprehensive family of products that protect, manage, and monitor corporate networks, and at last count had thirty-five consecutive quarters of revenue growth behind it.

Last Considerations: The Land of Mo . . . and Other Provinces

Starting as obvious Rule Breakers, each of the stocks discussed in this chapter enjoyed an extended period of outstanding performance: Cisco for eight years, McAfee for four, and Yahoo!, so far, for two. During these vast gains, the companies rather consistently sported relative strengths of 90 or greater, though there were occasional bouts of lost consciousness when they dove like Chuck Yeager at the end of *The Right Stuff*, falling 25 to 40 percent in value, for generally unpredictable reasons.

Same deal with America Online stock, which I purchased in the summer of 1994 and has been my best investment ever. The shares dropped 25 percent or more three times in 1995; in 1996, they absorbed a hit of 65 percent! And yet, look at a graph of the stock price now and you can't even detect those 25 percent drops—they're microscopic. The spanking the stock took in 1996 is, and will remain, quite evident. Nevertheless, those who held the stock all the way through—for most of which time, again, these shares carried a relative strength of 90 or better—went on to make thirty-five times their money from the summer of 1994 to the summer of '98. Just buying and holding . . . recognizing an obvious Rule Breaker and having fun watching it wreak havoc on the business and journalistic establishments, en route to putting up some of the best investment returns available during a decade of great investment returns.

Due to the third attribute, Rule Breaker investors will, by definition, live on momentum, or in the "Land of Mo." Anytime you live in the Land of Mo, your investment can be helped, hijacked, or both by the presence of Mo-mentum investors. These are, of course, the dandy fellows—traders all—who look Mo-stly—or *only*—at relative strength as they make their investment decisions. The implications are, in fact, Mo-mentous.

Success can feed on itself, thanks to momentum investors. As a stock hits new highs, some of the buying interest in our markets these days comes from people who merely buy stocks at new highs. No thinking there, other than a total reliance on Newton's first law, generally by people who have no real love or appreciation for Sir Isaac himself. Tsk, tsk.

Thus, you, the Rule Breaking investor, may wind up playing the male in a marriage of black widow spiders. You've passed your time happily enough these many days, clambering around under logs and stones, investigating the occasional trash heap. You've eaten your fair share of insects, puncturing their little bodies and sucking out the soft innards. *(Mmmmmm!)* Both your stock and your body size have been growing significantly as you've dodged insect predators—particularly wasps, those darned wasps—ever since you can remember. Successfully. You've been a winner. The market loves you. And now comes your *really* big day—you get to mate with Queenie. Queenie is literally four times your size. *Mmm-mmmm.* How excited you are, and how excited the market is getting.

Qrrrrrrrzhhhhha-qrrrrrrrzhhhha. Oonk.

(This is only a simulation; actual noises and sensations that occur during arachnid mating may vary.)

Wham!

(Ouch.)

Wh-wham-wham-wham!

(Flat-lined. Camera pans away to show tiny husk of male body disappearing down female's gullet.)

Yes indeedy, my encyclopedia confirms it. They are seldom seen, those males, as most of them don't live very long. And that's true of many momentum stocks, too—they're eaten by the great market matriarch, once their unjustifiable gains inevitably prove insupportable. By focusing only on stocks that move, rather than focusing more fixedly on businesses with staying power, momentum investors will usually receive their just deserts—or, rather, *be* dessert.

Rule Breaking investors must therefore be prepared to watch their stocks get snacked upon from time to time. It all comes from hanging in the Land of Mo.

This said, however, the question that naturally arises is how to know if a stock is just making a drastic but temporary drop like McAfee or America Online or doing the Tweener death rattle (see also chapter 9 on Tweeners, where it is explained how you can judge when a company is no longer a Rule Breaker). The answer is that one never does, for certain, though you greatly increase your chances of recognizing "fake-out corrections" by knowing a company's business model and its place in its industry. In cases where we're completely confused or on the fence, our maxim is "When in doubt, hold." If you've picked a true Rule Breaker, even if it's now a Tweener, this approach will work more often than not. (Just think of all those people who are today kicking themselves because they bailed out of a long-term monster like Microsoft or Dell early on, by cashing in their chips on a short-term dip.)

And, hey, if your supposed Rule Breaker, navigating the unpredictable and sometimes treacherous waters surrounding the Land of Mo, goes under and never really resurfaces? Well, that's why we diversify; we expect that, despite our best efforts, at least one in three of our skiffs will one day sink. Fortunately, in many of these cases, you will have bought in at a low price and your gains will have been significant enough that even if you are selling well below a virtually unreachable fifty-two-week high, you'll still be in the black—still having beaten the market.

Now, before we close, we must for a moment consider the Faker Breaker. Given this rather easy-to-understand third attribute, what would be a classic Faker Breaker? Let's make it the company that seems to measure up well on all other accounts, *except* that its stock doesn't seem to be doing well. Given that Rule Breakers by definition must have high relative strengths, the Faker Breaker's poor performance will never precede one's purchase of it. It's only *afterward* that one will begin to perceive the dastardly Faker for what it is.

One example comes to mind immediately. It's a Rule Breaker Portfolio entrant that from the get-go woofed its way out of the gates—and we ain't talking prize-winning greyhound here, either.

When we first purchased the stock of KLA Instruments (Nasdaq: KLAC), in the summer of 1995, we figured we had an out-and-out winner. The company was the dominant player in a key-industry niche, producing systems that monitored the semiconductor chip–manufacturing process. KLA's business was to provide monitoring systems that would increase the "yield" at semiconductor factories—enable them to more efficiently and dependably render chips from silicon. Given that semiconductor chips are manufactured in increasingly huge numbers—and that this is a long-term trend in KLA's favor—we confidently purchased the stock for the long term. KLAC was going to click.

Indeed, the business sported double-digit net-profit margins, margins that looked secure (and have in fact held up well) since the market for monitoring systems is not nearly as competitive as that of semiconductor manufacturing. Also to its credit, KLA's customer list reads like a roster of semiconductor blue chips, and the company was still well managed by Kenneth Levy, who had cofounded it twenty years before. In our initial buy report we noted that KLA "has a global business, new products, and technology answers that pay for themselves. To be frank, the only real problem we see here is Mr. Levy's posture in the photographs of him in the '94 annual report . . . he sits with his legs spread too far out!"

With our August 1995 buy, we did a brilliant job picking the near-term top. KLAC stock tracked the market through October, but took a horrendous dive at year's end, as purchases of new equipment in this decidedly cyclical industry began to slow and the market anticipated the worst. It would take more than a year—through a great bull market, no less—just to pull even on the investment again. Then, in February 1997, the stock began to soar. For a few charmed weeks, not only did we have a pretty profitable investment on our hands, but KLAC was in fact a market beater from the time of our original purchase!

Shortly thereafter, in May, bulls cheered KLA's merger with industry rival Tencor, for it created what is now called KLA-Tencor—a true industry leader. Since a glorious top in early autumn 1997, though, the bottom dropped out of KLAC stock while the market has continued to rise. Not at all coincidentally, the KLA peak just preceded news of the Asian recession of 1997. This "crisis" severely weakened one of KLA-Tencor's key markets.

As of late 1998, the S&P 500 index has roughly doubled since our 1995 KLAC purchase, but KLAC itself is off 40 percent. (You know, we keep encountering that figure—40 percent—in this chapter. More about that in a moment.)

KLA-Tencor turns out to have been a Faker Breaker. I'm not saying here that any stock that doesn't do well is a Faker, by the way—I'm saying that any stock that, *despite all the earmarkings of greatness*, begins to substantially and consistently underperform the S&P 500 deserves your most acute scrutiny. One can easily understand how the stock of a crummy company might decline 40 percent or more, but when this happens to something that looks dyn-o-mite, you best start checking the fuses.

What happened to KLA-Tencor is that the market kept looking ahead. The market always looks ahead; this is a Motley Fool maxim by now, discussed repeatedly in our writings. Novice investors are often perplexed when their company's blowout earnings report is ignored or treated rudely by the markets, but the answer is once again that the market had factored in that report months before. How far does the market look ahead? Well, consider that KLA's best earnings per share came out in the quarter ended March 1996. When did it hit its best all-time price, prior to that earnings release? In September 1995, six months previous. That six-month block accords with our general experience of the stock market, which is that, on average, the gaze of the market's "seeing eye" extends half a year into the future. This is a general rule with many specific exceptions, but it's quite elegantly and visually taught via our KLA-Tencor example.

As we noted, KLA is off 40 percent from its 1995 level, and 40 percent is a figure that's come up a few times now. That's not by chance. First off, if you can't stomach a drop of 40 percent with little to no explanation, you shouldn't ever invest in Rule Breakers. In this chapter we've already seen numerous examples in which drops of just this magnitude occurred periodically, and in some *great* stocks too; the successful long-term investor in those instances was the one who held straight through. But whenever one of your Rule Breakers drops *more than* 40 percent, two things must happen: (1) you need to breathe normally, drink a few glasses of water a day, and continue to treat friends and family with habitual good cheer because you were not unprepared for this, while (2) you take a good hard look again at the attractiveness of the industry and the company's place in that industry.

This approach will more often than not lead you to the right decision. It won't work infallibly, but note how well it worked with two representative examples from this chapter.

KLA-Tencor, in retrospect (and isn't it always easy to see things in retrospect?), had a couple of characteristics prohibiting it from being a true Rule Breaker. Number one, it operates in a cyclical industry. The market does not favor cyclical industries and never will, given that many other industries—particularly nascent, young, truly Rule Breaking industries—exhibit straight-line growth, often on a rather steep slope. Also, semiconductor equipment is a "heavier" business, with lower gross margins and inventory turnover than other manufacturing sectors. Thus, following the greater than 40 percent drop in KLAC stock, one might have decided to opt out of the stock on account of the increasing unattractiveness of this rather mature (less room for future dynamic growth), cyclical, and "heavy" industry. Had one done so and redeployed the money elsewhere—in an index fund, even—one would have been better off.

On the other hand, as a foil, consider the example of America Online. Even during its 1996 swan dive, AOL remained the undisputed leader in the Internet hookup business, a wild-growth industry with which the market would maintain a long-term love affair. Had one recognized these things and held, that nasty downturn would soon enough become only a minor blip on a long-term stock graph of unusual beauty.

Let's close by asking ourselves whether we would've bought young Sir Isaac Newton, were he a stock. Yes, of course we would; this is easy to see in retrospect. But what an amazing Rule Breaker! His family was agrarian and uneducated, and he was raised by his grandmother. You see, his father died three months before his birth, and his mother—early in his childhood—remarried and moved away. Born tiny and weak, Newton was not expected to live through the end of his first day of life. And yet he lived eighty-four years (far more impressive in those days than today), during which he became the first British scientist to be knighted for his efforts. And, like Cisco and McAfee Associates, Newton too had a couple of breakdowns—his version, I guess, of a 40 percent decline.

Anyway, great stocks like great men often require patience of those who associate with them. But the association itself is extremely enriching!

Chapter 5

Aubrey at the Helm

A plague of all cowards, I say.

—WILLIAM SHAKESPEARE,
HENRY IV, PART 1 (II, iv)

*You care not who sees your back: call you that backing of
your friends? A plague upon such backing.*

—WILLIAM SHAKESPEARE,
HENRY IV, PART 1 (II, iv)

I can think of few novelists whose work has inspired reference-
book companion volumes published during their lifetimes. Fewer still,
competing reference companions! But for eighty-four-year-old Irish-born
novelist Patrick O'Brian, whose Aubrey-Maturin series is still gloriously
expanding (the nineteenth installment appeared in September 1998),
there's a market out there. Though I do not yet own any of these
guides—and only recently finished just the third novel in the series—I
now sit squarely in the "target market." The affectionate adulation that
so many feel for O'Brian's historical fiction is now shared by me as well.

One need know little (in my case, very, very little) about the
Napoleonic Wars or nineteenth-century frigates to enjoy these books,
which detail the fictional maritime exploits of Jack Aubrey and Stephen
Maturin. Aubrey, a dashing young British Royal Navy captain, is the
hero, while Maturin (pronounced MAT-er-in) is his philosophical Irish-
Catalonian sidekick—a physician, a botanist, and a spy. Together, the
risk-taking Aubrey and the reflective Maturin form one of the more
memorable pairs in twentieth-century literature. And as the recipient of

critical *and* popular acclaim, O'Brian will find his place in the literary canon secured.

If these meager paragraphs inspire you to read the first book in the series, *Master and Commander*, I shall have accomplished enough. Once you get past—heck, even get *interested* in—the nautical jargon, you'll find yourself transported back to another time and place, floating peacefully somewhere out in the Atlantic Ocean, looking at your own life through the lens of Aubrey's glass as he scans the seas for friend or foe, and murmurs aside to his companion Maturin.

This chapter introduces the Rule Breaker's fourth attribute, which, like O'Brian's novels, celebrates and analyzes character. We may return to O'Brian later, but for now let's begin this most important and rather complex Rule Breaker chapter with a glimpse at a superb Faker Breaker.

Attending Annual Meetings: HospiTech

As a young investor, I held a firm, though rather untested, belief in the importance of attending a company's annual meeting, visiting its headquarters, and (to whatever extent possible) getting to know its managers. It made sense; when else can the small private investor ask a question of the CEO, be able to follow it up by shaking his or her hand, and then proceed to informal chitchat and an office tour? When else can you really look management in the eye?

And while I don't do too many of these visits anymore, I still believe in doing so—especially with small-caps.

The first annual meeting that I ever attended was of The Washington Post Company, in which my father was a "significant shareholder." I use that term jocosely: Dad was not a "big player" at the company, but, rather, WPO stock was a big player in his portfolio. Dad took me, the young teenager, into the room and we sat down near the front, right behind the first couple of rows which, as it turns out, were filled with quacks. That's another thing I learned early on: Annual meetings of large, significant companies typically attract professional hecklers who use the opportunity to draw attention to themselves. And the annual meetings of large, significant *media* companies attract self-styled watchdogs who read out a litany of stories they deem inaccurate or biased. I sat there and listened . . . and rolled my eyes at this part of the adult world. I *had* tended to believe that adults were much more worth listening to than children . . .

(That was also the day I first met and shook hands with Warren Buffet. Buffett has been a Post shareholder for a long time, but back in the 1970s, while he was important, he wasn't yet BUFFETT. Buffett adulation and the thick cloud of attention surrounding him were still in the unseen future. I'm not even sure whether the Sage of Omaha appellation had yet been coined.)

Now contrast this experience with my visit to HospiTech, a fictional stand-in for a very real small-cap company that I invested in a decade ago and which became one of my best early investments. Indeed, HospiTech was my monster stock for a time, and, full of the enthusiasm that that generated, I convinced my new bride Margaret to come along with me to its annual meeting, which was to be held inside company headquarters. So we both dressed to the nines, drove up the New Jersey Turnpike to South Cucumber, New Jersey (all names changed here) and located the company's office building. It was, as Margaret puts it, "parallel to the New Jersey Turnpike in more ways than one." (This would wind up being, to this point anyway, her one and only annual meeting.)

Entering the first-floor reception area, we explained that we were shareholders who'd arrived late by a few minutes for HospiTech's annual meeting. The woman behind the desk smiled slightly, and then she told us to take an elevator up to the third floor, where the meeting was being held in the executive conference room.

I opened the door to the executive room and was instantly surprised by its, well, coziness. To my right were three company officials seated behind a long table, while to my left were portable chairs set up in six rows of six. About ten of these seats were occupied. When we opened the door, we'd had no intention of butting in—actually interrupting the proceedings—but the very act of tardily entering a meeting so small called disproportionate attention to itself and, by extension, to *us.* Our embarrassment was compounded by the contrast of our own sartorial earnest with the informal attire of the meeting's attendees. While the three managers—all men—behind the table had donned an Italian suit or two for the event, the few other collared shirts in the room boasted logos on their chests reading stuff like "Budweiser," or, "I don't break for Pinkos."

But, you see, I *had* to dress up, or so I thought. At the time, I was a "significant shareholder" of the company, just as my father had been of the Washington Post. HospiTech was a big player in my portfolio.

HospiTech, a maker of computers that hospitals used to log patient data, had been on a roll. Its stock had doubled, split three for two, doubled again, split three for two, and on and on. The idea driving it—which had both sales and profits to back it—was that by keeping electronic records, hospitals could dramatically enhance their information gathering *and* lower costs. Brilliant. Anyone could see it. How could this *not* be the next big thing? Forget that part about "next"—this already was a big thing, if you were a shareholder. If you were a shareholder, you attended this meeting very happily.

In fact, if you had attended this meeting as a shareholder, that would have made three of us. In addition to Margaret and me, the only other people in the audience were, in fact, company employees.

The meeting, in any case, followed standard procedure, featuring a reading of the recent results, a proxy vote or two concerning the board or the accountants, an opportunity for management to talk some about future plans, and then the compulsory question-and-answer period. Upon reaching this final stage, all eyes turned instantly, expectantly, to my wife and me. That lovely young woman and her pinstriped sidekick. The *outsiders*. It was naturally expected that we had something to ask. Why in God's name would we have bothered to come, otherwise?

We didn't ask anything. The CEO peered back at us in the fifth row, paused, then lowered his chin and raised his eyebrows at us as if to say, "You sure? Nothing?" And when there was indeed nothing, he smiled and called the meeting adjourned.

At that, Margaret and I were immediately greeted by the amiable head of investor relations, who shook hands and introduced himself, and took us over to see the HospiTech system itself, on display. This was all pre-Windows interface, so I can still remember the black screen glowing with a jumble of numbers and a few text fields. Had I stared directly into that screen for a few moments longer and taken some quality time to reflect, I might actually have seen more deeply into the cosmos and, possibly, decided to sell my shares then and there—at a great profit. But let the record show that this did not happen, though within a year I would be out of HospiTech at a substantially lower price. The stock would shed 80 percent of its value during the next five years and eventually be bought out for a fraction of its high.

After the product demo, it was time to meet the president and the CEO. Both were older men, and both were very personable. The president had steel-gray hair and a huge paw of a hand; he clapped me a friendly clap on the back while treating me to a no-nonsense handshake. The CEO, who then led us into his office for that brief informal chitchat previously alluded to, was a more dour-looking fellow with warm, sad, brown eyes. Though dark haired—dyed, we surmised—he looked to have been in his early sixties. Standing in his shady office, he looked like nothing so much as a mortician. He did have a photo of a beautiful young woman (she posed like a dancer) displayed prominently on the very front of his desk; further inquiry revealed that this was . . . not his daughter. Again, I didn't know what exactly to make of this at the time, but had I just sold my shares then. . .

(A few months after Margaret's and my visit to HospiTech, *The Wall Street Journal* published an article stating that this man—this very man himself, on whose back my money was riding—had presided over a business failure years earlier, the fallout from which (according to the state government) included allegations from the state that his company had attempted to sell light bulbs that it falsely claimed were manufactured by handicapped people. And not only were these bulbs not made by or benefiting the disabled, but they apparently cost more than, and didn't work as well as, normal light bulbs.)

As I say, the chitchat was . . . brief. One thing in particular that I should have asked about, but did not, was HospiTech's relationship with its top distributor, which accounted for a commanding 40 percent of HospiTech revenues. Apparently, the distributor was selling only a small fraction of the systems necessary to cover the amount it had paid for the right to sell them. However, this and other warning signs about HospiTech had not yet come to light. Now that they have, hindsight reveals that neither HospiTech's product nor its business model were particularly well designed.

All that said, the HospiTech misadventure provides a good entree into the fourth attribute of the Rule Breaker. This one is by far the most subjective, and therefore the one most open to misinterpretation, confusion, and disagreement. Simply stated, you are looking for:

Good management and smart backing

Easily stated, but much harder to pin down and actually define, eh? The nouns are simple enough ("management" and "backing" are easy concepts to distinguish). But the adjectives—how do we define "good"? how do we recognize "smart"?

It's my hope that by looking at some real-world examples of past Rule Breakers that illustrate superior management and backing, perhaps we can then come up with some guiding principles that an investor can use as a litmus test of any management situation.

But first, consider this: Any Rule Breaker that fulfills the other five criteria explored in this half of the book *probably has* good management and backing. With stupid management and poor backing, it would be exceedingly difficult (1) to position yourself as the top dog in an important and emerging industry while (2) maintaining a sustainable advantage and (3) boasting a common stock that is whomping on the market averages.

Thus, our guiding principle when evaluating a company with regard to the fourth attribute is: "Assume that any company fulfilling the first three Rule Breaking attributes *also* fulfills the fourth, and spend any research time in questioning that assumption."

Now to our examples.

Recognizing What Customers Want Before *They* Do: Intuit

Incorporated in 1983, Mountain View, California-based Intuit introduced its first product, Quicken, in 1984. By now, whether they've actually used it or not, most Americans have heard of it. It's the personal-finance software that one can use to balance a checkbook, budget, pay bills, track investments, or tap into the Internet. When Quicken was first launched, it was but one among several dozen financial software products available. Today it is number one by far, owning 75 percent of the market.

Intuit was founded by Scott Cook and Tom Proulx. Both were in their twenties. Cook had attended Harvard Business School and did time for Procter & Gamble, where he served as brand manager of Crisco shortening. To Intuit and Quicken he brought the consumer-product marketing techniques that he had learned at P&G—applying those to software was pretty innovative fifteen years ago. Proulx, meanwhile, was a Stanford student and the computer programmer who coded the first version of Quicken.

As the story goes, Cook and his wife were sitting at the kitchen table way back when, he watching her pay the bills in the painstaking (read: pre-electronic) traditional manner. "There's got to be an easier way," or something very close to that, ran through his brain that night. (This is a classic statement that has sparked the creation of many a Rule Breaker!) Intending to advertise on campus at Stanford for someone who could help him develop that easier way, he bumped into a student and asked for directions to the campus jobs board. That student was Tom Proulx.

The two partners had lots of trouble selling the first version of their check-balancing software. Cook wanted to sell it through banks— y'know, banks . . . those high-visibility, high-excitement retail establishments. But banks didn't bite, and neither did any good publishers. Unable to find an outlet for their product, Cook and Proulx nearly went out of business in 1985. In fact, three of their seven staff members quit because Cook couldn't pay them. The ones who stayed didn't get paid either—Cook managed to convince them to work for free for six months. He had already spent the $300,000 he had borrowed to fund the business.

Quicken's eventual success came with Cook's decision to begin selling it directly to consumers, using a combination of buzz from good reviews and direct paid advertisements. Cook himself wrote those ads, which, according to *The International Directory of Company Histories*, "emphasized the benefits of the program as opposed to its features, unlike most software ads of the time. 'End financial hassles' was the key benefit touted in Cook's ads."*

Riding the mass-market success of Quicken, Intuit went on in 1992 to launch QuickBooks, a similar financial package for small businesses. Then, in 1993, Intuit bought out ChipSoft, thereby acquiring the number-one-selling tax-preparation software, TurboTax. Both moves were driven by the notion that individuals—whether average consumers or small-business owners—wanted more control over their own finances, but needed it made more convenient and comprehensible for them. In a world awash in accountants and unbalanced paper checkbooks, that's breaking the rules. It's also doing something right—today, each of Intuit's packages controls more than 70 percent of its respective market. Additionally, in 1995, Intuit added bill-paying services to its product roster, making it possible for people to pay their bills using their PCs, which was cheaper, timelier, and more convenient than traditional means. Again, that's a Rule Breaker.

---

* *The International Directory of Company Histories* reveals this nugget in its elegant summary of the company's early years. The *Directory*, from St. James Press, provides good capsules of many Rule Breakers' early years, and it is an outstanding—if expensive—source for anyone interested in reading more about the beginnings of many of the companies mentioned here.

Scott Cook is well known for his fanatical devotion to his customers. It's evident in the way he listens to them and serves them. Quicken's design owes its success to numerous focus groups, while Intuit's "Follow Me Home" program sent product developers to customer homes, where they observed how real customers used the software. And indeed, having had the pleasure of meeting him, I can personally attest to Cook's reputation. Cruising around the Internet together via a laptop in his hotel room once, I took him to our Motley Fool message boards. He of course wanted to see the Intuit discussion, which we read with a chuckle; there's nothing like sitting with a CEO as the participants in a discussion dedicated to his company are vehemently attacking management and complaining about the stock's performance. (Intuit stock was down in the doldrums then, in the summer of 1997, though it was soon due to double.) One woman expressed particular grievance, prompting Scott to click on her name and tap out a brief e-mail introducing himself and inquiring how she might be better served. One can only imagine this woman opening her e-mail at work the next day, pointing slack-jawed at her screen, calling over her coworkers. I wonder what her response was.

As it emerges from its past successes, Intuit appears today to be a Tweener. Will the company manage to maintain its leadership as its medium changes from software to the Internet? That involves, in part, a transition from good programmers toward good editorialists. Intuit needs to learn how to teach and entertain through language and other experiences, to engage its customers in ways that are alien to its past efforts. It's not just about balancing the checkbook anymore: it's about reinventing yourself as a media company. One bad sign: Intuit's current writers produce sentences like this one, lifted verbatim from the company profile posted on its Web site:

> Cook and Proulx believing that individuals had both the ability and desire to carefully manage their financial lives if only they had good tools to do it changed all that and nurtured their vision to reality.

We won't hold that against them *too* much—every writer can have a bad day, I suppose.

To show how forgiving we are (for now), we counter that with one good sign: Intuit has consistently been brilliantly managed. That augurs well even amid difficult transitions.

Youth and Vision:
Steve Jobs and Apple Computer

Here's another Rule Breaker: Apple Computer.

That line on its own may be considered controversial, so it bears some explanation. Insofar as I am championing the notion of Rule Breakers as great businesses and great stocks, some may consider it heresy or just bad form for me to include Apple in the group. But include it I must! Don't think Apple in the 1990s, when it pretty consistently failed to create any shareholder value during the stock market's best decade in this century—that was Apple as Tweener. Think golden Apple in the golden '80s—the go-go business that colorfully splashed its way onto the scene, broke all the rules about what computers were and how they should be marketed, and rang up substantial shareholder profits.

Entire books have been written on the growth of Apple from a mere seed planted in 1976 by two college dropouts who'd been making money by selling boxes that allowed customers to make long-distance calls for free (illegally). Given the breadth of information available about Apple's birth, growth, death, regrowth, and who knows what comes next, I'm somewhat at a loss to do the story justice . . .

But before I even start, I want to make a confession: I'm a Steve Jobs guy. Maybe it's my similarly receding hairline, but I think it's more than that. I first encountered him at a *Business Week* conference that we were both speaking at in San Francisco; he was the keynote speaker. He sat in a chair alone on stage and began his remarks, as best as I can remember, essentially like this: "I must admit, I've come in here today a little bit angry. I'm perturbed. You wanna know why? It's the Bells, the baby Bells. You guys," he said, leaning forward and pointing at the CEO of Southwestern Bell, who was in the front row, "are consciously trying to slow down use of the Web by trying to push ISDN on all of us. This is your pet technology, your 'solution' to faster Net access, and it's expensive and slow and it isn't going to work. You're just trying to save your butts, while you're hurting the rest of us and slowing down the useful and economical progression of the Web."

That's pure Jobs, right there. He's brash, he's a free thinker, he's thoughtful, he's entrepreneurial, he's much maligned, and, from a purely business standpoint, Steve Jobs—the adopted orphan who grew up, as he puts it, "in the apricot orchards which later became known as

Silicon Valley"—is a self-made billionaire. I do not here or anywhere else assert that whoever has the most toys wins, but I remain surprised at how much criticism the guy has taken for his business acumen, given not only his own personal net worth but also how much value he has created. I focus on the latter. Whether it's helping to found Apple, starting Pixar Animation (creator of such marvels as *Toy Story* and *A Bug's Life*), or one of his many other pursuits (which include some notable failures as well, like NeXT Software), Jobs has improved the lives of a lot of people, consumers and employees alike, through his products and businesses. In fact—and ain't *this* Dickensian?—he's aptly named. He has created many, many rewarding jobs, as would befit anyone tapped as *Inc.* magazine's Entrepreneur of the Decade for the 1980s.

The primary criticism leveled against Jobs is that he's terrible to work for, that he's an arrogant, stubborn, slavedriving manager who can burn out absolutely anybody. So, perhaps you can chalk up my fandom to my never having had to work for the guy.

Now, back to our observations about Apple's management and backing.

First off, Jobs, along with his engineer partner Steve Wozniak, broke rules from the get-go with his very conception of what a computer could be. These two were the first to create a real "personal computer," one that could be used by an average person, personally, in a personal work space. Prior to this, computers were either hulking monstrosities suitable for government and big business, or hobbyist boxes that only an engineer or an obsessive could love. Later, with the launch of Macintosh computers in 1984, Jobs broke all the rules again by conceiving of the Mac OS, an operating system that made the computer friendly—even fun—to use. It's no secret that this operating system would be copied (and eventually improved upon) by Microsoft and mass-distributed across millions of clone PCs, slicing Apple into pieces with its own innovation. But again, that was now—this is then.

Shortly after the launch of the Apple I in July 1976 (how patriotic), Jobs and Wozniak—both in their twenties—met with a fellow named Mike Markkula, who had been referred to them by a venture-capitalist acquaintance. Markkula had previously managed marketing for Intel (read: smart backing), and he helped the two entrepreneurs draw up a business plan that aimed to take Apple to $500 million in ten years. (Ambitious, you say, with just one nascent product? Maybe, but Apple would surpass that target in *half* the projected time.) Shortly after devising this plan, Markkula invested $250,000 for a third of the company and assumed the chairmanship.

The Steve Wozniak-designed Apple II of 1977 gave Apple its standard. This contraption could output to a color monitor (a television set), with the initial impetus for that capability being the desire to create a good machine to play games on. (Wozniak had programmed the early video-game hit Breakout for the Atari.) And while color was certainly a breakthrough, the Apple II had a number of other features that set it far ahead of its competitors. One was that it had an expansion slot, with which users could enhance the machine's capabilities. Also, it was rather elegantly designed: in an age of "homebrew" computers with wires and screws sticking out, Jobs modeled the Apple II after the Hewlett-Packard calculators whose sleek design he admired. He felt that the look of the Apple II was very important, and made it a smooth, beige box. Indeed, the machine's many attractive features quickly translated into the first $1 million in sales while spurring the development of a software library that would eventually number over 16,000 available titles. Apple's sales rocketed into the hundreds of millions of dollars, and it went public in 1980 via Hambrecht & Quist and Morgan Stanley (read again: smart backing). AAPL debuted at an underwriter's price of $22 but traded up to $29 on its first day, in so doing achieving a billion-dollar valuation. Sales were $335 million in 1981 and rose 74 percent to $583 million in 1982. Jobs and team had created a top dog and first-mover in a significant, emerging industry, and Apple's sustainable advantage could be clearly demonstrated by simply penciling in a graph of the company's straight-line-up business momentum. Apple even managed to survive the deaths of the Apple III, a defective product released prematurely to compete with IBM's domination of the office market, and the Lisa, which had the world's first mouse—the sort of friendly technology that Jobs was always pushing—but, unfortunately for its long-term viability, carried a $10,000 price tag.

I say Apple survived this, but the stock plummeted in 1983, prompting Jobs to call in John Sculley from Pepsi-Cola to become the president. Together, the two would launch the Macintosh in the face of an IBM PC that had come on the scene two years earlier and had actually already bypassed Apple in sales. Apple was still a billion-dollar company, but the PC clearly presented a challenge. In response to Big Blue's advance, Jobs and Apple created the famous 1984 Super Bowl commercial, in which a female runner eludes presumably evil pursuers and hurls a sledgehammer through the huge projected image of a Big Brother–like figure. The Mac was the revolution, the bomb, and its customers were revolutionary co-conspirators. (The ad aired just once, but at the time of this writing, it was available to anyone who wanted to relive the memories again, at http://www.apple-history.com/movies/1984.mov.)

It worked, and the Macintosh was an immediate success. Apple followed up with a number of upgrades and peripherals enhancing the machine's capability and visibility. But a power struggle ensued within the company, and Sculley won out. Jobs became persona non grata; he was considered to be too much of a loose cannon, too disruptive, too interested in visionary technological innovation to listen to his customers' needs. In Sculley's and the Apple board's opinion, he was a leadership liability for a huge public company.

Our story can end there for now, because by this time Apple was no longer a Rule Breaker. The final rules were broken with the launch of the Macintosh, and much of the story after that is of a failed Tweener. It's depressing, and doesn't involve Apple's original founding rule-breaking management anyway. Apple rode the success of Macintosh for a few great years through 1988, and the company hit a new stock high in 1991. Then somebody apparently stepped on a mirror, because following that came seven years of bad luck. Anyway, as I say, none of this was about rule breaking, so it doesn't concern us.

Relevant aftermath: Jobs is currently back at Apple as interim CEO (he had served as chairman from March 1981 to September 1985, but never as CEO). Since the resignation of the last official CEO, Gil Amelio, in July 1997, Apple's stock has as of fall 1998 risen from $14 to $37, an increase of 164% that outperforms the S&P 500 by a factor of five. Whatever happens—and I'm actually a bull here because I believe in The Man—it's a darned interesting story to follow.

Nucor: Technology and Risk in the . . . Steel Industry?!

OK, we've done the ten-minute refresher courses on the management histories of two Rule Breakers. Let's add one more by stopping off at the rather spartan Charlotte, North Carolina, headquarters of Nucor.

Seventy-three-year-old company chairman Ken Iverson recently wrote a book full of his unusual advice about running a company. It's called *Plain Talk*, and it's all about how Iverson eschewed job descriptions, performance appraisals, committees, and special privileges for executives as he built Nucor into a world-class steel-industry powerhouse. This from a *Fortune* 500 chairman—but by now you're probably not surprised by this, able as you are to spot a Rule Breaker as soon as it swaggers into the saloon. Iverson broke rules at Nucor as soon as he took over a profitless incarnation of it—called Nuclear Corporation of America—in 1966.

(I wish I had some fun story or two about how I knew Iverson early on, and what a card he was, but I was *born* in 1966 so in this case have little to add.)

Before getting into the story, it is worth first revisiting what steel is: a low-cost alloy of iron (usually 98 percent) and a slight amount of carbon (usually 2 percent), the latter providing substantial additional strength and hardness. Steel is used in skyscrapers, bridges, and cars: It is the very model of a modern metal structural. We're talking here about an industry that's probably going to stick around for a few more decades. Annually, the world produces forty times as much steel as it does the next most popular engineering metal, aluminum.

But how would Nucor, a tiny and troubled steel producer when Iverson took it over, be a Rule Breaker? Where's the first-movin' top dog here?

The answer involves new technology and new ways of thinking as much as anything else.

You see, Iverson determined, first of all, that to turn his business around he would have to *produce* steel, not just manufacture steel products. He knew this because the most stable part of the failing company was Vulcraft, the subsidiary that Iverson had managed prior to taking Nucor's helm. Though it held only a 20 percent share of its market, Vulcraft was *the* top seller of steel joists to the construction industry. But Vulcraft was vulnerable nonetheless, because its key cost, the price of steel, was variable and out of its own control, fixed by outsiders. To remedy this, Iverson, with the daring that marks great rule-breaking management, determined that Nucor had to begin producing its own steel. What made this proposition particularly daring and challenging is that the huge costs of entering that business were well beyond the company's meager resources.

In addition, if Nucor *were* going to enter the steel-manufacturing business, it simply had to be able to produce quality steel as cheaply as foreign producers could. (Pardon me—me, ever the anti-protectionist— as I applaud in between keystrokes.) Unless the company could succeed at that, it was set up to suffer a long-term decline, along with the rest of the American steel industry, as a result of inroads made by low-cost non-Yanks. So the new CEO was faced with a huge challenge, the solution to which was technology.

Rather than produce steel in huge and expensive traditional factories employing higher-cost labor, Iverson in 1968 conceived of a distinctively novel approach: "minimills." Minimills would cost much less to build than the typical steel factory, as they would house simpler electric furnaces that would not make new steel but instead melt down *scrap steel*. The liquid steel from the melting process would be constantly drawn into continuous-casting machines (another recently developed technology), where it would be cast (molded) as it cooled. Compare this cheaper and more efficient procedure to the traditional Bessemer process; Bessemer mills pour liquid steel into huge molds that produce ingots weighing *seven tons*. These ingots must then be removed from their molds and reheated using a massive additional amount of energy. Why? So that they can be reprocessed through a "blooming mill" that renders much smaller constituent parts ("billets"). Billets, finally, are rolled into steel rods and beams.

In contrast, by using continuous casting Iverson's minimills turned the liquid steel directly into billets. Only 2 percent of the steel produced in 1965 was continuously cast. By 1990, that percentage had risen to 64 percent.

Iverson's first minimill went up in Darlington, South Carolina, in 1969. To build it, Iverson borrowed $6 million—$6 million, when the company's total assets for 1968 totaled only $11.5 million. He would surely have been much comforted at the time to know that "minimill" would one day appear in dictionaries, with its first use (whose, do you think?) traced back to 1969. But back then, no such comfort—yet rule-breakin' Iverson did it anyway. And he succeeded. Writing of the decision to manufacture steel by this new approach, in 1998 *Industry Week* observed that "That event can be regarded as a turning point that ushered in the modern era of electric-furnace minimills that have revolutionized the steel industry."

Because a single machine could now do more of the work, Nuclear

Corp.'s labor didn't need to be as skilled or expensive as in the past. So, as *Success* magazine put it, Iverson

> recruited farmers, sharecroppers, and salesmen to do the dirty, often dangerous work of making steel. High technology and untrained troops made for a volatile mix, and delays and catastrophes caused stock prices to drop to pennies. But a legendary company culture was born: inventive, resourceful, team-oriented, inspired by impossible challenges.

That's risky. And on a couple of occasions over the past three decades, those challenges did prove too much; industrial accidents have tragically killed a handful of Nucor workers. In no way do I mean to excuse those incidents, nor did the company do so, but the fact remains that Nucor's safety record in the steel industry has been better than average. And it's evident to anyone who studies the industry that Nucor treats its employees with respect and rewards them better than most of its counterparts do theirs. Nucor has been a great boon to the United States of America.

Contributing to the company's culture and success is that, while traditional steel mills had to be located next to natural deposits of iron ore, minimills could be situated wherever scrap steel was available. Thus, Nucor has positioned its factories in rural locations within range of industrial regions. So, like Sam Walton's Wal-Mart strategy, Iverson chose to build in small-town America, where the labor costs would be lowest of anywhere.

In addition, in a time when so many industrial manufacturers employ unionized labor, to this day Nucor remains a union-free company. How? By offering its employees far better options than most union workers ever see. Nucor offers an incentive package to even its lowest-salaried employees. In fact, the incentive package makes it possible for workers to earn more than twice their base wages should they exceed their production goals. Also, Nucor offers guaranteed college scholarships for employees' children. And—what union has ever been able to achieve this?—no Nucor employee has ever been laid off. In lean times (and there are always those), everyone "shares the pain" (that's what they call it) by coming to work for fewer hours during the week. Over the decades, Iverson has instituted these policies and numerous others; all emerge out of an egalitarian spirit, some are unusual, and all are in place today.

The minimills were the key, though, and by 1972, Nucor (Iverson changed Nuclear Corp.'s name that year) found itself in the midst of a strong profit rebound, and its minimills threatened the industry's prevailing powers. But, as we discussed in the introduction to Rule Breakers, the powers that be are often slow to evolve—much to the delight and survival necessity of Rule Breakers. So, throughout the 1970s, as its competition lumbered along, Nucor produced steel joists at such a low cost that the company began running its competition out of business. And it didn't stop there: Nucor diversified into producing other steel products, like decking, that complemented joists. By the end of the decade, Nucor had multiplied its annual sales from 1968 by nine times, and its earnings had risen to 55 cents per share from a couple of lousy pennies. Yet despite all this growth, it had only just breached the steel industry's top twenty.

Today, Nucor is the second-largest steel company in America, its sights set on overtaking U.S. Steel Group (NYSE: X—part of USX Corp.). It left the status of Rule Breaker about a decade ago, following perhaps its greatest rule breakage of all: its opening of a thin-slab casting mill in Crawfordsville, Indiana, in 1989. Nucor had been making inroads into the steel-sheet business, and right around then the U.S. government was planning to fund a five-year study to interest steelmakers in pursuing this thin-slab casting technology. The technology would conceivably produce continuously cast steel sheets of just two-inch thickness, as opposed to the standard eight-inch. Nucor surprised everyone by purchasing outright a West German prototype of the technology, one which had never been tested or installed. The million parts were assembled at the Crawfordsville mill into a contraption that exceeded three football fields in length! As this was proceeding, the company received extremely negative press for breaking these rules—Nucor's bigger competitors were full of critical statements. (A great sign for investors, of course.) When it began operating at full capacity in 1990, the Crawfordsville mill cranked out flat-rolled steel at $45 less per ton than its competition—and did it in one-fourth the time. Nucor had the last laugh.

In a world that's still made of steel—not silicon!—Nucor should maintain its dominance and may become a true Rule Maker in its industry. Financially strong, Nucor's stock has returned shareholders 17.5 percent annualized over more than thirty years. Given that this is a *steel* company, and *not* a silicon company, this is even more amazing.

Or, given what we've learned, is it?

Smart Backing: John Doerr

We've looked at management—now let's briefly cast an eye on backing. Almost every start-up company needs some form of financing to fund its early operations. It costs money to develop and manufacture a product line that may or may not eventually score big profits, to say nothing of renting office space, hiring a staff, and kicking back money to the OSHA inspector so she'll overlook your office's thirty-nine-inch handrails. (OK, kidding with that last one, but can you believe the Occupational Safety and Health Administration's imperious uniform standards? OSHA Regulations, 29 CFR, Standard Number 1910.23 [e] [1]: "A standard railing shall consist of top rail, intermediate rail, and posts, and shall have a vertical height of 42 inches nominal from upper surface of top rail to floor, platform, runway, or ramp level." What would our Founding Fathers think?)

Entrepreneurs who lack such financial resources must either borrow money or (more likely) sell an initial portion of their company to gain the necessary funds. Those who opt for the latter may take on a partner, sell a stake of the start-up to a larger company, or, as traditionally happens, turn to venture capitalists.

That's why smart backing is a component of our fourth attribute. Business is not just about who's parking in the CEO slot in the garage. Investors can learn almost as much by following the people who fund a business as they can by studying the management of the business itself. And Silicon Valley venture capitalist John Doerr provides us the perfect example of the guy you want funding a business in which you might invest.

First of all, though, in case it's not already clear, know that the entire world is tilted toward the state of California, or, more precisely, toward Silicon Valley in Northern California. Over the past twenty years, the amount of wealth created in the hundred square miles surrounding Palo Alto is absolutely staggering. Doerr himself frequently refers to it as "history's largest legal creation of wealth," and it's probably the fastest, too. The vast majority of this growth comes from technological development—the innovations and ongoing cost-cutting they enable—which will no doubt continue to spur capitalism well into the coming century. (With much of that global technology development centered in Silicon Valley, its friendly environs are at the least a real sure bet to be—among many other things—a good buy-and-hold real estate investment!) The

Valley's first successes occurred in computer hardware—hence Silicon—but today we might do better to rename the region "Internet Valley," given the shift of money and interest away from hardware toward networking and all its possibilities.

The best-known and most powerful venture-cap firm in the world is called Kleiner Perkins Caufield & Byers, and John Doerr is a partner in that firm. He has guided and helped fund Compaq, Amazon.com, Sun Microsystems, Lotus, Intuit, Netscape, Excite, and At Home, virtually every one of them a true Rule Breaker past or present. (In this book we've already dealt at some length with Intuit and Amazon.com.) No surprise, then, that John Doerr is our model for smart backing.

Networking is what Doerr does, in more ways than one. Not only do many of his companies specialize in it, but it's also a big part of his modus operandi as a businessman. A 1997 *New Yorker* feature, for example, portrayed him as "a highly caffeinated Clark Kent," "wired to the hilt," his days "filled with a procession of board meetings, phone calls, vain attempts to cope with endless e-mails, [and] trips to industry conferences." The aim of all of this activity? *To meet the best people.* People are what Doerr looks for; people with great new ideas, people who can develop great ideas, people who can manage those people, and people who just happen to know all of these people. By funding many of these folks' businesses, Doerr and Kleiner Perkins have fashioned their own much-vaunted *keiretsu*, or interlocking network of business relationships. (The word is Japanese, and this sort of business arrangement is very common in that country.) As best it can, Kleiner Perkins attempts to link its various businesses to form a united Dream Team. If you have Kleiner's money riding on you, you can expect that Doerr and the firm will be working hard to find the best people and business relationships to help you out, all drawn from Kleiner's web of partly owned companies, its *keiretsu*.

The stock market has consistently rewarded Kleiner-affiliated companies, blessing them with great initial public offerings, sometimes (as in the recent example of At Home) doubling the offering price on the first day. A Kleiner Perkins IPO not closing its first day of public trading higher than its offering price is virtually unheard of. That's the degree of respect that this smart backing has earned.

Amazon.com was one of Kleiner's great IPOs. Early in that company's life, after John Doerr and Kleiner Perkins paid $8 million to obtain a 15 percent share, Doerr brought Scott Cook (the Intuit guy—remember, it's the people) onto the company's board so that Cook could work with young Jeff Bezos to help fulfill Bezos's entrepreneurial vision. Next, Doerr and company identified the key slots to fill, the ones that would count most in Amazon.com's own distinctive business. The dynamite management team that they assembled ended up including top information-technology guys from Wal-Mart and a top logistics guy from Federal Express. Thus, with a strong board and strong management team, Amazon.com was primed for success. And when the company went public in May 1997, it was valued at $500 million—making Doerr's stake worth roughly ten times what he paid for it two years before. As of this writing, Amazon.com is now worth $6 billion—twelve times Doerr's initial investment. Fifteen percent of Amazon.com is today worth $900 million.

Amazon.com is not the only company to benefit from Doerr's expertise. Top Internet analyst Mary Meeker wonders where Excite, for example, would be today without Kleiner Perkins. The answer is implicit and understood: It would probably still be the Internet's number-six search engine. But instead, through numerous KP-orchestrated partnerships and collaborations, Excite has vaulted into second place among search-engine companies, and boasts a valuation of $2 billion.

Every investor should look at his Rule Breaker candidate's sources of initial capital as well as the ongoing big money. It's not hard: just get a copy of the company's prospectus (if brand new) or a recent 10-K annual report from the Securities and Exchange Commission. These latter are all available via the many online sites, including www.fool.com, that offer comprehensive SEC filings. Then begin by checking to see whether Kleiner Perkins has a stake in the company. If not—and this, of course, will be true in most cases, because KP doesn't make many investments and is only one firm!—ask *why not*. Is any Silicon Valley money in the company, money perhaps from one of Kleiner's impressive competitors, many of which are also located on Sand Hill Road in Menlo Park, California? Again, if not, why not?

So many sources of capital exist today that it would be impossible to examine all of them. All we can do in this chapter is describe generally what might constitute smart backing. Through your own research, you can and should find out other ventures in which outside capital investment has played a large role. Any notable successes, ones you've actually heard of? ("Microsoft" counts, but "backed Wooden Nickels in the fourth at Greyhound Raceways" does not.) There is, of course, some pretty smart money outside Northern California, too. One such example is Softbank, a Japanese firm that initially garnered a reputation for throwing way too much money at the Internet. Irresponsible, observers pronounced. But then, when the Internet began to take off, Softbank's endorsement suddenly became smart backing, and the company began to establish its own *keiretsu*.

If you're going to go into business and plan to challenge the giants and the way things have always been done, you need to have good leadership and smart backing. I think that the backing is fairly easy to define: go for well-established pedigree in venture cap and investment backing. You don't need a rookie or novice backer, and, indeed, a company that couldn't attract the attention of anyone *but* some unheard-of backer is probably not going to be the next Rule Breaker in the business world. Do your due diligence on the backgrounds of those involved as investors in a company; tend to regard as suspect and a potential weakness anyone with no associations that you recognize whatsoever.

Good management, by contrast, is often going to have come out of nowhere, is often going to be "first-time." But I'm getting ahead of myself, so it's time to close up this section.

Conclusions: Principles of Good Management and Smart Backing

It's incredibly difficult to write a chapter on evaluating the quality of management when most of us won't have the opportunity to get to know a company's manager face-to-face. In fact, this is the first Motley Fool book to even consider management—our previous works have been quantitative more often than qualitative, focusing on analyzing financial statements and valuation measures, and compounding out growth rates in credit-card debt versus the stock market's annual return. And yet the qualitative aspect of business counts for so much. Consider again successful investors like John Doerr who believe that *people* are the strongest assets of all. Given this, I couldn't conceive of the Rule Breaker anatomy without including—and then having to somehow analyze—people. People really matter. The quality of a company's management, and the pedigree of its big-money backers, can be incredibly telling.

To repeat, the difficulty arises in evaluating character, particularly that of people whom one may never actually meet. To take up this challenge nevertheless, we have presented in this chapter several examples of good leadership after leading off with one bad one, the fictionalized HospiTech. A number of common threads run through the stories, and these can be distilled into four principles, quite useful in evaluating corporate managers, even from far away. Let's set them forth now.

First, Rule Breaker managers are usually young and daring. Reflect on the companies discussed in this half of the book and consider the ages of their founders. Think of young Scott Cook and Tom Proulx, the Stanford student Cook bumped into when looking to put up an ad for a programmer. (And speaking of Stanford students, how about Yahoo!?) Think of Jeff Bezos, who left a cushy job to start something on his own—he became a billionaire by his mid-thirties. Think especially of Bill Gates. And remember the youthful bravura that characterized the founding of Apple Computer. Revolutions are rarely started by old men or anyone among last year's *Forbes* 400. "The world was made to be wooed and won by youth," wrote Winston Churchill, and the more one becomes acquainted with Rule Breakers, the more clearly one perceives the truth of the prime minister's words.

This isn't to say that youth is an *absolute* prerequisite. The case of Kenneth Iverson—who has run Nucor during the latter half of his life—provides a good counterexample. But if you're not going to be young, you'd better be unconventional, and probably daring as well; Iverson has been both. Investors who fail to locate *any* of these qualities in management are probably not looking at a Rule Breaker. The best sign of all, of course, is Rule Breaker managers who are young *and* daring. How I wish I had read those very words prior to attending the HospiTech annual meeting!

Second, Rule Breaker managers are driven by a vision, something they have seen before anyone else has. And, for the purposes of successful long-term investment, the wider in scope that vision, the better. Steve Jobs wanted to make computers friendly. Ken Iverson wanted to create—from a tiny and irrelevant starting position—a great steel company by building plants economically and running them efficiently. Scott Cook started with a check-balancing program but wound up ten years later with market-dominating software products in personal finance, small-business finance, and tax preparation.

Now hold on there, you say—how could anyone have predicted that? Well, Intuit's mission statement calls for the company "To revolutionize the way people manage their financial lives." So, if you liked the Quicken product, believed in Scott Cook, and inquired into his company's mission statement, you'd have been that much closer to making a winning investment.

Look at a company's mission statement. If there is one, it's likely to be prominent in the annual reports and on the company's Web site. (If you can't find one, e-mail the company's Webmaster and ask why.) The reason I love to read and use mission statements when evaluating management is because, often, great visions can be stated simply in very few words. Mission statements force management to confront, nakedly and tersely, just exactly what they'll be trying to do—and force management to communicate that effectively to the investing public. Note the built-in public accountability created by the declaration: Once familiar with the mission, private investors of all kinds become able to evaluate a company's prospects of achieving its mission, and the passage of time will generate empirical data for you to use in comparing a company's actual performance against its stated aims. Mission statements are intended to serve as guides for long-term success and should be considered in that light. They are, in Scott Cook's own words, a way for anyone to "tell how the company defines its opportunity and how compelling [the opportunity] is. If it's compelling to you [as management], you can bet it will be to recruiting employees, customers, and partners. If not, look out." (For more reading on mission statements, consult *Built to Last*, by Jim Collins and Jerry Porras.)

Third, Ruler Breaker managers must communicate well. Companies communicate frequently and directly to customers, employees, shareholders, the media, and Wall Street. We just considered one way in which they do so: mission statements, which are designed to be circulated mainly among employees and shareholders. The effectiveness—clarity—of a mission statement says a lot about a company. Numerous other examples of company communication exist. When possible, take the time to see company managers interviewed, whether it's on CNBC, in the *Wall Street Journal*, or at the Motley Fool Web site.

What do you want to see? *Good managers are always honest, above all.* Listening for honesty must therefore be your primary focus. Fortunately, anyone who cultivates a love of the English language can listen closely to or read carefully the words of a company manager. And as you do so over time, you'll wind up with your own pet list of things to watch for. (For instance, anyone who refers to himself in the third person or who frequently uses the phrase "at this time," as in "There are no earnings at this time, but . . . ," sparks strong distrust in me.

Good managers also generally exhibit self-knowledge and know their own limitations. I like to ask direct questions like, "Which of your strengths has most benefited your organization, and with whom have you surrounded yourself to compensate for your weaknesses?" The answer to that is so much more revealing than the one to, "Are you comfortable with earnings estimates?" To reiterate: honesty above all else.

Being honest often goes hand in hand with managing for the long term. Nucor's Iverson demonstrated this elegantly when he told *Industry Week*,

> These days, you can't swing a dead cat without hitting some corporate executive whining that Wall Street won't let him run the company for long-term growth. But . . . you have to choose your master—the investor or the speculator. What's the difference? Time. Over a three to five-year period, the success and growth in equity of a business will be reflected in its stock price, rewarding the investor. . . .Speculators, of course, believe in the fast buck. They wave the capital in your face and expect you to abandon common sense. The amazing thing is, it works! Time and again, executives dance to their tune. At Nucor, we refuse to do it. Every decision we make as managers is rooted in long-term perspective.

That's the sort of plain talk I'm trying to talk plainly about.

Fourth, most Rule Breaker managers really know their marketing. Today's more sophisticated consumers are searching avidly for both quality goods and the best price. There's no longer a cushion in the price to reward wasteful middlemen. The result: Efficiently priced products are an ever-more-prevalent marketplace reality today, and this trend will only continue. Take automobiles as an example: Identical models used to be sold on open-air lots at wide price ranges via bartered transactions, but today the mass-retail superstore model is creating more uniform prices than traditional dealerships can offer, while online consumers are increasingly exploiting the Internet's information resources and numerous vendor choices. As a result, it's a safe bet that as time goes on most companies will have a harder time winning on the basis of price advantage alone. This makes the attractiveness of a product's design, and the catchiness and "stickiness" of its advertising, count more than ever. Plus, now that Web sites provide a dirt-cheap way for companies to communicate directly with customers—even, in some cases, clinching deals via e-commerce—every company needs to become a media company of sorts.

Marketing matters. And, once again, our list of Rule Breaker companies and managers do a great job at it.

Jeff Bezos of Amazon.com brilliantly "branded" his online store, starting with the choice of company name and going all the way down to the attractive bookmarks and refrigerator magnets included gratuitously with his customers' orders. Scott Cook and Intuit got to know their customers' likes and dislikes by following them into their own homes, then used that knowledge to design software as well as to create a highly successful advertising campaign for it, the first-ever direct-marketing effort for a piece of consumer software. And Apple Computer demonstrated some of the best marketing ever done by a young technology startup: Jobs and Wozniak, having worked extensively on computer games before founding Apple, knew how important the element of fun would be in the products they designed. Back in the late 1970s, that was both visionary and timely, for fun was badly needed at a time when computers were on the short list of products even less user-friendly than VCR programming controls.

The list of marketing experts running Rule Breakers *not* mentioned in this chapter is extensive, including the likes of Steve Case, the man responsible for flooding the world with the 3.5-inch America Online disks that provided convenient access to a friendly, one-price-fits-all consumer online service. Also there is Charles Schwab, who via all the traditional vehicles relentlessly advertised his firm's increasingly numerous advantages over full-service brokerages: This established an upstart name that people could trust in an industry—financial services—that would soon be following Schwab's lead and moving online en masse. And Starbucks gave America a new synonym for "coffee" through Howard Schultz's attempts to create brand ubiquity—a Starbucks on every corner (that condition actually exists at one intersection in Vancouver), Starbucks coffee beans in your grocery store, Starbucks ice cream in your fridge. A typical quip about Starbucks (from *The Onion*, an online humor publication) stated that it would soon announce plans to open up its first-ever store *within the men's room of an existing Starbucks.* Cheap real estate, captive audience.

To conclude this near-treatise—it is lengthy, no?—on evaluating management, some final considerations. Please note first that this chapter presupposes that, at bottom, people really do matter. While Tolstoy contended that history's annals overrated the role of individual leaders, who he declared were more often than not simply "manufactured" by the spirit of the age, I do not see history that way. In Tolstoy's view, history comprises an infinite number of small decisions made by everyday people whose actions are overlooked because they don't make good copy. On this he may have a point, but it does not follow that the work of individual leaders could have been accomplished by anyone happening to be in the right place at the right time. Yes, electronic commerce would have come about whether Amazon.com ever existed or not. However, the efforts and vision of Jeff Bezos and the people who worked with him not only sped this process up, but also embossed Amazon.com's own distinctive stamp on the medium's present and the future. Entrepreneurs who do something right—really right—contribute to social progress in ways much more powerful than other entrepreneurs who, in screwing up an opportunity, bring ill will down on their industry or the technology that they advocate. Such screwups, and their fallout, are in fact harmful to economic and social progress.

Furthermore, it's important to recognize that any attempt to tell corporate stories as I've told them here—to tell "history"—necessarily engages in some oversimplification. Beyond any shadow of a doubt, and without even knowing whom specifically, I have left out various executive vice presidents and junior managers and many humbler unsung heroes, all of whom contributed to the success of great rule-breaking companies. Also, I've consciously drawn on a lot of real-life experiences here, from the Washington Post Company to HospiTech to Intuit to observing Steve Jobs. There's a good reason for that: there's no substitute for personal experience. I've already acknowledged that it may be difficult for the average private investor to reach these people, so maybe any experience can be the next best thing—

Wait a minute, there. What's that about the average private investor? I wrote about attending the annual meeting of the Washington Post; about my drive up to South Cucumber, New Jersey, to visit HospiTech; and of seeing Steve Jobs speak at a business conference. There's nothing exclusive about any of those experiences. Plus, most of these experiences occurred *before* the advent of the Internet, before the dawn of a networked world that greatly facilitates remote research. So now, even if you don't want to drive to South Cucumber, you can team up with people at The Motley Fool and research a company's management and backing together. (One of them probably lives in South Cucumber, and will offer to visit HQ and report back on his experience.) Think how much easier this is to do! I like to think that if the Internet had been around back then, I wouldn't have been a "significant shareholder" in HospiTech. By working together with others, you can now go much further in assessing the character, motivations, and abilities of a company's managers—and of the money behind them.

Our examination of managers would not be complete without recognizing that different stages of companies' evolution often call for different sorts of managers. One always likes to see a company's original founding team stay in place for as long as possible. However, it may be that in the end, a person like Steve Jobs is a great Rule Breaker manager, but may not be capable of holding the same reins of a Rule Maker. Running a Rule Breaker has much to do with passion, risk-taking, and alternative views of what the world could be, while helming a Rule Maker often involves being dispassionate, minimizing risk, and walling off all competition—for that competition will inevitably try to change the rules. Different disciplines will usually call for different people.

So, finally, to close the book on the fourth attribute, good rule-breaking management helps companies evolve through the rapidly changing conditions that typify the modern-day business world. The speed by which business is done, changes, and can disappear is constantly accelerating. This means that rule-breaking managers need to be nimble, always ready to adapt to new or shifting environments. This is their advantage. Larger ships take a much longer time to come about.

And when we speak of ships, I'm reminded again of the navigator theme introduced with Columbus in chapter 2, and, of course, of Patrick O'Brian's books, with which we led off this chapter. The parallels between nautical exploration of uncharted realms, and running a rule-breaking corporation run deep. And the more I think about it, the more parallels I see between O'Brian's heroic duo and the two components of the Rule Breaker's fourth attribute, management and backing.

In O'Brian's books, Lucky Jack Aubrey is the young sea captain who must act, while his sidekick Stephen Maturin is allowed to think. Aubrey, the manager, verily *lives* in his ship—in the same way that many young entrepreneurs practically live in their offices. Maturin, the backer, already has his own Spanish castle. Furthermore, he's a spy—he must *know* people. That conjures up for me the image of John Doerr getting out and shaking hands at conferences, flashing his bright smile as he soaks up information. Aubrey has much less use for information: he must rely more on instinct and vision, and takes the bigger risks based on intuition and gut. Both men benefit tremendously from each other, and their respective strengths make the partnership work.

The best combination in business involves established smart money backing a daring, upstart management. It's just much more fun to think in terms of a harbor, where painted ships glide high like lunar moths, and your cash rides on one of them, guided by a young captain called Lucky and his crafty, introspective devotee.

Chapter 6

The Artistry of Campbell's Soup Cans

I would to God thou and I knew where a commodity of good names were to be bought.

—WILLIAM SHAKESPEARE,
HENRY IV, PART 1 (I, ii)

So, it's time now for some word association. What's the first thing that pops into your mind when you read *Campbell's soup cans?*

OK. Duly noted. Now let me try out another phrase on you. What's the first thing that pops into your head when you read the words *Marilyn Monroe?*

Indeed! Now, a final test. Put the phrases together and see what comes to mind:

Campbell's soup cans and Marilyn Monroe

The man was brilliant, wasn't he? Many people blurt out his name right off the bat in answer to the first question: Andy Warhol. Other typical answers include "red and white," or some variation of "mmm-mmm-good." In answer to question two, most answer "blonde" or "JFK" or "Joe DiMaggio." But in answer to question three, it's hard for most people not to think again of Andy Warhol.

Imagine that! We link together two icons of Americana, a consumer product and a sex symbol, and the thought that comes to many people's minds is "Andy Warhol."

Andy Warhol, of whose art I am *not* a fan, was a dyed-in-the-wool, no-holds-barred Rule Breaker. Born to Czech parents in 1928, Andrew Warhola graduated from the Carnegie Institute of Technology in 1949 and shortly thereafter got his first big break: he was chosen by *Glamour* magazine to illustrate a feature piece. When it appeared, the credit listed him as "Warhol," and in the typically arbitrary way he would treat his life and his art, he just let the name stick. A handful of years later, Warhol emerged as New York City's most successful commercial artist on the strength of both his illustrations and his advertisements.

In 1961, Warhol began the breakthrough work that would immortalize him. His friend Muriel Latrow set the ball rolling when she suggested to him two subjects for paintings: (1) the thing he loved most in the world, and (2) something so common that everybody sees and recognizes it every day. In Warhol's world, the first of those things was a dollar bill; Warhol loved money as much or even more than he loved to promote himself. The second, as it turned out, was a can of soup. So, subjects decided, Warhol began painting both the very next day. By 1962, he was shocking the world by exhibiting his portraits of Coke bottles and other pop-culture icons as serious art. In so doing, Warhol was asserting that his work was no less artistically valid than High Renaissance art, while at the same time he was undercutting— almost mocking—the pretensions of his own avant-garde contemporaries.

The man was an iconoclast, and he wrote a new chapter in the book on shock value. Warhol took commercial-culture icons like Popeye, Marilyn Monroe, Brillo pads, and Superman and called them art, then went on to mass-produce their images in lurid colors using a silk-screening technique of his own invention, cashing in on his, and his subjects', popularity. He was a business, really: Warhol Incorporated. He knew it. He loved money, and he saw a way to make lots of it.

Warhol broke rules of all sorts. He shot twenty-five-hour-long "underground movies" that explored concepts like repetition and boredom. In 1968, he *was* shot—three times in the chest—by an insane female groupie. Arriving at the hospital, he was pronounced clinically dead, but was then revived (perhaps the ultimate Rule Break). "I think everybody should be a machine," was his motto. Lines like this—and his penchant for answering only "uh" and "yes" and "no" in interviews—were ways to grab attention through abnormal behavior. Attention: that's what it was all about. When the Apollo 12 lunar module launched in 1969, it was to have a tiny computer chip secretly attached to its hatch as a prank. Casting about for what to put on it, Warhol eventually decided to merely scribble in his initials: "Just in case there are people up there . . . might as well start the PR now."

Believe it or not, talking about Andy Warhol is a perfect way to begin a chapter on corporate and product branding. Warhol's art drawn from the consumer world translated directly into consumer appeal. And in this regard Warhol's tactics serve as a superb model for the fifth attribute we need to see out of our true Rule Breakers, which is:

The stronger the consumer appeal, the better: to attract, to habituate, to profit, and to protect.

In fact, Warhol was full of good investment tips. Anyone who actually purchased stock in Campbell Soup Company (which today owns Pepperidge Farm and Godiva Chocolate) when Warhol first put its can on canvas would be very rich today. The same goes if you'd picked up a hundred shares of Coca-Cola when he first exhibited his bottle painting.

Is this surprising? Merely coincidental? Emphatically no.

Which leads us directly to an investment lesson we'll teach over and over again: Businesses that can put their products in the homes, pockets, or minds of *millions* of average people typically represent the best long-term investments. Warhol's Americana art put on lurid display brands that would over the next several decades prove to be some of the best investment opportunities in existence. The guy simply has never been appreciated for that—until this paragraph.

Speaking of that paragraph, I dipped into a bag of Pepperidge Farm Goldfish as I wrote it. That inspired me to tap into Campbell Soup Company's Web site, where I discovered that "a third of all American households with children [mine among them] now eat Goldfish." That's the sort of statistic that leads to great investment returns.

But back to our attribute. In this chapter we'll be exploring brand. Tom has a full chapter on the subject in the Rule Makers section, and says some similar things in a different way. But I don't mind any redundancy: Few concepts are better to hit readers over the head with, hard. *(CLONK!)* Brands are integral parts of most successful businesses, whether Breakers or Makers. Here, we'll examine the four advantageous functions of a successful brand.

The Power of a Brand: Starbucks

Founded in 1971, Starbucks was a specialty coffee-bean seller that sold coffee by the pound until 1987, when Howard Schultz acquired it and installed himself as CEO. Schultz focused his energy on the creation and expansion of Starbucks retail locations, on selling coffee by the cup. Back then, Starbucks had just six stores and fewer than a hundred employees. Today, the company has nearly 2,000 stores (at last count) and 30,000 employees—and it's growing. As it has expanded, Starbucks has built and maintained a constant presence in the minds of many people, even those who never drink coffee. The company's attractive green logo, quality coffee, and friendly store interiors accomplished what it needed to in a consumer retail world: It created mindshare.

"Mindshare"?! OK, time for more word association: I say cola, you probably think Coke. I say soup, you think Campbell's. I say coffee, you think . . . ? (No fair answering "Taster's Choice.") That's mindshare.

Like many good brands, "Starbucks" as a word has no direct relation to its product. While this would seem counterintuitive, it works well for getting a customer's attention. When a business can make the average consumer think twice about the name ("Why the name? Why *that* name?"), it's often on the right track. In Starbucks's case, the name derives from the first mate of the *Pequod*, the ship in *Moby Dick*. The logo depicts a siren, the mythical woman whose irresistible song would draw sailors to their deaths. Both name and logo make one think . . . coffee?

It makes sense, though, really. After water, coffee is the second most-consumed liquid in the world. No surprise there. It draws us not only with the mystique of its long history and its delicious taste, but also with its caffeine content, which makes it addictive. (Is this sounding like Coke?) Thus, in the mind's ear of millions of Americans every morning, the siren's voice sounds. For a growing number of those folks, it is the siren of their local Starbucks.

The name, the logo, and the mindshare that they have created comprise the first function of a successful brand: It *attracts*. Name attracts customers. "Why is it called that?" the customer wonders. "And what is this attractive logo all about?" Or, "Is this the store that is so ubiquitous that people make jokes about Starbuckses opening up across the street from each other?" All of these funnel curious new customers to a company.

And, given that through 1997 Starbucks had spent a tiny $10 million on advertising in its history, you can see how powerful this brand has been. (Of course, good-tasting coffee and myriad convenient locations didn't hurt, either.)

Indeed, Starbucks itself doesn't necessarily need to advertise—others do it for them. United Airlines, for example, recently spent big bucks flacking Starbucks on national television. United, in fact, built a whole campaign around the fact that when you fly United, *you get Starbucks coffee*. The Starbucks brand, the name, the logo, and the atmosphere they connote exert a magical power of attraction over customers so strong that United was willing to spend millions telling people that that was what differentiated it from its competitors: Starbucks. No surprise to see that Barnes & Noble bookstores do much the same; they have little Starbucks coffee outlets built right into their stores.

The second effect of a powerful brand is that it *habituates*. The key to Starbucks's and many other brands' success is its repeat-purchase business. People become habituated to using the product. It's the very opposite of one-timer decisions like . . . well . . . how about finding an estate and wills lawyer? (Of course, many people skip that decision altogether.) When a business can induce its customers to become regulars, to come back time and again and buy, every new customer represents a great long-term cash-flow opportunity. Indeed, customers become walking annuities, delivering regular annual payments to the businesses that "invested" to acquire them. Habituation creates large long-term cash flows from individual customers, whether we're talking about people who, their whole lives long, buy Charmin, Cheerios, Chiclets, Chock Full O'Nuts, or Chubb.

The third result delivered by great brands is *profit*. This isn't about repeat business. Rather, strong brands confer *pricing power* to the companies behind them, giving those businesses the power to charge more than their competitors without losing significant market share. That pricing power leads directly to profit. This occurs everywhere; think of any industry or business you know well. A recent example: I was in a New York delicatessen a few months ago, looking for some juice to complement my donut. I instinctively reached for Tropicana orange juice. After paying for it at the cash register, I actually stopped before exiting the deli and reflected on what I had just done: Mindlessly, without regard to price, I had gone to the drinks refrigerator and pulled Tropicana off the shelf. So, right then, I marched back to the deli's fridge to discover that right next to the Tropicana, and at a cheaper price, was another orange juice, something called Just Pikt. (Yes, that *was* the spelling.) I hadn't given Just Pikt any consideration whatsoever, not even a look, as I reached for my Tropicana. Do you think Tropicana doesn't know that and expect that? (How about the deli owner?) Same too for Starbucks, and hundreds of other products and businesses. It's no surprise that neither Tropicana nor Starbucks is the low-cost alternative in its product category. They don't have to be. In fact, they'd be dumb to do that. Brand names confer the power to price higher, which generates profits that can be deployed to build the brand further and wipe out the competition.

The fourth and final result of a redoubtable brand is tied closely to the second one, habituation. The fourth is *to protect*. Strong brands create moats around a company's castle. You see, once people become habituated to using a product, competing products and businesses must suddenly offer a truly compelling reason to try out (and eventually switch to) their alternatives. The onus is therefore on the competition to create these compelling reasons, which are difficult to conceive profitably. The standard tactic is to offer lower price, but the lower the traditional price of a given product, the less room there is left to earn a profit and stay in business. So, the cheaper the item, the wider the moat it must cross. For instance, we have enough other stuff to worry about in life than whether or not our brand of paper tissues is five cents cheaper than the alternative. In all but the rarest cases, five cents is not a sufficiently compelling reason to change anyone's habits.

Alex Schay, a member of our crack Fool News team, recently wrote something that brings these thoughts together. "The power of brands is not *pure* magic," he observed. "If it were, Apple wouldn't have served up zero shareholder value for most of the 1990s." This is true, of course, and is one good reason why we have *six* attributes that a true Rule Breaker must fulfill, not just one or two. But back to Alex—this is the good part: "Branding is about pricing power and about walking across the street to get a certain product if a store doesn't offer the brand you like. And, most importantly, branding is about building a sustainable business franchise from which a management can generate returns on capital above and beyond the cost of capital invested in the business." In this concise statement, the reader can recognize all four of the advantages bestowed by a strong brand.

Starbucks CEO Howard Schultz wrote a book called *Pour Your Heart into It,* and in it he devotes some ink to branding. While his comments pertain to Starbucks, they can be used by any investor to get a better handle on the general subject. Among Schultz's comments:

We never set out to build a brand. Our goal was to build a great company, one that stood for something, one that valued the authenticity of its product and the passion of its people. In the early days, we were so busy selling coffee, one cup at a time, opening stores and educating people about dark-roasted coffee that we never thought much about "brand strategy." (p.244)

Great brands . . . have a distinctive, memorable identity, a product that makes people look or feel better, and a strong but comfortable delivery channel. . . . To succeed, you need to be in a category large enough to be robust and vibrant and to have a clear and original vision. (p. 245)

In this ever-changing society, the most powerful and enduring brands are built from the heart. . . . Mass advertising can build brands, but authenticity is what makes them last. If people believe they share values with a company, they will stay loyal to a brand. (p. 248)

Great brands always stand for something far bigger than themselves. The Disney name connotes fun, family, and entertainment. Nike signifies superior athletic performance. Microsoft aims to bring a computer to every desktop. (p. 260)

The Power of a Brand: Further Thoughts

Whether you're talking about nondurable-consumer-product companies like McDonald's or Nike, computer companies like Dell, or service companies like Federal Express, brand is often the powerful differentiator that enables companies to attract, habituate, profit, and protect. And given that we now live in a world in which every company is conceivably just a mouse click away on the Internet, brand counts for even more. Out of a hundred Web sites offering movie reviews, for example, the few that will eventually "win" (account for the lion's share of business) will be those with the best-recognized brands. Same goes for weather reports, stock quotes, and sports scores, as well as for transactions—electronic commerce in all its many forms. Who has the name? Who makes the customer, as Howard Schultz puts it, "feel better"? Who manages to be a topic of conversation for its own sake?

For investors, this fifth attribute of Rule Breaking couldn't be more intuitive or more welcome. Can you imagine how off-putting the stock market would be if the best-performing stocks were all ones you'd never heard of, selling obscure or complicated products you'd never tried? The beauty is that it's quite the opposite: *The great secret to long-term wealth in the market is recognizing that it's the "obvious" choices that win out.* This pertains even more to Rule Makers than it does to Rule Breakers, since rule-breaking investors are not always going to want to buy and hold their Breaker ad infinitum. However, for whatever period you own a Rule Breaker, recognize that it's often the power of the brand that can create and sustain its success.

As I mentioned, Tom handles branding more extensively in his own section, in chapter eleven. So it's not worth pressing the point anymore here. However, there's still one thing I need to make clear about branding and Rule Breakers: Rule Breakers will have varying amounts of brand power, so what is important is that you value this attribute and the companies that most possess it. Some few Rule Breakers will have little brand recognition—at least at the broadest level of the mass market.

A sterling example of this is Glenayre Technologies (Nasdaq: GEMS). Glenayre was a raging Rule Breaker in the mid-1990s, rising from a split-adjusted $1 in 1992 to over $50 at its peak in 1996. Most people had not heard of Glenayre Technologies then, and probably still haven't. But during its glory days, this company tore up the market by dint of its efforts in developing a popular new rule-breaking technology: pagers. Pagers were floating around everywhere, many of them given away virtually for free by companies that cared much more about the steady cash-flow streams from monthly service fees than they did for the technology itself. Meanwhile, Glenayre was churning out net profits approaching 20 percent of sales as it advanced the state of wireless communications, and no aggressive knowledgeable investor in this field would have wanted to miss out. Consequently, Glenayre Technologies is a company that had created no meaningful buzz among consumers yet was still a Rule Breaker.

That's why this fifth attribute is so very loose, so subjective. Companies with technology leads don't always need to own mindshare.

All of this said, if a rule-breaking company is going to survive its Tweener stages and go on to become a Rule Maker, it will *have* to be a brand. Consider again Glenayre Technologies, which has lost nearly 90 percent of its value over the past two years, doin' the Tweener death rattle. Sales kept expanding, but profits narrowed and finally disappeared as the world increasingly switched from pagers to cellular phones—some of which now include paging functionality. Then Glenayre's sales began to drop off as well. Numerous factors have contributed to its decline, but had the company ever managed to achieve name recognition—a direct relationship with consumers—we can at least speculate that the fall would not have been so hard. But without ever creating this habituation, long-term cash flow did not head toward the company's headquarters in Charlotte, North Carolina, and GEMS lost its glint. After sitting near the top of the list as one of the great stocks of the mid-1990s, Glenayre looks today more like a has-been; it's lost its looks and its star power.

Ah, star power . . . perhaps the case of Andy Warhol and the art world can instruct us further on brands. Think of a brand and ask yourself this question: Were Warhol still with us today, could you picture this company's logo among his many framed works? Again, this may be truer of Rule Makers than Rule Breakers, but ask yourself whether down the road you could ever envision the company in question having its logo silk-screened and mass-produced, sold at Christie's for a million bucks. Will the company be famous for more than the proverbial fifteen minutes?

Ironically, in the end, Warhol himself was a brand. Indeed, most successful artists become just that. A beautiful seventeenth-century Dutch portrait is a beautiful seventeenth-century Dutch portrait—until the knowledge that it's by "Rembrandt" (brand!) induces people to pay a *lot* more for it. If you're still not convinced, ask yourself if you would ever in your life pay thousands of dollars for a silk-screened image of a Coke bottle . . . if it *weren't* by Andy Warhol?

That probably says it all.

Chapter 7

Percentages, *Not* Points!

FALSTAFF: *An old lord of the council rated me the other day in the Street about you, sir, but I mark'd him not; and yet he talk'd very Wisely, but I regarded him not; and yet he talk'd Wisely, and in the Street too.*

PRINCE: *Thou didst well; for Wisdom cries out in the streets, and no man regards it.*

—WILLIAM SHAKESPEARE,
HENRY IV, PART 1 (I, ii)*

Even despite his ubiquitous media coverage, the philandering American president was not the only big story to arise in the late summer of 1998. Two other domestic events simply couldn't be crowded off the front page. Indeed, on their biggest days, either of these national news stories was capable of pushing every other story down below the fold of any of our largest and best-known newspapers. Let's spend a few minutes looking at each—preparing the way for our sixth attribute of Rule Breaking to emerge naturally at the end.

The first was the record-setting season of baseball sluggers Mark McGwire and Sammy Sosa. Their feats made news all summer, but they created quite a stir when first McGwire and then Sosa broke Major

---

* Certain liberties taken with capitalization.

League Baseball's thirty-seven-year-old home-run record. In their run up to and past the record, their exploits received more extensive day-by-day media coverage than the whole game of baseball normally does even during the World Series. (Of course, a few heroes never hurt to offset demoralizing revelations about the executive branch of our government.) It was great to see baseball reestablish itself in the minds of Americans again. The old game had been getting a bit dusty, truth be told.

The home-run record had been held by Roger Maris, who hit sixty-one in the summer of '61. Unlike McGwire and Sosa, who received copious kudos from the press, Maris had mostly been reviled for breaking Babe Ruth's mark of sixty, established back in 1927. Ruth was such a legendary and beloved figure in American culture that few people wanted to see his record surpassed. In addition, Maris's standard-setting season ran 8 games longer than had the Babe's, as baseball extended the schedule from 154 to 162 games with that 1961 campaign. Yet Maris had managed only one more home run. That led baseball's commissioner, Ford Frick, to stick an infamous asterisk next to his mark in the record book.

No such problems dogged 1998's poster boys. Both hit their sixty-first and sixty-second homers well within a 154-game window, and were media darlings to boot. The conventional wisdom about McGwire and Sosa, reinforced everywhere at the time of their feat, is that the two players had each managed to pull off the greatest single-season achievement in baseball history. For thirty-seven years, this mark had stood—since before men set foot on the moon, or the war in Vietnam started. No statistical genius, I nevertheless couldn't help noticing an irony that few in the media or the world at large pointed out: Namely, a record that had stood untouched for thirty-seven years just happened to be broken in *early* September by *two* different guys. This smelled a bit fishy.

So I went back and looked at 1927, the season in which Ruth hit sixty home runs. That year, the sixteen major-league teams managed to hit 922 home runs overall, or an average of 57.6 per team. Ruth hit more home runs than the average team! Behind Ruth was his Yankee teammate Lou Gehrig with forty-seven, and then for third you had to go all the way down to the thirty hit by Hack Wilson in the National League. Tony Lazzeri, who finished third behind Ruth and Gehrig in the American League home-run race, had just eighteen homers.

By contrast, in 1961, while Maris was hitting 61, the eighteen major-league teams combined for 2,730 home runs. That comes out to a per-team average of 151.7, or more than double Maris's own total. But perhaps more interesting to me was that the American League, home that year to a number of sluggers who hit forty or more homers, had added two new teams to its roster before the season: the Los Angeles (now Anaheim) Angels, and another edition of the Washington Senators. (The previous edition had just moved to Bloomington, Minnesota, where it became the Minnesota Twins. I know this particularly well because the team's minority owner, who fought unsuccessfully to keep them in Washington, was our grandfather, H. Gabriel Murphy. Despite that setback, he's still going strong today at ninety-six—hi there, Grandaddy!).

Now, I ask you, what happens when a league expands? It adds another fifty players who would not otherwise have played in the major leagues. These players are by and large of lesser caliber than the players already there; the year before, most of them were in the minor leagues. Commonsense logic dictates, then, that in such an environment the performance of outstanding players will improve, as they'll be the ones who excel most against an influx of weaker opponents. To put it more succinctly, in 1961, Roger Maris got to tee off on some pitchers he would never have faced had the league not expanded. It therefore stands to reason that 1961 would've been a great year to predict that someone might challenge Ruth's record. Indeed, the year before (1960), the five best home-run hitters in the American League totaled 183 home runs. In 1961, that figure swelled to 252, a 38 percent increase.

Flash forward, and please note that in 1998, two new teams—the Arizona Diamondbacks and the Tampa Bay Devil Rays—entered the major leagues, one in each circuit. Thus, it would've been a good year to predict that someone might challenge Maris's record. And as Maris had in an expanded league before them, both Mark McGwire and Sammy Sosa posted career years. (In fact, in addition to his home-run totals, McGwire set the National League record for walks, while Sosa led the NL in runs batted in.) For the 1998 season through September 15, thirty teams hit a combined total of 5,064 home runs, an average of 168.8 per team.

Now take the key numbers presented above and let's shift from gross totals (the mass media's way of reporting and understanding) to percentages (the Fool's) shown on the opposite page.

As is evident from the average, Ruth's achievement is in a category by itself. The other three sluggers run at a consistent clip of approximately 40 percent of the average team's total for their respective eras.

Is 40 percent impressive? Absolutely! In most seasons, the home-run

Player	Home Runs	Home Runs per Team (Average)	Player's Home Runs as Percentage of Average Team
Ruth '27	60	57.6	104.2
Maris '61	61	151.7	40.2
McGwire '98	70	168.8	41.4
Sosa '98	66	168.8	39.1

king's tally as a percentage of the average per-team total will be closer to 25 or 30 percent. So, are *all four* hitters we've discussed to be lauded and cheered for their achievements? Certainly! Should Mark McGwire and Sammy Sosa have been on the front page of newspapers for their efforts? Yes! Are Mark McGwire and Sammy Sosa to be credited with the greatest home-run seasons in baseball history? No . . . that's where any right-thinking Fool will hop off the bandwagon. Not only are McGwire and Sosa's accomplishments in line with Maris's but they are as nothing compared to Babe Ruth's achievement in 1927. On a gross-totals basis—if you're counting just points—the 1998 twin towers are the best ever. But on a relative basis—where percentages afford us a more informed look—we see the heroes of 1998 in line with the hero of 1961, and all of them only a blur of headlights in the rearview mirror of the Babe.

Look at it this way: What would happen if any number of factors conspired next year to push the average team home-run totals up to 230? The answer is that you'd expect the top slugger in the game (who normally would hit about 30 percent of that) to hit seventy home runs and that, by our analysis, would be an *unremarkable* top-slugger effort. His "points" would threaten to smash the record again, but his percentage would actually be well below what was achieved by Ruth, Maris, Sosa, and McGwire.

The meaning of this chapter's title, and its theme, should now be becoming evident, even as we turn to the second other big story from the late summer of 1998.

In August and September 1998, the world's stock markets experienced one of the more volatile periods in their collective history. The American stock market's drop of 20 percent from the high it set in July looked paltry, compared to the spanking taken by many stock markets (and currencies) around the rest of the world. Global deflation, economic crisis in Asia, and political crisis in Russia, along with the usual

1,001 other factors, all contributed to the American market's tumble. "Worst week in stock market history," one CNN headline blared. That was followed a few days afterward, though, by "Best one-day gain in stock market history," as the Dow roared back up some 380 points.

The conventional wisdom at the time held that we were witnessing the most shocking shifts ever seen in the stock market's history, one after another, worst following best following worst. The headlines shouted it, the news telecasts led with it. But, in reality, we didn't have anything near so bad as the worst week in stock market history, and that 380-point one-day gain was nice, but not unprecedented. Again, what was lacking was the fundamental recognition and understanding that to comprehend what's actually going on, one must look at *percentages, not points.*

The mass media are excellent at capturing and delivering images and moving pictures, and are generally OK at words. And that is debatable. What is *not* debatable is the mass media's inability to handle numbers correctly. Putting numbers in the hands of the average reporter is usually akin to handing a blowtorch to a six-year-old. Many misconceptions—some outright dangerous, others harmless—result from the media's efforts to make numerical sense of the world. And the impression being created by coverage of the summer 1998 stock market was as fundamentally flawed as the coverage of the concomitant "greatest single-season home-run performances of all time."

Points are facts.
Percentages are *context.*
Context puts facts in their place.

(If you could take only three lines away with you from this chapter, I'd recommend those . . . and request also that you let CNN and Dan Rather and *Nightline* and ESPN know about them, as well.)

With all this ignorance being spread around the world in real time, the common Fool probably wonders whether there isn't some profit to be realized by somebody who recognizes misreporting for what it is. (Now, would I be wasting your time with this stuff if there were not? Never!) The very same misunderstanding and misuse of numbers that we now hold to be self-evident routinely characterize the coverage accorded rule-breaking stocks by media pundits and gooroos. Not only can you profit off that, but here's how: You actually use it to help you find your next Rule Breaker. And so the curtain rolls up to reveal the final attribute, attribute number six:

> **Grossly overvalued, according to at least one significant constituent of the financial media.**

That's right. Your newest Rule Breaker prospect may have met all five of our other criteria, but in order to anoint it a true Rule Breaker, you're going to have to obtain documented proof from one of our nation's financial magazines, financial TV shows, financial radio shows, or financial newspapers that the stock in question is *grossly overvalued*.

It shouldn't be too hard. Among the press, there's enough envy of success, enough of a desire to shoot down anything that reaches toward the heavens, that you won't have to look too far. Hey, if it exhibits our other five attributes, the company in question will already be doing so many things *right* that you can just bet that that alone will rub some financial journalist *wrong*. Stocks that go up "too much" have that effect on the Wise.

Barron's: A Helpful Starting Place

While the publication itself is often chock-full of attribute-six possibilities, the lead columnist of *Barron's*, who for years has written page one of what is the nation's highest-circulation printed financial weekly, deserves a special award. To go back and attempt to unearth every bearish misstep from such a huge body of bearishness would consume roughly the same amount of time as it takes light to travel from here to Betelgeuse (six hundred years, if you're counting). Still, after numerous painful hours reading through years of old columns, we found a host of incorrect market calls. This wrongheaded investment "advice" (in a neat journalistic trick, always credited to others) was published with no real accountability or follow-up, no acknowledgment of error, and, worst of all, no indication that the writer might have learned anything from his missteps or the market. It's just a constant, consistent stream of decaying, condescending (albeit sometimes witty) prose, with its higher-than-thou royal "we" and its lower-than-thou performance.

For rule-breaking investors, it is critical that you both understand and appreciate what's going on in these columns. The following themes are seen again and again: Average-joe investors are gullible simpletons; the market has been doing too well, is bound to drop, and those who are predicting this are stylish and intelligent, always to be lavishly praised and complimented; the stock market *can* be predicted, by the way, *of course*, and it's very useful to do so; stocks that have done well have been blindly driven by momentum investors (those "gullible simpletons"); the columnist claims that he would *like* to see the market do well, though to the reader his fanciful writing and constant predilections of doom indicate quite the opposite; one can derive an almost salacious enjoyment of totting up the money lost by investors during downturns.

Perhaps it would be helpful, particularly to those unfamiliar with such work, to see a few examples:

> [T]he drill for three years has been that a rising tide of liquidity lifts all equities. So it might be a touch difficult for a flock of innocents who have forsaken CDs and passbooks for stock to contemplate an ebb tide with serene equanimity. *(October 25, 1993)*

> Speculative excess is very much on the mind of our old pal and market prophet, Marty Zweig. . . . He's brooding about two possible scenarios . . . both rather depressing. The first is a stretch of, say, five years that includes three "moderate bear markets" punctuated by a "couple of upswings." At the end of this lively half-decade, the Dow might be at 3000. . . . The other prospect is for a market decline similar to 1973–74, by any definition a major bear move, in which stocks, as Marty ruefully pictures it, "go down 50%." *(March 16, 1994)*

> For over three years, the markets had everything going their way, and they grew complacent and cocky even as they grew fat. It's sobering-up time and after so long and so wonderful and so wild a party, the sobering up might just conceivably go on for a while and cause more than a modest discomfort. *(April 11, 1994)*

> Jim has appeared in the pages of *Barron's* on a number of occasions, the subject of some astute and stylish profiling. . . . Jim's kind of a Renaissance Investment Man: he's run a hedge fund, been a broker, written a newsletter. He peruses charts and immerses himself in fundamentals. He has a historian's perspective and a market timer's up-to-the-minuteness. What he lacks are blinders and biases. . . . When it finally does head for the hills, he thinks the Dow Jones Industrials will be at 2,000. At that point, we have a hunch, not everyone will be smiling. *(June 27, 1994)*

[U]ntil the Fed relents and rates go south in earnest, stocks shape up as more than a trifle vulnerable. And however much follow-through the recovery in the stock market manages to generate, November's ugly decline, we'd hazard, is a foretaste of things to come. *(November 28, 1994)*

You may have noticed that all of these quotes come from late 1993 and 1994—the eve of the strongest four-year stretch in stock-market history, during which the indices surged to a gain of more than 100 percent. But from whatever period, these would all be rather trivial rantings, except that they have "served" investors for years from the front page of the nation's most-read financial weekly. Make of that what you will.

What we'll make of it *in this chapter* is to point out that such commentary perfectly fulfills the sixth attribute: "grossly overvalued, according to at least one significant constituent of the financial media." *(DING!*—that's the bell that lets us know that we've fulfilled the criterion.) Except in this case, the comments were about the market overall, rather than any individual stocks. We'll get to those in a sec, but just notice what a superb green light *Barron's* has been flashing at investors: Here you had a significant media constituent calling the *whole market* grossly overvalued. And last I checked, the tune remained the same . . . even if it may now sound more played out and stale than ever.

Now to individual stocks.

In January 1996, if you were holding computer-peripheral manufacturer Iomega (NYSE:IOM), a classic Rule Breaker that was the subject of the introduction to our *Motley Fool Investment Guide* (1996), you may already have been very happy. The stock was the Nasdaq's top performer of 1995, and had also already received its fair share of negative press. But if, as a rookie rule-breaking investor, you'd somehow missed that and were looking for some documented proof in order to prove the sixth attribute, you got it in *Barron's,* on January 22, 1996.

In his distinctive way, the *Barron's* lead columnist, after reading the disclaimer section ("Risk Factors") of the company's prospectus, suggested that Iomega's stock was grossly overvalued. *(DING!)* That's one of the standard disingenuous sources for a bearish article: When you quote from a disclaimer, you can make *anything* look bad; you can make champagne sound lethal, if you like, now that bottlers are including a warning to those who pull the corks. Anyway, the primary issue here was the columnist's statement that "it is likely that in some future period, the company's operating results will be below expectations of investors, which would likely result in a significant reduction in the average price of its common stock." Scary stuff, I know.

Exactly four months later, the stock had gone from its January 22 close of $3⅝ (post-split) to a close of $27 on May 22, a gain of over 600 percent. Voilà, and vive la sixth attribute.

Then there is America Online, one of the great Rule Breakers of the 1990s, and a company that may today be positioning itself for Rule Maker status. (We shall see; Tom says that it ain't yet so, because of low and inconsistent margins.) You have to work pretty hard to find a good, legitimate company that was more maligned by the press in this decade. Do a LEXIS-NEXIS search of the headlines and you'll find the company disparaged as "America Offline" or "America On Hold" with amazing regularity. Reading the stories, you'd think that no one *ever* managed to sign online with AOL. And, if they did, it was probably on the day that the service went kaput for nineteen hours (which, after it happened, made the front page of the *New York Times* and *Washington Post*). Throw in how "overvalued" the stock was, the accounting "irregularities" (deferring costs of subscriber acquisition), the privacy violations, class-action suits over charges being rounded upward to the nearest minute, the lame Web browser, and the numerous newsgroups with names like alt.aol-sucks, and you have a stock under siege.

Yet, as of this October 1998 writing—with AOL off a bit from its fifty-two-week high—the stock has risen from $1 (accounting for splits) at its 1992 initial public offering to today's closing price of $127. So $1,000 became $127,000, and $10,000 became $1.27 million. Not too bad an investment for a Fool who could keep his eyes closed to the vitriolic short-term press coverage and instead focus patiently on the long-term business prospects. And not only just on those, but simply on the way that the world at large was developing.

Although I numbered myself among AOL customers for a few years before it went public, I did not buy the stock at the initial public offering. Idiot. In fact, I kicked myself for two years as it quadrupled. Finally, I knuckled under in 1994 on the premise that the past doesn't matter—the future's what counts in the public markets. (This is also before I had conceptualized Rule Breakerhood, so I wasn't yet able to see how evidently the stock was a Breaker.)

About that time—in fact, a few months before I bought—*Barron's* did a story featuring AOL prominently. Entitled "Short On Value?" the article appeared in the April 11, 1994 issue. On the byline was newsletter writer Will Lyons, who otherwise did a creditable job with his other three short picks. For AOL, the story's lead stock, Lyons predicted "at least a 35% decline from here" *(DING!)*, based on "new competitors on the horizon, waves of price cutting and future growth rates that are 'iffy.' " The valuation, he maintained, was "grossly [there's that word!] inflated . . . more than 7 times sales and 120 times earnings." He dismissed the notion that AOL might be bought out, suggesting "that it would be far cheaper for a potential acquirer to build a system from scratch," because, as he goes on, "Technologically, it's not difficult to do." Ironically, however, his next line is, "The key to an online service is good marketing." (That, in hindsight, is probably the best advice and insight in the article: AOL went on to market its way into the record books.)

AOL stock closed that day at $3^{13}/$_{16}$.

In considering Lyons's comments, note, if you will, his use of the wrong metrics in drawing his conclusions. Lyons focused on AOL's P/E ratio at the time (which is a favorite measure for rule-breaking investors trying to locate that sixth attribute, since many Rule Breakers lack significant earnings and sport ridiculous-looking P/Es as they emerge), when he should've paid more attention to the growth rate. It's what our "percentages *not* points" decree warns against; Lyons's evaluation of AOL exemplifies a situation in which one number is isolated out of context, while poor analysis of the company's industry and its position within that industry leads to erroneous conclusions. The *Barron's* lead columnist and his intimates, on the other hand, focus relentlessly on a combination of past stock-market performance and current bullish sentiment. Their technical analysis is finely tuned to historical comparisons and takes as an article of faith that bullish investor-sentiment readings are a contrary indicator of real import. Back in 1993 and '94 (as well as today, for that matter), they instead should have been watching the movement of interest rates and paying real attention to what was going on in the economy—particularly the liquidity flowing into the markets from home and from abroad—a constant movement of cash into stocks—during an era featuring some of the most impressive governmental fiscal discipline exhibited this century. But that's what technical analysis will do to you: It's just bad numbers.

(I got a funny note from fellow Fool Scott Hunter recently, who pointed out this from a news story: " 'I do feel the bulk of the near-term gains are probably already in the market, and that's looking both technically and rationally,' said Joseph Barthel, chief investment strategist at Fahnestock & Co." Quipped Scott, "The implication is obvious: technical analysis is not rational!")

Other Financial Sources

Dozens of other sources exist for those seeking out that "grossly overvalued" label applied to their favorite stocks. The advantage to using written sources is that they save you the need to monitor the airwaves in hopes of encountering the sought-after opinion. Using the Internet, you can do text searches for your companies. Or, if you follow your stock on the Motley Fool message boards, you're practically certain to see that fated article, as someone else posts an online link to it. Over time, you will develop your own favorite sources.

Often, you can find all you need in the headline alone. As an Amazon.com shareholder, I felt great as soon as I read "Why Barnes & Noble May Crush Amazon" in the September 29, 1997, issue of *Fortune*. Accompanying the article was a graphic showing a book ("Barnes & Noble Online") falling hugely and swiftly through the air, poised over a tiny computer displaying Amazon's logo. That headline and picture was all it took. *(DING!)* Sure, I could've gone on to read the article, too, where I'd have been treated to analysis that included harping on the wrong numbers (Amazon's most recent quarterly loss of $6.7 million, at a time when the company's emphasis on sales growth was far more important than near-term profitability) and mentions of low barriers to entry (as if almost *anyone* could start up one of these things). In fact, it's pleasing to note that both accusations—lack of profitability and low barrier to entry—were the exact same criticisms leveled at America Online years before.

Anyway, on the day that the *Fortune* article hit the newsstands, Amazon's stock closed at $24¹/₁₆. In less than a year, it would top $140, up almost 500 percent. Even after it got pretty much cut in half a few months later during the market selloff, the shares were still a nice-looking triple dating back to the appearance of that article. And Amazon's sales rate was still ten times that of number-two online competitor Barnes & Noble.

At the bottom of this article on *Fortune*'s Web site, the editors saw fit to link in another article: "Amazon.com Stock Soars After IPO . . . But Can the Good Times Last?"

This one was from even earlier, from back in May '97, shortly after the initial public offering, and it came from *Money*—another great source for "grossly overvalued" opinions. The headline alone is not enough to fulfill old number six, but you better believe that the rule-breaking investor would be on the scent, her nostrils flaring, based on that headline. And, in fact, she needn't have even read down very far to encounter this line: "Clearly, though, there are many reasons to think that Amazon.com is overvalued at Thursday's closing price of $11³/₄ [postsplit]" *(DING!)*. Again, consider from strictly a humorous standpoint that this "overvalued" stock would be worth twelve times that price by the end of the following summer. We bought at $19; I wish we had seen that article.

The examples could run on and on till the cows die (that's long after they come home). Every single Rule Breaker mentioned in this half of the book has had at least one such article written on its behalf. Most have had dozens. Back in the late eighties, Microsoft was "overvalued." In the seventies, it was Wal-Mart's turn to be "grossly" overpriced. And yet each of them went on to make gains of 200 to 600 percent in the following years.

Obviously, this method is not infallible. I mean, maybe at some point all this clucking about high price-to-earning ratios and low barriers to entry will cease, as financial journalists wise up. But I doubt it: Most of those guys are just mouthpieces for the institutional investors they interview, many of whom are either short sellers with significant financial positions, or stodgy investors wed to book value. Plus, writing about how overvalued the latest and greatest growth stock is sells magazines. This is all very much the stuff of convention. And conventional wisdom is the very opposite of Folly and Rule-Breaking.

Now, If You Can't Quite Find the Perfect Proof . . .

The examples discussed thus far were all rather easy to spot, requiring only that one take the time to visit a few obvious places and cast about through the refuse. (And I mean "refuse" strictly literally—only perverse people like me go back and actually read old issues of financial magazines; for most people, if it's even a month old, it *is* refuse.) It really isn't too hard to find your bearish documented proof. After all, if you actually *do* take the time to read back issues of financial magazines, you'll see how frequently the gooroos change their minds—you can almost always catch them on a flip-flop. But however and wherever you do it, once you do find your "grossly overvalued" evidence, make sure you cut it out and pin it up for posterity.

Now, in rare instances, you may have difficulty (for whatever reason) in finding your sought-after proof. And in these instances, the enthusiastic and hungry rule-breaking investor who has confirmed the other five attributes may become frustrated as he scans the headlines day after day, cursing his bad luck in not being able to find *any* influential media source telling him that the stock's overvalued.

Fear not; you can bend the rules a little bit, in *two* ways. One, find a "perma-bear," an author whose dour market opinions are so well known that, for you, they color his otherwise harmless or neutral commentary bearish. That works for me. For instance, if you'd been looking at Cisco and the best you could do was to turn to the lead columnist of *Barron's* writing, as he once did, "A melancholy casualty in point is Cisco Systems, once a certified momentum favorite, which, from peak to bottom, has been neatly cut in half,"* that still suffices. Because there he is, ignoring the business—the crucial, dynamic industry of which Cisco is the leader—and writing the whole thing off as a "certified momentum favorite." *(DING!)*

Perhaps unsurprisingly, many of the journalists who've held such decidedly negative views of computer and Internet stocks were themselves unfamiliar with how to use computers and the Internet! Which leads to the second way in which you can bend the rules: If you can find a journalist who writes skeptically (though without saying "grossly overvalued") of a dynamic growth stock whose business he quite evidently does not understand, that stock is also fair game. I'm talking here not just of the mere misapplication of numbers, but of a blatant or total lack of familiarity with a company's product or industry.

Some people are never going to be able to look at a stock like Amazon.com and see anything but numerous egregious violations of value

* That was in the June 27, 1994, issue. Since then, the stock has traced an almost blip-free upward slope from $5 to $60, a gain of 1,100 percent in the succeeding four years.

investing as taught by Benjamin Graham. That's fine. That's what can keep these stocks a bargain. Furthermore, few to none of the financial magazines will ever come out with a big bullish article about a stock that has recently doubled or even tripled in value on little to no earnings. While it's clear from the examples used here and throughout this book that this is often exactly the sort of article that *should* be written, it simply won't happen. Most editors at these magazines and financial papers would think it irresponsible, bad journalism. Much easier to go with the formulaic stuff like "eWidget.com Is the Home Page of the Moment, But Will It All End Badly?"

That too will help keep these stocks a bargain.

This is all worthy of a brief meditation. Despite the conventional wisdom that it is liberal, the press is in fact essentially conservative. One can see that by observing how it covers business. With its constant skepticism and not infrequent condescension toward upstarts, the press effectively defends the ramparts and cathedrals of the status quo against the incursions of barbaric business invaders, newcomers who are naturally suspect by virtue of their unfamiliarity alone.

It probably doesn't help that—as we pointed out in our chapter on managers—Rule Breaker managers are often youthful and daring, and the companies themselves much the same. It stands to reason, therefore, that journalism's conservative old men will write critically of them. Age has always arrogated to itself wisdom, and treated youth as naïve (those who fail to see any envy in this may ignore it at their own peril). So, again, *of course* the senior elements of the business media talk down these stocks and miss out. This is also yet another factor that can keep these stocks a bargain.

There are many good journalists in the United States, positive people who are aiming to teach their readers about what works in business and investing. But some few others consistently display no such ambition, and it is their work that is so valuable to the rule-breaking investor: Think seriously about going where they won't. For years they have played the critic, ever the critic, which always puts me in mind of one of my favorite quotations from Theodore Roosevelt:

> It is not the critic who counts; not the one who points out how the strong person stumbles, or where the doer of deeds could have done them better. The credit belongs to the person who is actually in the arena, whose face is marred by the dust and sweat and blood; who strives valiantly; who errs, and comes short again and again, because

there is no effort without error and shortcoming; but who does actually strive to do the deeds; who knows the great enthusiasms, the great devotions; who spends himself or herself in a worthy cause; who at the best knows in the end the triumph of high achievement, and who at the worst, if he or she fails, at least fails while daring greatly, so that his or her place shall never be with those cold and timid souls who know neither victory nor defeat.

Now to close. Throughout our first two books, we repeatedly pointed out that you didn't need much more than fifth-grade math to tackle investing and understand the Motley Fool books. It is therefore ironic that in this chapter we have been looking at the misuse of simple numbers, misinterpretations of figures, by our broadcasters, journalists, and pundits, showing how it can happen anywhere—in sports or investing or what have you.

Which leads to two final thoughts.

The first: Investing is beautiful because it affords you a rare opportunity actually to *capitalize* on this tendency to misinterpret numbers. With sports, all one can really do is point something out to one's family or friends, or shout at the TV set. Not very profitable—or healthy, frankly.

And the second thought:

What was so tough about fifth grade?

Chapter 8

Rule Breakers Summary

Thus far, with rough and all-unable pen,
Our bending author hath pursued the story.

—WILLIAM SHAKESPEARE, *HENRY V* (V, ii)

All the elements are in place; the table is set. We have reached the culmination of our section.

Rule Breakers are companies that, without exception, fulfill all six of the criteria we've set forth. Let's bring these requirements all together.

A Rule Breaker *must* be *the top dog and first-mover in an important, emerging industry.*

It *must* possess *sustainable advantage gained through business momentum, patent protection, visionaries, or inept competitors.*

The Rule Breaker's stock will have demonstrated *strong past price appreciation equivalent to relative strength performance of 90 or greater.*

That's a nice testament to its *smart management and good backing.*

And *the stronger its consumer appeal, the better it will attract customers, habituate them, profit off of them, and protect its business.*

Finally, given this confluence of positive factors, you *must* find documented proof that *it is grossly overvalued, according to the financial media.*

Now, reflect for a second not on what the attributes *are*—we've already been doing that, for pages and pages—but on what the attributes *are not*.

Notice how we ignore quarterly earnings reports, Wall Street estimates, brokerage ratings, and the number of runs the Yankees scored last year in night games. Notice how we ignore numbers in general. Instead of any sort of rote commitment to numerical measures, we're asking qualitative questions that force us to familiarize ourselves more deeply with a company, its business, and its industry. That's far more important than whether a company just beat its last consensus earnings estimate by more than two cents, even if Mr. Market doesn't think so in the short term.

Notice also how we ignore valuation criteria altogether. Indeed, the only valuation consideration is that a stock must be called *overvalued* by the media! No ratios, no multiples, nothing pulled off the balance sheet. Why is this? Precisely because true Rule Breakers are nearly impossible to analyze using traditional valuation criteria. Their industries are dynamic and unpredictable, and their leadership in those industries translates into unpredictable growth, as well as a potentially large and influential scope. The best companies will constantly smash all the little boxes into which naysayers will keep trying to fit them. Typical examples of those boxes run the gamut from reductionistic labels like "It's just a bookseller!" (Amazon) to misapplied valuation metrics like price-to-earnings ratios ("It's got a P/E of infinity!").

This all calls to mind an e-mail that I received while writing this chapter. Wrote fellow Fool Dan Amerena:

> I'm relatively new to stockpicking and have read a handful of books (including *The Motley Fool Investment Guide*) on the subject. Most of what I'm getting out of this is how to "conventionally" value a company—look at earnings and earnings growth, look at the balance sheet and the company's financials. Finally, judge whether the stock is currently expensive or cheap. But this method is pointing me away from companies such as Pfizer, At Home, AOL, and others I would call "special situations." These companies don't have very impressive balance sheets, often have negative earnings, but sometimes become big winners (to date, AOL has *yet* to post earnings that amount to a hill of beans, but over the last five years the price has gone from $4 to $100). Using such criteria as the Foolish Ratio would cause me to want to short these stocks more than actually buy them. Now, I know that Warren Buffett probably shies away from the AOLs of the world,

choosing instead to grab Philip Morris or Coke when they get cheap enough. I also know that I would probably do OK in the long run if I did the same. But in the meantime, me and Warren are missing out on a lot of great companies! How on Earth can I spot great stocks that defy "conventional" valuation?

The Rule Breakers are our long answer to that question. But the short answer is that when it comes to Rule Breakers, you should ignore conventional valuation altogether.

What?! *Ignore* conventional valuation?!

Absolutely. Picture an investor who is blind and deaf—utterly insensitive—to everything except for our six Rule Breaker attributes to guide him in making investments. It is my conviction that such a fellow's portfolio will outperform virtually every mutual fund in existence.

Now It's Time to Break Our Own Rules

In the best tradition of rule breaking, I'm going to close the section on Rule Breakers by breaking a whole bunch of rules that have been drummed into readers by previous Motley Fool books and online writings (refer again to Dan Amerena's e-mail). But before the bemused reader asks, "What? Break all of your own rules? It makes no sense!," we must first understand it all in context. To provide that context, I'd like to turn to the game of bridge.

Ever played bridge? Derived from whist, it's an elegant four-hand card game whose every deal gives rise to an auction between two competing partnerships to establish, and then execute, a contract. Learning the rather complicated bidding system used to set the contract poses the biggest initial hurdle for newcomers to the game. Novice players must acquire and master a precise point-based system in order to evaluate their own hand and make necessary inferences about the composition of their partner's hidden hand. The first fifty hours spent with the game will usually be focused on understanding and memorizing the system and bidding rules.

But now obtain an intermediate quiz book on the game, or consult your newspaper's daily bridge column. Many, if not most, of the problems presented in either involve—surprise!—a conscious decision to *break* one of the "rules" of the game's standard bidding system. Doing so is the only way you can win the hand, the only way you can get the problem right. Those condemned to following the letter of the laws they've been taught are doomed to failure in the game of bridge . . . and eternal frustration with the bridge column in the daily paper.

I use this analogy because it explains exactly what's going on when I subvert what we've written in previous Motley Fool books: *In no way do the precepts taught in this chapter and this book obliterate what we've taught elsewhere.* An expert bridge player, after all, does not render a rule meaningless just because he breaks it in a given hand. (Indeed, without its bidding rules, bridge could hardly be played at all.) As the old saying goes, exceptions prove the rules. And Rule Breakers are the exceptions, very rare birds swooping and diving out there over the investment landscape. Unusual stocks call for unusual measures.

Investing in Rule Breakers requires that an experienced practitioner of an art—choosing stocks—consciously break his or her elementary rules in the interest of anticipated benefit. It has always taken an experienced eye to perceive when that benefit exists, and this will always be so. The intent of this book is to increase the number of experienced, capable eyes: We want to bring you into that Foolish intelligentsia by making the process a bit more transparent and easier to understand. Back to bridge: Just as the daily bridge column always provides a solution revealing the full rationale for the breaking of whichever rule, so have we done all book long. And why stop now?

Let's break five Fool rules, pertaining only to these Rule Breakers:

THROW THE NUMBERS OUT

This point was already made earlier this chapter, when we examined the emphasis on the qualitative over the quantitative. With Rule Breakers, we're throwing the numbers out, particularly when it comes to valuation.

Leave it to the market and the pundits to tell everyone what your Rule Breaker should be worth. Let them confuse themselves as they misapply valuation metrics and arrive at incorrect conclusions. From your point of view, whatever level you bought in at, you own one of the best entrepreneurial up-and-comers in America, a company that got there because it was run by people who possessed more smarts and chutzpah than the journalists critiquing it. You have the top dog in a key new industry, and you can bet that even the institutional research being conducted on the company has no real good idea of what its profits and sales will look like beyond two years out. You want to criticize the company's P/E ratio? Gimme a break. Let the lead columnist at *Barron's* do that. Throw the numbers out.

Our next transgression will make throwing the numbers out even easier. . . .

THE EFFICIENT MARKETS THEORY IS *RIGHT*

In earlier books, we've taken some shots at the Efficient Markets Theory. We stand by those, in the context of when that theory is used to conclude that picking individual stocks to beat the market over time is impossible. However, a bad application or excess of that theory does not ruin all of the theory itself.

The fact is, our markets *are* pretty darned "efficient" these days, and with every passing day they're getting more so. In fact, years ago—during the first few weeks after The Motley Fool's online debut—Tom and I jokingly mused that our first marketing campaign should be built around the slogan "The Motley Fool: Making the Markets More Efficient." It was evident even then that the massive amounts of information shared by millions of people over our message boards would fundamentally alter the information wars between Wall Street and Main Street—and an inevitable result would be a more efficient market. (Of course, we didn't expect "millions" of people back then—we were only dreaming. Sixty people showed up on that first day online.)

Well, what does "efficient" mean? In this context, it simply means that the current bid-and-ask quotation for any given stock is "accurate," in the sense that it factors in all known information affecting the stock. As soon as anyone hears anything new that would affect the stock price, he or she writes an article about it, or announces it over the Internet, or trades the stock in order to profit from the news. Each of these reactions, in turn, causes the market's resulting price to incorporate that information as well, keeping the price "accurate" and the market "efficient." Today, thanks in large part to the Internet, the speed with which information hits the wires and becomes part of the collective knowledge—and part of the current stock quote—is indisputably faster than ever before.

I strongly disagreed with this interpretation of the market's behavior several years ago, based simply on my own observations. For example, take my erstwhile investment in The Stephan Company mentioned earlier in the book. At one point in the early nineties, the stock took an inexplicable dive in which it gave up about 25 percent of its total value over a couple of days. I was flabbergasted. The company shortly put out a press release: "The Stephan Company," the thing ran (I'm paraphrasing), "is in no way affiliated with Stepan Co., a chemical manufacturer that had an industrial accident this week." Responding quickly, Stephan stock returned to its previous perch, much to my delight.

Aha! I thought. There you are. So much for your efficient markets, Dr. Malkiel! (Burton Malkiel is the author of *A Random Walk Down Wall Street*, which expounds the efficient-markets theory.)

Similar errors can still occur today. The Internet will never eradicate human error. However, corrections (pun intended) now occur much more quickly, leaving less room for arbitrage. Go back a century and introduce that identical error, and it would've taken twice the time to sort itself out, or longer. You can now see which way things are trending, and why I believe that the efficient-markets theory as I've outlined it so far is right.

To reiterate what the theory implies: The price of any given stock at any given moment is "right." If it weren't right, whoever knew that would quickly correct it by trading as appropriate, taking advantage of the "free money" that briefly becomes available due to a temporary price differential between actuality and rationality (a condition known as arbitrage).

Given this, however "overpriced" or "underpriced" a stock seems to be, *it is, in fact, "fairly priced."* Do you see now how little the valuation work of the pundits matters, as you take those numbers you're reading about your Rule Breaker and throw them out (or pin them up for posterity)? If not, picture the collective intelligence of the market as a huge brain that is constantly—second by second—scratching its own encasement in an effort to come up with a better price for the stock. As soon as any neuron or synapse or whatever it is introduces new information, the brain quickly factors that in and adjusts the price.

That huge brain is nothing more than all of the buyers and sellers in aggregate, working together in a dynamic to arrive at that "right" price.

All of that said, the market is good and efficient at pricing stocks in the short term, but is next to useless much beyond six months out. This is especially true of Rule Breakers, and *it is this nearsightedness that gives rule-breaking investors their advantage.* Dynamic growers look *much* different (often, look much bigger) with every passing six months, relative to most of the sleepier businesses the market is better at pricing. Exploiting this myopia is what we rule-breaking investors are doing.

INVEST LIKE A VENTURE CAPITALIST, NOT A BANKER

Bankers are smart. Who (besides the Vatican) built up the greatest wealth during the Western Renaissance? It wasn't the kings and queens of Europe—it was their bankers. The Medici and Fugger families made a *ton* of money by lending vast sums to kings and queens, who were constantly (over)spending it trying to protect or expand their domains. The crowns were chronically in debt, and would regularly pay off those debts by granting to their bankers full trade and manufacturing rights in particular industries. The Fugger family, for instance, lent the future emperor Maximilian more than 200,000 florins in 1491 in exchange for exclusive rights to the copper and silver mines in Tyrol. While Maximilian would spend those 200,000 florins quickly enough as short-term financing for his wars, the Fuggers instead wound up with a lucrative long-term asset that contributed toward their establishing near-monopolies in Europe on the sale of copper and silver. This way, bankers became the true power brokers of Europe, as the historian Lisa Jardine writes, responsible for "significant alterations in the power balance between princely houses (depending on who could raise the biggest loan)." The Medicis and the Fuggers were smart, and in my opinion make far more interesting historical reading than what most students get in their European history surveys (y'know, like having to study and memorize the otherwise unnoteworthy exploits of King Freddie XXVI of Genoa).

As I say, bankers are smart. They're superb at evaluating risk. They have many numerical measures that they use to do so, then they attempt to minimize it prior to loosing their purse strings. They lend—they do not buy. In a sense, we've been teaching Motley Fool readers to invest like bankers: invest—lend—long term; your dividends and profits are the interest you earn.

Investors in Rule Breakers must discard this mentality. Rather, they must think like venture capitalists. They must feel comfortable occasionally losing ALL their investment—possibly going belly-up three times in a row—in pursuit of the occasional great white whale. Bankers shy away from such prospects, and in sympathy with that, the creditors of liquidated failed businesses are always paid off before the partners.

Venture capitalists buy ownership, and do so more qualitatively. They use their guts to find people with guts, and they buy into them. That's one of the clear themes of my half of the book.

This approach to investing is not for everyone—bankers need not apply. (Sorry, bankers, but I'm just not a big fan. Not that you need *me*, anyway, you rich rapscallion dogs.)

BUY AT THE IPO

This one's simple. We have for years been telling people to stay away from initial public offerings, particularly the proverbial "hot IPO." Our reasoning has been that the few truly good companies that come public usually see their shares in such demand that the price skyrockets, even as the institutions sell out huge blocks of shares on the first day and wait on the sidelines to sell more.

There's some truth to this. However, let's turn things around for a moment. Use hindsight as your counselor. When was a great time to buy just about any of the great long-term stocks that we've discussed in this book? Day One. In retrospect, if you could've had Microsoft on its first day, or Yahoo!, or the Gap, wouldn't you have wanted to? Wouldn't you want to have bought and then just held?

Sure, there's the old investing maxim about how a year after they go public, most IPOs stand at lower prices. But do remember that a minority of them do not: They go higher. And concentrated in that smaller number are some of the great Rule Breakers and eventual Rule Makers that investors will have the opportunity to find in their lifetimes.

If you're an experienced investor who's found a company that appears to exhibit most of the properties of a true Rule Breaker (relative strength won't be available yet), we are countermanding our previous orders. If you find a true Rule Breaker, sure, heck yes, buy at the IPO.

BE A STAR AT COCKTAIL PARTIES

Finally, in the past we have been outspoken critics of the cocktail-party stock tip. How much money is lost year in and year out by idle chatter exchanged over pinot grigio? "Do not listen to such talk!" we have insisted—and, by implication, do not contribute to it.

Toss away that tacit advisory. You see, as a Rule Breaker investor you are now ideally positioned to be a star at cocktail parties. The companies that you follow are *sexy*. It's hard to get anybody terribly interested in you as you explain your shareholdings of General Electric or the merits of Coca-Cola's balance sheet. But in 1994 tell someone that you owned America Online, in 1996 you owned Iomega, or in 1998 you owned Amazon.com and you're making a statement. Depending on your own approach to life, you're saying one of three things:

1. "Go ahead . . . knock this battery off my shoulder. I dare you."
2. "I'm so darned saucy . . . aren't you dying to know more about my opinions on everything?"

or just . . .

3. "I'm a Fool. Let's talk."

A few other things you need to know before you head to the party: You're even better looking than you were before. You're a card. You've got that confident twinkle in your eye. People will flock to you. You're a free spirit. You're someone who's going to make a mark on the world, rather than vice versa. And you don't need alcohol to be hip.

During their tenure as Rule Breakers, your companies enjoy the spotlight's glare. And as a part owner, that spotlight shines on you too.

To sum it all up, let's return to the very phrase that we used to conclude our introduction: *Be the sauce.*

Rule-Breaking Industries

In the future, the search for Rule Breakers will be a search for rule-breaking industries as much as for companies themselves. If you can anticipate what the next big thing will be, you simplify your search process dramatically, because then all you need to do is identify the top dog and first-mover, and begin to apply our other tests from there. Remember: smart management and good backing. Remember: the stronger its consumer appeal, the better. Don't neglect these. But if it otherwise checks out, you've found a Rule Breaker. The point is that at least some of the time you can take an industry-based approach, rather than an individual stock–based one. Here's the distinction: You'll take a stock-based approach when you see an upstart company doing something uncanny in an existing industry. You'll take an industry-based approach when you see a whole new industry being born, and want a mover and shaker in it.

The latter approach begs for a broad-brush list of industries in which one will find future Rule Breakers: biotechnology and genetics, communications, Internet applications and functionalities, commercialization and development of outer space, energy alternatives, computer software and hardware, alternative medicine, retail innovation, and forms of business that may emerge with new social orders and practices. The total list will no doubt be far more exhaustive than this meager collection—yet this short list as it is doesn't look *that* meager—it's probably enough to comprise a lifetime of compelling investments, a few of which will make forward thinkers filthy rich.

When Is a Company No Longer a Rule Breaker?

What brings about the end of Rule Breakerhood? *When's it over?* How can a rule-breaking investor figure out when she is no longer dealing with a true Rule Breaker? And what are the implications for investors?

These are crucial and deep questions. After all, I just advised you, dear reader, to "Invest like a venture capitalist" . . . well, venture capitalists always have exit strategies. From almost the beginning, they develop a plan to sell, and you'll need to consider yours, too.

To Tweeners . . .

 **PART II**

Tweeners

*Marry, I wad full fain heard some question
'tween you tway.*

—WILLIAM SHAKESPEARE,
HENRY V (III, ii)

Chapter 9

The Death Rattle
or the Crown?

Heir to the crown?

—WILLIAM SHAKESPEARE,
HENRY IV, PART 1 (I, III)

There comes a time in every Rule Breaker's life when it ceases to be a Rule Breaker. At that point, it becomes a Tweener: It enters a pupal stage from which it will either emerge as a glorious Rule Maker . . . or will not.

Perhaps there's a better metaphor, from a different science (I've always disliked insects): astronomy. A main-sequence star goes through predictable life cycles as it converts its hydrogen core into helium. Eventually, the star winds up with a hot helium core and expands massively, turning into a red giant. From that point, the star either cools off, becoming a *white dwarf* (this is what our sun will do, in five billion years), or—if it's a more massive star—it converts into a *neutron star*, a million times denser than a white dwarf. If it's even more massive, it can become a *black hole*, the densest entity of all.

Black holes are Rule Makers. They're actually not holes at all, but singularities (points of no volume and infinite mass) so incredibly dense that even light cannot escape their gravitational pull. *This* is the influence of the Rule Maker. (It'll eat you up.) Neutron stars are also-rans; think of them as long-running Tweeners, uninteresting fodder for eventual acquisition. White dwarves, on the other hand, have exhausted their nuclear fuel and cool down irreversibly, undergoing, in succession, white-, yellow-, red-, and brown-dwarf stages, eventually ending up at black dwarf, a cold and lifeless vestige of onetime stellar glory. That, in essence, is the full course of the Tweener death rattle as well.

This chapter looks at the transition that companies endure as they move from Rule Breakers to Tweeners to Rule Makers (or otherwise). The first challenge for an investor is to understand and define when a Rule Breaker is no longer a Rule Breaker. Before we do that, though, let's riff very briefly on the nature of rule-breaking investing as art, for this perspective will help us as we address the question of "When a Tweener?"

Art

By now, I hope it's evident to the reader that investing in Rule Breakers is something of an art. The subjectivity, the lack of numerical precision, and the vision that rule-breaking investing sometimes demands are all suggestive of art, not science. (Science is the Foolish Four Approach, taught in previous Fool books.) Actually, the very act of taking charge of one's own finances and building a portfolio is itself an inherently creative act. So too is the founding of a company. Thus, investing in Rule Breakers—themselves the result of someone else's creative vision—is an expression of creativity.

It's all art.

But "art," such a small word, is fraught with all sorts of implications, so I owe it to you to define what I mean by it. Whole books and philosophies have been writ just to answer that question. I'll try to keep it simple; I don't mind risking oversimplification in this context.

I define art in three ways, all of which work here and shed light on where we're going in our investigation of when Breakers become Tweeners.

The first is the all-inclusive definition included in *Understanding Comics*, a delightful book by Scott McCloud. McCloud asserts that we have three impulses in life: survival, reproduction, and creativity. *Any* actions that fall outside of the first two satisfy the third, and are thus art. Whether it's doodling, hang-gliding, whistling, or picking stocks (assuming that you're not doing so out of sheer survival instinct), *that* is art. It's an extremely inclusive and somewhat low-brow definition, but it provides a useful perspective.

My second definition of art is one that I first encountered in *Memoirs of a Superfluous Man*, by that cranky old journalist Albert Jay Nock. Nock's take on art is as pithy and to the point as McCloud's, but Nock is more restrictive. "Art makes you better," he says. Thus, art isn't just what you do when you're not eating ("surviving") or reproducing. (In fact, eating and reproducing may well fall under Nock's purview of art.) It's the stuff that you do or experience that makes you *better*, whether that's watching Greek tragedy or (to pull a page from McCloud) making cookies for a friend. Conversely, movies that encourage hatred, or architecture that cramps—both of which could be considered art by McCloud's reckoning—are not art in Nock's view.

Now, let's see. The act of making your own decisions about your money has nothing to do with survival or reproduction, and it makes you better in several ways: (1) you gain confidence, (2) you escape dependency, (3) you learn, and (4) you have more fun. People who manage their own money are being creative, and creativity makes them stronger. That's another way of saying that it makes them better, which means that by both the above definitions rule-breaking investing is "art."

But there's still a third perspective I see art from, and it's one step more restrictive. It builds off the other two, and it is my own. Art is not survival or reproduction, it makes you better, *and* it possesses an ambiguity that forces you to think it through. Without putting too fine a point on it, Shakespeare's greatest art (*Hamlet*, for instance) is great because of its ambiguity; you can't ever quite tell whether the ghost is real or not, or whether or not Hamlet actually loses his wits. You are challenged to think it through, to make up your mind by yourself. Likewise, whether a given company exactly fulfills the requirements of being a Rule Breaker or not—and, later, whether the company has progressed to Tweener status or not—these are all things that also involve ambiguity, and they force you to think things through. Force you to be creative. Make you better. Take you away from worrying about survival and reproduction. All of these things.

Now then, that said, we return to tackling the first critical question—namely, when do Breakers tween? (Never in my wildest dreams as a student of English literature did I imagine getting my own book published with a sentence like *that* in it; I'm shaking—whether in awe or for shame, I know not.) You can now understand the reason for our digression into art: the approach we use to determine when a Rule

Breaker becomes a Tweener is, like art, subjective, inexact, intuitive, imprecise. The point that I hope you'll take away is that it can never be otherwise. I'm not going to propose a single, numerical, scientific solution. There *is* no single solution. And the use of a numerical signal, while useful for some companies in certain situations, would clearly not apply to other Rule Breakers in other situations. It's a rule that would fall down before it could ever stand up.

Thus, the curtain rises . . .

Going Tweener: "Legitimate Business Alternative"

Tweener status looms for any Rule Breaker when a "legitimate business alternative" shows up to compete with it. For the first time, the once-upstart company is being challenged directly and impressively by another business with similar pretensions to the throne.

Simply by having its approach mimicked, the Rule Breaker converts from being a Breaker of others' rules into an aspiring Maker of its own. The key word here is "aspiring": at this point, it is truly neither. Those Breaker days of being an outsider, a guerrilla, a marauder—they're gone. The company now has its *own* turf to defend from a competitor who's playing the company's *own* game by rules that were its *own* invention. What was once radical and revolutionary has now instantly been made, in a sense, *conventional*, with a legitimate business alternative. At the same time, though, it lacks the power of a Rule Maker. It is now a Tweener.

For illustrative purposes, Coca-Cola provides a straightforward, general example. Coke was a Rule Breaker of the first order when it converted—all of a sudden—from being a medicinal drink under fire from the government into a "soft drink," a drink one would sip for pleasure. Following that, Coke did not have a legitimate business alternative until Pepsi-Cola showed up and became a national brand. When it did, Coca-Cola passed on to Tweener status. Would it become a Rule Maker or an also-ran? (We know the answer to that one.)

Pepsi's arrival and Coke's transition took a long time, though; others, today especially, take less time. Dell Computer, with its direct-to-consumer sales of computers (via mail-order and the Internet), was a classic Rule Breaker. It changed its industry's rules, rules that had previously been established by Compaq. But when Gateway 2000 (NYSE: GTW) mimicked Dell's model, it made Dell a Tweener. This does not mean, by the way, that Gateway duplicated Dell's model successfully, or that Gateway is positioned to put Dell out of business. Far from it. The point is *not* that a better competitor shows up, but simply that a legitimate business alternative has arisen. (Dell, incidentally, appears well positioned to graduate from Tweener to Rule Maker someday, if it has not already.)

And just as the Internet has sped up the pace of change, Internet-based businesses are rocketing to Tweener status, due to the relative speed and ease of setting up new, competing online sites. Thus, Yahoo! was a pure Rule Breaker only for as long as it took Excite to set up a legitimate business alternative. Like Yahoo!, Excite also now offers a search engine, personalization features, and an advertising-based model. Whether it is better than Yahoo! as a service or an investment is not at issue; neither is its lower relative valuation than Yahoo! (on this point go back to chapter 3, where I document the disparate valuations for the first and second companies in a bunch of different industries). So this doesn't mean Excite is as good a business or an investment as Yahoo!, or that it is "undervalued." What's important is that Excite pushed Yahoo! into the Tweener category when it created something comparable, an acceptable alternative.

Another way to help us decide whether the legitimate-business-alternative dictum has been fulfilled is to imagine what the world would be like if we snapped our fingers and caused the Rule Breaker in question to disappear. Would something else immediately grab most or all of its business? If so, it's a Tweener. If not, it's a Rule Breaker. Were Yahoo! to disappear in the very instant you're reading this sentence, for instance, Excite and some of its other competition would snap up pretty much all of its business. Legitimate business alternatives exist, and customers would not be particularly put out, or feel tragically bereft if it disappeared. By contrast, if you were to do the same with Amazon.com, I don't believe that the same thing would happen. As of this writing, no business is presently offering as convenient and useful an online site with the same wide selection of books, CDs, movies, and software, as Amazon.com. It remains a Breaker.

So, would people drink Pepsi if Coca-Cola disappeared? Sure. I mean, many people (I, for instance) don't like Pepsi very much, but if Coca-Cola had been completely obliterated early on, Pepsi would now be the choice of *all* generations. Legitimate business alternative.

A corollary to this is that one must make sure that the alternative is *real*. A competing company announcing a new product that won't be on the market for months is *not* a legitimate alternative. The alternative must be alive, tangible, well distributed—it must have raised consumer awareness comparable to your existing Breaker. It must be capable of competing on the Breaker's own playing field.

Figuring out whether a company has tweened is not always easy or clear-cut. For instance, has Amgen faced a legitimate business alternative? Amgen began as a Rule Breaker, turning biotechnology discoveries into new treatments. Now, there are certainly many companies conducting biotechnology research, but do these provide legitimate alternatives to Amgen? The answer—because Amgen is a company that depends on two products for virtually all of its revenues—is that you have to look at its products themselves, Epogen and Neupogen. Do these products have legitimate alternatives? (Here's more evidence that you really have to know the industry when you're investing in a Rule Breaker.) If not, Amgen's still a Rule Breaker. Amgen is by far the largest, most dominant company in its industry . . . and yet is it still a Rule Breaker? Well, fragmented industries—industries that are loose conglomerations of hundreds of different players all doing similar things with different goals—often have no Maker.

Here was another toughie: In the mid-nineties, America Online bypassed Prodigy and CompuServe as a consumer-oriented service with one-price-fits-all convenience. It broke rules to bypass those two in the first place, then vanquished them both. Then, the Microsoft Network (MSN) debuted amid a lot of hype and featuring a similar business model to AOL's. But MSN in its original incarnation fizzled, unable to match—by any stretch of the imagination—AOL's growth, scope, and size. Would you have wanted to count that as a legitimate alternative? By 1997, it appeared that there existed *no* legitimate business alternative to AOL. But as Internet popularity and use expanded further, Yahoo! began to look like a legitimate business alternative—your friendly guide to the Internet. Today, most of the things you can do with AOL, you can do as well (some better) with Yahoo! Most, but not all. Fifteen million people still get online with AOL and pay it a monthly fee; none do so for Yahoo! In fact, when Yahoo! tried to sign a deal with MCI to provide Internet-access service as MCI/Yahoo!, the deal failed. Does AOL therefore have a legitimate business alternative? Does the Internet in aggregate (as opposed to any given company) function in this way? Has AOL been a Rule Breaker all along? Or is it instead a

Tweener? (And at what point might AOL qualify for Rule Maker?) These are all complex questions, and are very debatable.

Again, it's art.

You can work on your artistic skills by reading, and perhaps contributing to, the information exchange and debate found on the Motley Fool message boards. They provide great forums to test out your theories about a company and its position within its industry, and with the publication of this book, the message boards will begin to fill not only with the new terms we're using here, like "Rule Breaker" and "Tweener," but also with the concepts that underlie them. Foolish investors will be thinking in new and more complex (and useful) ways about dynamic growth stocks.

You now have the skinny for how we at Fool HQ determine whether and when a company has tweened. Let's now consider the investment implications.

Rule Breaker to Tweener: Investment Implications

Rule Breakers can and often do provide outstanding short-term returns, sometimes even on the order of several hundred percent over periods from six months to a few years. As they slide over into Tweener status, they often maintain appreciating stock prices, though the rate of appreciation will usually slow significantly. In many cases, though, Tweeners suffer significant declines in their share prices. This is why knowing when a company tweens is important.

Why do Tweeners often stumble? Two main reasons: competition and success.

First, the most exciting Rule Breakers earn high premium valuations partly because *they don't have any meaningful competition*. When this condition disappears, so does the premium. To take an example I use frequently (because it's so well known and clear-cut), Amazon.com's business was only a tiny percentage of the bookselling industry, but Amazon earned a multibillion-dollar valuation—larger, in fact, than those of Barnes & Noble (NYSE: BKS) and Borders Group (NYSE: BGP) combined. This occurred for two key reasons: (1) Amazon's e-commerce business model held out the eventual likelihood of higher profit margins than bricks-and-mortar retail, and (2) it had *zero* legitimate business alternatives within that "space." Amazon had by far the best-organized, most active e-commerce site (with many more customer reviews than any other—which are themselves an important draw), and offered unparalleled product selection. These factors, along with a first-mover advantage that could probably never be chased down, resulted in AMZN transacting ten times the online sales of its nearest competitor (Barnes & Noble) by the middle of 1998. No meaningful competition equals high premium valuation.

If and when a competitive true alternative does show up, the market is almost certainly going to temper its enthusiasm about Amazon.com's multiples. Thus, in many cases when a company is perceived to tween, it'll trade down to a lower multiple, maybe for a while, maybe for good. That does *not* mean that it'll be a bad stock, or that it won't continue to put up market-beating numbers in the future. It *does* mean that it'll have a hard time expanding its multiples back to previous, competition-less levels. And the company may often get whacked. But if not, it goes without saying that if the company can manage to vanquish its near-term competition, and/or become a Rule Maker, it should reexpand its multiples and dramatically outperform the market once again. So, the appearance of competition is the first factor that can cause Tweeners to stumble.

The second reason that Tweeners often stumble is simply that break-through success is very difficult to sustain or duplicate. The prosperity of any great stock can create unrealistic expectations that the future will mirror the past. Such expectations can be reflected in the stock price, as happy shareholders get greedy. Further, the institutional pressures—pressures that will brook no exceptions—begin to mount for *ever-higher* quarterly earnings driven by *ever-higher* quarterly estimates. However, as a company matures, its growth rate inevitably slows as increasing size begets increasing inertia. There comes a point, often, where these two competing forces—the escalating expectations of Wall Street and the diminishing growth rate—collide, and the business reality (the diminishing growth rate) generally wins out. The stock is suddenly devalued, often (as we saw in chapter 4) on the order of 40 percent. That might be akin to a shift in the price-to-earnings ratio from 100 to 60, or from 40 to 24; it's the same corresponding shift in the price-to-sales ratio—or whatever valuation measure you favor.

Given that tweening can throw shareholders for a significant loss, we must all ask ourselves whether or not to sell. More-conservative investors may wish to do so, escaping with all or just a portion of the amount they have invested. After all, if a better investment can be found—say, a new Rule Breaker with potential for greater returns—money would be well placed there. If you sell out a portion, you can always keep some money in the Tweener on the chance that it'll continue to crank out strong returns and possibly wind up making rules. And as we Fools continue to favor the buy-and-hold approach—even through Tweener status—this is generally our own approach. Indeed, the prospect of a company rising to become a Rule Maker—and the tax-free returns that will accrue over decades to patient investors in those stocks—is extremely attractive. Buy-and-hold investing, which protects your money from capital-gains taxes and protects your quality of life as well, remains the preferred Foolish approach.

That said, the goal of this book is not to teach investors how to "time" the market, because neither Tom nor I makes any pretension to understanding how to do so. Indeed, we're pretty skeptical that it can be done successfully and consistently. The goal of my half of the book has been to help you identify monster stocks of the sort that we have added to our online portfolio and been successful with, stocks that do so well that they wind up carrying a portfolio on their backs. (We've also discussed the occasional nosedive, because those are very real too.) If aggressive investors read this book, agree with many of the precepts, but wish to pile out of rule-breaking stocks as soon as they depart from rule-breaking status, that's their business. There will certainly be other Rule Breakers out there, and, heck, some Tweeners are in fact going to be dead money or something like it. Perhaps what you'll pay in taxes can be recouped by another winning investment.

So, in the end, one's sell strategy vis-à-vis Rule Breakers should mostly conform to one's existing sell strategy, toleration for risk, and overall approach to life. Remember our definition of art, and its application to this form of investing. What works for one person may not work for another. There are many ways to paint a great picture, many styles. Find your own.

The Last Word on Rule Breakers

The first attribute chapter, "First to a New World," spent some time looking at Christopher Columbus's achievement. In the course of doing more reading into Columbus, I was surprised to learn about his ultimate demise. The man who was the first European to "discover" the New World, the man who from 1493 on had a right to one-tenth of all the gold exported from Hispaniola, the man who navigated the entire Caribbean and missed finding the Pacific route through Panama by a hair's breadth, the celebrated mariner and navigator—Columbus—died a Tweener. Not only that but a Tweener on the way down, doing the death rattle.

Columbus spent his last year or two chasing King Ferdinand around Spain (Isabel had died), hoping for an audience at which he could ask for more credit, a better deal, because he'd been shortchanged. Fourteen years before, he had been the talk of Europe. Now, his bones were moved around and buried (three different times), finally coming to rest in the Dominican Republic.

Columbus died a Tweener. This is instructive. It can happen to anyone, and it can happen to any stock.

A few chapters back, I briefly mentioned Iomega, another great Rule Breaker. The first couple of pages of *The Motley Fool Investment Guide* identified Iomega as a company that was discovered by investors at the dawn of the Internet era. Using a medium that had never existed before, these investors were able to share their experiences as consumers, their expertise as engineers, and their combined efforts as researchers to locate and invest in this Rule Breaker–to-be well before it hit Wall Street's radar. The story was reported everywhere. A lot of people made a ton of money! At its peak, Iomega's stock increased thirty times in value for us, just one year after purchase.

Since that time, which has seen a flurry of splits, Iomega is today an $8 stock. It's lost 80 percent of its value since the heady days of its brief, explosive high. A lot of people lost a lot of money. For our own part, the Rule Breaker Portfolio wound up making only a fraction of what we might have made had we sold out earlier: In April 1997, we sold half our holding for a two-year gain of 650 percent; as of September 1998, we continue to hold the other half at a cost basis of $1.28, marking a still-substantial return on our investment. Iomega's story is so instructive because it shows what can happen to a Rule Breaker that was once trailing clouds of glory. Iomega has been demoralized, its star CEO having quit, its profits dried up (for the moment, anyway), its lawyers having fought numerous lawsuits, and its managers having made an ill-timed stock-split decision—one split too many—partly responsible for the shares today sitting at such a low level. So IOM is off Wall Street's radar once again, but this time with its momentum going the other way. I scratch my head sometimes and try to count on one hand how many other companies I can think of with more than a billion dollars in sales and a stock price at $8. Not many. Then again, I can't think of many other explorers who've discovered a continent and yet died, if not in complete anonymity and penury, in at least something not terribly far from them.

I see a lot of Columbus in Iomega, and a lot of Iomega in Columbus, though with at least one difference: I'm not sure that Iomega, to this day, has ever tweened. Columbus tweened. By the year 1500, you could have hired any number of legitimate alternatives to explore the Seven Seas for you. But Iomega, which revolutionized computer data-storage technology with its Zip drive, still hasn't had any company come along and provide a legitimate alternative to that benchmark product. (That's really why the Rule Breaker Portfolio is still holding a position in the stock.) Instead, it just made a host of poor decisions, failed to get new products to market in a timely manner, and lost the market's confidence. But it *didn't* tween.

This closing note therefore serves as a cautionary tale to warn that in some cases, some companies never do become Tweeners, though that's not necessarily good. While they remain Rule Breakers, they may still do the death rattle. Columbus did not die in shame, but his fame was but a pale shadow of what it had been only a few years before. Iomega has not died, but otherwise it too is today but a pale shadow of its former self.

If we had to do it over again, we would of course have sold everything at the very top. Flawlessly. Every investor's fantasy. In practice, things rarely, if ever, play out that way. That's why each individual investor is best served to stick with his or her basic approach to portfolio management and selling strategy—whatever it is—and to stay diversified.

We have no regrets (even with our worst investments—and we have our fair share!). No regrets on Iomega. In fact, even after seeing the stock drop 80 percent, we've still handily beaten the market with that one!

I scratch my head and try to count on one hand how many stocks I could ever make *that* claim about . . .

. . . And Tom Takes the Stage

Phew! I've been waiting for 150 pages.

My task in this brief section on Tweeners is both impossible and dangerously subversive. I'm expected to spell out in just a few paragraphs what developments take a company from adolescent success into rule-making authority. I am to reveal the entire second half of this book in an instant.

Unfortunately for you, I can't. But I will still try.

Rule Makers are companies that can afford investors excellent returns at moderated risk. The classification can be boiled down to five intuitive principles, and these may be tended to like a checklist as you investigate investment possibilities. That's because—logistics being what they are—the larger a company becomes, the more predictable and the more trackable is its progress. As the business evolves from breaking all the rules toward making all the rules, it gradually transforms from being a mostly artistic venture with many nonmonetary ideals into an operation driven by scientific artistry and the methodical pursuit of profit. While starting up a rule-breaking business, or investing in one, is a creative act, managing or owning a Rule *Maker* is a calculating act, more plodding than passionate.

You can locate companies engaged in that journey from passion to poise just by typing a random stock ticker into your online quote service or playing blind man's bluff with the newspaper stock pages. Thousands of public companies at this very hour are attempting this passage from art to science, attempting to climb out of the sometimes mawkishly sentimental leadership of a Breaker into the cold-eyed, big-sticked, worldwide management of a Maker. They are doing everything in their power to rise up from the underground, to rule from a castle, to metamorphose into being *the* overdog from a former life as underdog.

Underdogs are erratic and captivating, like the political efforts of Ross Perot; overdogs are methodical and cool, like the cinematic pose of Clint Eastwood. The second half of this book is going to suggest that you cheer loudly for the underdogs in life, and definitely throw a few Rule Breakers into your house of investments. But it's also going to counsel that you invest heavily, and, if need be, quietly, in the overdogs—perhaps neglecting to confess as much to your friends (particularly if they program software for a direct competitor of Microsoft). I believe that the bulwark of your investment portfolio should be fashioned around those companies successfully navigating the latter stages of tweening and beginning the early phase of true market dominance.

Following are five attributes that I look for in companies trading the Tweener ballcap for a crown.

Five Signs That Your Tweener Is Beginning to Make Its Own Rules

The first and most easily discerned characteristic of a company ascending the throne is its *manifestation of a tireless commitment to either absorbing or dismantling every one of the pretenders to that same royal station*. For a business to begin making its markets' Rules, it has to embrace the simple idea that there will be only one leader per category, one monarch per monarchy. Accordingly, the competition that pressed your company out of its rule-breaking status into Tweenerville must now be fitted out as a prince or a pauper. The ascending Maker must present its competition with a stark choice—cooperate or be demolished.

The second and most important quality of the Maker of Rules is classic turtle *patience*. As a company ages, it must begin administering to its markets rather than trying to roil them. Winning the industry's pole position is not an immediate thing. It's an endurance game, and for any company it involves external as well as internal threats to triumph and prosperity. Any number of second-rate companies can win a single pitched battle with the quick delivery of one hot product and the brief attention of the madding crowd. But making rules in a market demands sustainable growth—an earnings line that traces a steady northerly path, from one decade to the next. That advancement relies upon corporate patience, not corporate greed; it depends on the self-control to let other jockeys win the first fifty yards of the steeplechase and bask in the glory that it brings, in exchange for a commanding lead and rule-making authority down the stretch.

To measure this progress, investors need to assume their own rule-making stance, and to divert their attention from the income statement to the balance sheet. They must, over time, come to understand the manufacturing guts of a business that reaches out to the whole world, and they need to follow its product and capital management. Because, as we'll see in the later stages of this book, even as a company's sales, earnings, and popularity are on the rise, its balance sheet can disintegrate into rubble, a grim reminder of what may really have never been.

The investor scrutinizing the balance sheet (not as tedious as it sounds) will gain some clear alternatives to simply guessing at the futures of his Tweeners. He'll know to sell Christopher Columbus as it becomes apparent that, while once a rule-breaking maritime genius, Columbus now is just a drunken, vainglorious lout, an ambitious pillager whose pride alienated his men and who is now doomed to die without honor. We'll leave the rest of that tale to the historians. In stock-market investing, the balance sheet is our historian.

The third and most quantifiable attribute of Rule Makers is the *consistent improvement of their financial outlook*. I'll be concentrating on consumer-product companies in this book, and I'll be searching in them for easily measured mathematical successes: high gross and net margins, a growing base of addicted customers, the elimination of debt and the expansion of cash reserves, and, above all this, the ability to finance its own efficient operations without interference from Wall Street bankers.

There is one other numeric I look for, the simplest and cleanest of all: I don't consider for Rule Maker status any operation with less than $1 billion in annual sales (set inflation at 3.5 percent per year to calculate the baseline in future years). Size is certainly not the only measurement of success; if it were, we'd all still be shopping at Woolworth. But size is definitely one key element of rule-making success. Any company with less than $1 billion in sales is either a Breaker or a Tweener.

The fourth and most lucrative aspect of any business shedding Tweenerhood and beginning to make the rules in the consumer space is an *absolute commitment to convenience*. In one mass market after another, royal business authority has been fashioned out of accessibility. Picture a Gap store on every corner in every major urban area in the world. Imagine Microsoft products being preloaded onto every computer device sold across the globe. Open your eyes again and look for Coca-Cola cursive an arm's length away—it's there from Poland to Pittsburgh, from Westminster to the West Indies. Convenience rules the consumer landscape. There's a gas station at every highway exit, a telephone in your pocket, dinner in the microwave, and 457 channels' worth of entertainment in the living room. There's even a database for locating and ordering books (and a lot of other stuff) available via the personal computer in your den—and they'll deliver it all to your doorstep. Convenience wins.

The fifth, final, and most colorful truth about a company coming into law-writing authority in its industry is that it's *probably involved in a nasty, loud lawsuit brought by one or many of its smaller competitors.* You've invested in a *potential* Rule Maker if Pepsi is suing it for buying out one of its bottlers in Latin America, if content providers are suing it for removing them from its online service, if the designers of computer peripheral products are suing it for emulating and embedding their products.

When the competition cries mercy from behind squadrons of lawyers, the media may embrace them, but the markets do the opposite. Well-promoted, vocal lawsuits from smaller competitors, coupled with the four elements above, indicate that you've found an organization that is at least moving toward the throne. To know for certain, you'll have to keep reading.

Over the next few chapters, I'll present a filter that will help you to latch on to the greatest American businesses and to discard the mediocre ones. The filter is framed as a ranking system, with the highest score being a 60 and the lowest score being a big, fat goose egg. First we'll measure out the strength of the company's brandname. We'll follow that along with an assessment of its financial standing. Then we'll track the forward operational momentum of the business. And our final stop will take us through an appraisal of how powerfully monopolistic the business is in its industry.

As you travel through the chapters, you'll notice that you're on a gradual ascent in the ranking system from lesser to greater values. In the opening section on brands, companies can score up to one point for excellence in marketing. Then by the final chapter, as we measure the degree to which companies dominate their markets, each mark of success can earn them up to four points. Again, the end result of the overall review is a system that will crown as Rule Makers those companies scoring between fifty and sixty points overall. In my estimation, they will make for consistent market beaters for years, or decades, to come. At the same time, this study will show companies that score less than thirty points for who they are—*phony kings on a naked walk through the public marketplace.*

 **PART III**

Rule Makers

The game's afoot!

—WILLIAM SHAKESPEARE,
HENRY V (III, i)

Chapter 10

Rule Makers Introduction: Authority

But tell the Dauphin I will keep my state,
Be like a king, and show my sail of greatness
When I do rouse me in my throne of France.

—WILLIAM SHAKESPEARE, *HENRY V* (I, ii)

The aim of the second half of this book is simple: to replace the heavy costs that Wall Street has been dishing out in the form of mutual-fund fees and brokerage commissions. The Rule Maker solution buys stalwart businesses and relies only on simple numerics, common-sense logic, and your patience. It's an investment model that is as convenient as a mutual fund, but which offers above-average performance and lower expense. Remember that, today, mutual funds are cutting into shareholder value with stiff annual expenses. The investor with $100,000 in a stock fund that charges the average 1.7 percent annual expense ratio will pay out $1,700 in fees this year. If, instead, that investor could find ten to fifteen great companies with authority in their industry, buy them through a discount broker, and hold them for a decade, he could spend as little as $25 per year and likely outperform the fund manager.

The strategy about which you'll read over the next hundred or so pages is designed to do just that—to lay a foundation of five to ten superior companies which can be bought and held in ten-year increments. Details of the approach have been outlined in our online site at www.fool.com, on *The Motley Fool Radio Show,* and in our weekly syndicated newspaper column—but this is the first full feature of it. The idea behind it was born on a lazy, hot evening in the summer of 1995, with crickets whirring and the night air still. During a Baltimore Orioles broadcast, I spotted one of those handsome television advertisements from a big financial firm extolling its mutual funds. The ad not-so-subtly implied that *you,* the individual, neither have the *time* nor the *discipline* nor the *ability* to learn anything about your investments, let alone manage them. Something about that particular commercial at that particular hour struck me and my dinner guests as particularly absurd. Rolling by on the screen were the staples of any financial pitch—the open field before a sun-sparkling lake, a father holding his infant in the air, kids flying by on a swing set, while the voice-over from an old Wise man spoke of the great complexity of investing, saying, in essence, "You can't do this. So don't try."

Two years later, in the midst of a consumer revolution against financial dependence on the big banks (and their 19 percent credit cards and front-loaded mutual funds), the vice chairman of Merrill Lynch was still spouting the same party line as that television ad, claiming that "the do-it-yourself model of investing, centered on Internet trading, should be regarded as a serious threat to Americans' financial lives." For some people, with no schooling in the subject, such promotional messages from the Wise ring true. Naturally. Because for some in America, the words "finance" and "investing" bear profoundly negative associations, calling to mind things like a 788-page reference book. Or the crooked-fingered, sallow town miser. Or the arrogant corporate executive's son back in high school. Or utterly foreign and intimidating terminology, like "industrial development bonds," "gas futures contracts," "odd lots," "equipment trust certificates," and "Fibonacci." Or maybe the word "investing" conjures up visions of wild-eyed traders shouting ticker symbols in a rave, rather than two bare feet on the edge of a fishing boat and the tranquil ownership of businesses. Or maybe the word "finance" is a token reminder of professors scrawling remote equations on the chalk board yonder . . .

$$X = shareholder's\ equity \sim /37tLY \times beta< R2^{nd+17p}\{fx - X7\% \sim \sim /2\} > +1$$

. . . and the red marks subsequently slashed across a midyear exam.

For many people, "finance" and "investing" are wearisome words, their subjects just so inconvenient and obscure that common fools accept the promotional pitch from Wall Street with a sense of deliverance. "Just to be done with it all!" their inner voice shouts as they sign the financial consultant's contract. They've accepted the notion that the slog of money management really is best administered to by the dark suit before them opening a case of colorful charts and graphs. They've accepted that this suit can be trusted to perform its fiduciary obligation, to allocate the assets, sidestep the recessions, participate in all the bounties of the next bull market, and shepherd them to some satisfactory retirement—or, hell, *just not lose the money.* And they believe that maybe that suit will even transport them into the painted-screen advertisement of the lake, the swing set, the warm embrace, the glistening daylight, and that sleepy retirement.

But before you go on believing it for another second, give up a few pages of your time. Pause for a moment in front of the suit before signing away your savings, and skim the remainder of this book. Because . . .

Billy Joel Shouldn't Have Gone Bankrupt

The commingling of someone's boredom, ignorance, and careless faith can quickly enough turn the color black into red and their savings into someone else's. Evidence of that appears even on the television screen. Though maddeningly absurd, it's a fact that some of our nation's celebrities, our greatest successes, with tens of millions of dollars to their names, have nevertheless wound up in or near bankruptcy. The *why* of it is simple: They naïvely signed away the rights to their financial affairs.

Billy Joel, a guy who by 1990 had sold 75 million albums; Burt Reynolds, among the world's top box-office draws in the 1980s; Kareem Abdul-Jabbar, possessor of a handful of NBA Championship rings; Kim Basinger; Toni Braxton; Kenny Rogers; Hammer; Willie Nelson; the list goes on. All were dropped in or near bankruptcy court after accumulating a fortune from their success. Whether it was the result of a lack of time, boredom with the subject, or natural financial illiteracy, their careless faith in managers who proved unscrupulous sealed their fates. All told, though, it was a lack of simple money education, not fate, that consigned them to some measure of despair and financial ruin.

It never had to happen, and it probably hasn't happened to you. But, to lesser extents, it has happened to all of us, and for much the same basic reasons—early indifference to the subject of money drives one into credit-card debt at exorbitant interest rates, or into the foolish purchase of a new automobile at the sticker price, or into any of the expensively priced and underperforming mutual funds in a 401(k) plan, or into the arms of a full-service broker richly (and oddly) compensated more for *trading* accounts than for creating value. Lacking education, and with no clear alternative but to believe financial advertisements, we fall prey to the paring away of our assets by an industry that *so far* has had little exposure to public accountability in America.

Take some account of the financial-management industry's performance, though, and you too might not be able to control laughter during their next thirty-second TV spot. For while they preach security, they practice expense. And even as they ooze confidence, they demonstrate underperformance. In the 1990s, more than 90 percent of all managed stock funds in America have been worse than just average, yet still charged annual fees eight times greater than the cost of the all-market index fund that guarantees the average.

The people's ignorance has so far painted many radiant dreams on Wall Street—a world, it seemed, of escalating plenty.

Nightmare on Wall Street

Into this maze of conflict, where Wall Street toys with America's ignorance with a series of images but cannot reassure the trained financial mind with even a single statistic, it is time to introduce a methodical and effective approach to common-stock investing for people of every age. It is time for an investment approach that, aiming for maximal long-term profit, will recognize that the public markets offer actual businesses to own, not stock prices to trade. Such approach will be a strategy for common-stock ownership that needn't take more than ten hours a year, can be established and held for a decade, carries total fees of less than $150, no matter the size of the account, and is underpinned by logical and mathematical accuracy.

That Wall Street nightmare, an approach bearing the name Rule Maker, is revealed over the next five chapters. It will haunt well-heeled financial consultants (a.k.a. the brokers) in their sleep, because it demonstrates that assembling a stock portfolio is no more difficult, no more time consuming, and no riskier than buying from the universe of managed mutual funds. Quite the opposite, in fact: Our thesis for this entire book is that individuals will, on average, spend less time worrying about money, have greater control over their destiny, and substantially improve their results if they choose common stock over mutual funds.

My case for that thesis actually began back in July 1995 at The Motley Fool Online. A few days after viewing the aforementioned advertisement, I decided to present to our online community a portfolio of ten companies, each of which I proposed to hold for ten years without transaction. My aims were simple: to dramatically curtail commission fees, defer capital-gains taxes, and substantially reduce the time costs of investing, all while beating the market. And what I proposed was not the work of Harry Houdini or a Flying Wallenda, nor was it a design from Stephen Hawking's masterful mind or the work of Nobel-laureate economists. Rather, it came from a Fool armed with a junior high school math book, framing a plan that will demand patience, not labor.

It all seemed reasonable to me, even if Wall Street thought it insane that any individual would undertake the task of directing his or her own financial affairs.

Of Freight Trains and Bulldozers

I called it the Simpleton Portfolio. I designed it to include primarily larger—and thus stabler—growth businesses. In terms of pricing volatility, the portfolio would act more like a mutual fund than like the Rule Breakers described by David in the first half of this book. It would rely on companies that generated superior returns by plodding along, eating through opportunities and grinding out profit, rather in the manner of a bulldozer or a steamroller, or perhaps a freight train. It seemed the perfect mix, offering a consistent above-average performance, without requiring that an investor follow the portfolio each day or cough up heavy investment fees in the form of commissions and capital-gains taxes. We published the selections in Fooldom's haunt in July 1995.

As of this writing, the portfolio just moved into the fourth of its ten years. These returns do not include cash dividends, though they do include the 25 percent drop in the markets' value since mid-July 1998.

THE SIMPLETON PORTFOLIO

Company	Purchase Price (July 1995)	Present Price (Sept. 1998)	Total Gain
Dell Computer	$ 2.68	$ 63.25	+2,260%
America Online	$13.28	$112.38	+746%
Cisco Systems	$12.28	$ 64.88	+428%
Gap	$11.59	$ 54.00	+366%
Microsoft	$23.91	$110.13	+361%
Sun Microsystems	$12.69	$ 51.00	+302%
Intel	$34.13	$ 85.25	+150%
Texas Instruments	$35.47	$ 54.13	+53%
Hewlett-Packard	$39.94	$ 53.38	+34%
Silicon Graphics	$43.25	$ 10.00	–77%
Simpleton Returns	n/a	n/a	+462.3%
S&P 500	556	1,043	+87.6%

As you peruse the numbers, consider the following:

1. Without a single trade in thirty-eight months, the Simpleton Portfolio is 374 percent ahead of the S&P 500. During that time, over 90 percent of all managed mutual funds have lost ground against the S&P 500, while still charging substantial fees. The Motley Fool Online has been free.

2. The entire portfolio required a flat up-front discount-brokerage fee of $100 at $10 per trade online; the size of each position didn't matter. Beyond that charge, the account now exacts none of the annual "management" expenses that every mutual fund imposes.

3. None of these investments has incurred capital-gains taxes beyond its insubstantial quarterly dividend outlays. And given that the average stock fund carries a turnover ratio in excess of 70 percent, this portfolio's sidestepping of the taxes incurred by mutual funds today is not trivial. Yes, the average stock fund trades seven out of ten positions each year, delivering substantial capital-gains taxes to its investors.

4. The portfolio has one dog: Silicon Graphics, which is down 77 percent. I can now understand a few of the mistakes made in selecting it—not following the balance sheet closely enough, not fully under-

standing the business—but a few losers come with the territory. If every dog has its day, then I'm comfortable believing that every portfolio should have its dog (which then has its day). Thankfully, the poor returns of one investment haven't much slowed the superior performance of the rest of the portfolio.

5. The Simpleton Portfolio fundamentally subverts the basic messages sent to individual investors every week by the mainstream financial media as well as the investment banks on Wall Street ("You can't do this. So, don't try it"). They would have you put this book down now and not look back. Yet this portfolio's performance will suggest that individuals *can* manage their own money, that money management needn't take more than a few hours a year (if that), that fees can and should be held to an absolute minimum, and that the average professional money manager is *extremely overrated.*

Two years after we established the Simpleton Portfolio, we began fielding requests for a collection of ten more companies to hold for the long-term, a portfolio with less exposure to technology (nine of the ten holdings in the Simpleton Portfolio could loosely be classified as technology ventures). It sounded like a reasonable idea, so I set up the Money-Heavy Portfolio, so named because these businesses boasted powerful operating models that steeped their corporate headquarters in cash. (I also thought that the name sounded like a heroine from a James Bond movie, and that carried with it a host of good associations.) The Money-Heavy stocks were published in May 1997. A year and a half later, the portfolio is winning, and winning with style (like the good guys in Bond). It is substantially outperforming the S&P 500's return. Here's an accounting of the ten businesses, with their performances through September 1998.

As you sort through the numbers, consider the following:

1. The Money-Heavy Portfolio is leading the S&P 500 by 29.8 percent.
2. Arf! Like the Simpleton Portfolio, these ten stocks have also been saddled with one real dog—Oxford Health (read: "Stealth") Plans, the HMO that missed estimates and showed *(gasp!)* unexpected accounting irregularities. The stock has fallen 83 percent, underperforming even the 77 percent loss by Silicon Graphics in the Simpleton Portfolio. But, as in the Simpleton group, this dog has not deterred the account from delivering market-beating returns.

3. This collection of companies is much more balanced than its predecessor. It features corporations in the technology, health, consumer nondurable, and even biotechnology industries. While diversification is overrated in the financial world, it's still comforting to know that a number of great businesses may be found in a number of different industries.

THE MONEY-HEAVY PORTFOLIO

Company	Purchase Price (May 1997)	Present Price (Sept. 1998)	Total Gain
Dell Computer	$18.40	$ 63.25	+244%
Gap	$22.83	$ 54.00	+137%
Cisco Systems	$29.67	$ 64.88	+119%
Microsoft	$62.94	$110.13	+75%
Johnson & Johnson	$58.88	$ 78.75	+34%
Pioneer Hi-Bred	$23.21	$ 30.50	+31%
Intel	$81.88	$ 85.25	+4%
Gillette	$43.88	$ 39.25	–11%
Coca-Cola	$67.50	$ 56.75	–16%
Oxford Health	$65.13	$ 10.75	–83%
Portfolio Returns	n/a	n/a	+53.4%
S&P 500	844	1,043	+23.6%

THE RULE-MAKER REAL-MONEY PORTFOLIO

With the Simpleton and Money-Heavy Portfolios chugging along, in early February 1998 we decided to launch a real-money portfolio for our members, enabling them to track the ongoing performance of the account, providing them with careful reviews of each company's quarterly earnings report, and offering a daily strategic report.

Launched and managed with the help of three Fools—Rob Landley, Al Levit, and Phil Weiss (a computer programmer, a pension-fund actuary, and a tax accountant, respectively)—the Rule Maker Portfolio has also been outperforming the market. Through late November 1998, the portfolio has risen 25.5 percent versus S&P 500 gains of 18.5 percent.

Our best-performing investments have been Microsoft, Pfizer, Cisco Systems, and Schering Plough; we've been wounded slightly in the short term by the heavy international exposure of American Express and Coca-Cola. All told, this portfolio is following the lead of its predecessors, moving toward doubling the market's average return. Then doubling it again.

Right about now, though, you may be asking yourself, "Will I ever learn how the investments above were selected? Is this guy ever going to stop rolling out portfolios of stock and gloating over their performance? Isn't The Motley Fool's stated mission to teach folks how to use a rod and tackle rather than just throwing them fish?"

Yep.

How Were These Businesses Selected?

Over the next few chapters of this book, you will read a good deal about consumer companies with whose names you are surely familiar, about companies with enormous cash reserves, about businesses that exhibit superior operational management, and about ones with five to ten years of public-market success. In effect, you'll be reading about the juggernauts of American business, led by aggressive marketing and sales teams, and financed by minds shrewd enough to know when to punch down the accelerator and when to tap the brakes. These leading businesses all carry more than $1 billion in sales over the past year—as stated earlier, I don't consider any corporation with less than $1 billion in sales as qualifying for rule-making status.

To be sure, the Rule Maker style of business is very different than that of the Breakers, which you've lately mastered. The Rule Breakers' success and their charm rely on our natural fascination with revolutions—the amazing new product, the captivating speaker on C-Span, grassroots thinking, and the power that human frustration has to force a solution. The Motley Fool loves the excitement of Rule Breakers. But let's remember that when the wrong Rule Breaker slides its head under a Tweener cap, it's not long before it also sets its neck into a noose, bound for the dreaded death rattle.

That's because not every revolution leads to royal authority.

Netscape's didn't. Apple didn't obliterate IBM and Microsoft and

Intel in the 1980s, despite its aim of owning the whole industry. Boston Market didn't knock down McDonald's. TCBY Yogurt didn't end ice cream. And Iomega hasn't changed personal computing forever. There is plenty of roadkill along the course from Rule Breakerhood to Tweenerville. The public markets feature grassroot efforts aplenty that, for want of organizational discipline, patience, or the interest of the people, collided with destiny and broke apart like a glass bowl dropped on a cement floor.

Rule Breakers offer companies that could very easily explode into nothing more than wizard's dust; Rule Makers offer the opposite: businesses promising steady, predictable growth, and the march of their services and merchandise across the globe. And while Rule Breakers hold out the potential for mind-rattlingly positive returns, too many of them in a single portfolio can demand hours of your attention, as well as delivering to you the occasional antacid supper. Conversely, Rule Makers—with billions of dollars in sales and a more gradual rate of advancement—take little effort and are all relatively painless to follow. I personally favor a portfolio of businesses that, at the outset, is composed of 10 to 20 percent Rule Breakers and 80 to 90 percent Rule Makers, after which I'd sail my catamaran (if I owned one) toward the evening sunset.

So what companies are these Rule Makers? They're the consumer giants, the market stalwarts, the companies that write the rules in industries that serve millions, or billions, of buyers each month.

Cash Is King

What distinguishes one billion-dollar company from another? How do you know whether to buy Microsoft or Motorola, Gap or Gucci?

That's the primary aim of our investigation.

The rule-making strategy favors those companies that manufacture products and provide services bought every day or every week by tens of millions of people the world over. That means that I will not be focusing on the powerhouse distributors—like Wal-Mart and Home Depot—that have amassed fortunes for their shareholders by collecting all the merchandise known to man, stacking it in warehouses on the edge of town, and offering it to consumers at discount prices. Those are the Merchant Kings, and while the business model is a very attractive one, it's not the focus of this book. (It is, however, the subject of ongoing discussion at www.fool.com/rulemaker.)

Instead, I'll concentrate here entirely on rule-making manufacturers—on companies that make and sell a few convenience products into heavy demand. This repeated sale of the same profitable item, over and over, results in the methodical accumulation of a mother lode of cash on a Rule Maker's balance sheet. Finding these consumer giants, with sustainable operating models, is a piece of cake: The work is highly intuitive and rooted in common sense. Buying and holding them for market-beating returns, at virtually no cost, is just as easy.

Conclusion

Before charging headlong into the second half of our book, I want to reiterate—with no legal intent—that we don't recommend that you blindly follow any investment approach, whether it be ours or anyone's but your own. Through the remainder of this book, I'll make some controversial points; I may already have said a few things with which you disagree. That's the beauty of any market: civil disagreement and open discussion. Those are the foundations of our online service. Accordingly, my strongest request is that you bring your critical faculties and thinking Fool's cap into the pages that lie ahead.

Also, as you make your way through these chapters, you're going to run across a fair number of calculations, a steady flow of measurements (few demanding more than the harrowing task of adding two round numbers together, or multiplying one by the other). As discussed earlier, the search for Rule Breakers is a very creative act, while scouring for Rule Makers is a calculative one. To find the very best Breakers of Rules, investors have to intuit the accelerated development of smaller businesses. To find the best Makers of Rules, investors have to assess the gradual development of large corporations. Given that these businesses have billions of dollars in sales, broad product lines, and a stream of consumer brands, trying to measure their performance item by item is impossible. Instead, we'll use financial statements to guide us to the treasure. I suggest that you take notes along the way. But if you don't want to build this model on the pad of paper next to you, then go to www.fool.com, where we offer a Foolish spreadsheet that allows you to store and track dozens of businesses based on this approach.

Finally(!), you'll note that throughout the next few chapters, the words "I" and "we" are interchanged. I've done this because the investigation of Rule Makers would never have been possible without the community contributions at www.fool.com. Everyone, from my three fellow portfolio managers—Rob Landley, Al Levit, and Phil Weiss—to thousands of investors in their dens across the world, have helped to fashion a spectacular strategy for common-stock investing, one that I believe is profoundly simple and rewarding. It anticipated the problems at Nike, it forecast the fall of Callaway Golf, it presaged the collapse of Nine West Group, and it has foreseen the successes of companies like Microsoft, Schering Plough, Dell, and Cisco Systems—and all only because it employs the plainest sort of logic. It is simply the best way that I know of to evaluate stalwart companies. And it's a model that would not exist without the online participation of professors, doctors, lawyers, accountants, mathematicians, historians, and a collection of extremely Foolish money managers, who would love to see their industry reformed.

The work that follows is my thanks to all of them.

Chapter 11

The Names
We Call Our Own

Where is the number of our English dead?
Edward the Duke of York, the Earl of Suffolk,
Sir Richard Ketly, Davy Gam, esquire;
None else of name.

—WILLIAM SHAKESPEARE, *HENRY V* (IV, viii)

An old friend—just mentioning his or her name brings a smile to your face. Is there anything more relaxing than hunching over coffee, curling up in a hammock, or sitting out in the woods with an old friend? And I'm not talking about the summer-camp girlfriend from Sweden, either. I'm referring to those tried-and-true friends like your worn-out, faded-and-torn blue jeans, a good novel, and a cup of coffee or a glass of lemonade. For many, that means Gap jeans, a Tom Clancy thriller, and Starbucks brew or Minute Maid lemonade. Just the four of you, splayed out in a hammock.

And this is where our search for great businesses to invest in for the next ten, thirty, and fifty years begins. The first of our four Rule Maker qualities is an old schoolyard currency—popularity. Those who want to set the rules down on the playground, in their community, or as a business across the world, first *have to be known*. The people need a name, something to hold on to, an old friend. For a growing business, though, the route out of obscurity into recognition is a brambly, uphill jaunt. It must move one town at a time, with one foot in front of the other, one year after another—an excruciating voyage. The truest Rule Makers make that journey into brand recognition, and they, as well as their shareholders, are duly rewarded for it.

For evidence of the value that popularity bestows on a manufacturer, avert your eyes from the corporate world and gaze instead on Hollywood, the most magical brand-making machine on earth. Over time, a name like Clint Eastwood became synonymous with Western heroism; Audrey Hepburn, grace; and Humphrey Bogart, masterful cynicism—they are but a few of this century's Rule Makers in film. Leave Hollywood and tune into the wireless, where Ray Charles, Bob Dylan, Frank Sinatra, and Ella Fitzgerald have helped to write the musical rules this century. Or turn to sports, and watch Tiger Woods with a driver from the rough, Larry Bird hitting a fadeaway jumper, Chris Evert at the baseline, Pelé brushing off defenders in stops and starts down the soccer field. When you heard their *names* called, you could expect excellence to follow.

Hunting down the great businesses to invest in is often as simple as identifying the obvious greats by category. In this section on rule-making business, we'll go in search of the names that we naturally associate with success. We'll pursue the drivers of mass popularity, we'll embrace enduring excellence, and we'll toss out the passing fancy. After all, our culture creates and forgets countless names, like so many faces floating by on Park Avenue, pages torn from an old calendar, overnight sensations gone before the hangover. Living in America means witnessing the winking-out of an endless succession of stars, as each one-trick pony gives way to another.

Who among us will remember Beanie Babies in a decade? I think I spotted a Cabbage Patch Kid with its head chewed off under a Dumpster in Spooner, Wisconsin. I guess it wasn't a collector's item after all. And what happened to those BABY ON BOARD signs? When's the last time you swallowed a goldfish, or danced the macarena? I grew up with girls wearing Luv's Baby Soft perfume and Bonne Bell lip gloss, but haven't heard of those products since. And, lo, though I walk from one street corner to the next, eager for their familiar faces, I still can't find the intersection where the New Kids on the Block hang out.

Faddish celebrities, gimmicks, hedge funds, lottery stubs, the rush for instant cash—we aren't going to waste our time or your money looking for the one-week or single-season Rule Maker. Our Foolish manner of investing is too much defined by the sleepy principle of compounded growth for us to place short-term bets on junk certificates. The mathematical principle of compounding proves that $10,000 today growing at 13 percent per year will be worth $11,300 next year. Nothing special. But at that rate, in ten years the investment will be valued at $34,000. And in thirty years, it will have expanded to $391,000, at which point the following year of 13 percent growth will generate $50,000 more.

Wealth isn't gathered overnight, unless you're Rip Van Winkle. It's a long process—like an avalanche that begins from a single drop of water that loosens one shard of ice, which then loosens three more, and so on until one day the entire mountainside comes undone. And while your clearest route to financial security, as an individual, family, or community, is through our nation's stock market, should you bring hubris and slathering short-term greed to it, the market will eventually clap your head and throttle your heart. Because while stock investing is a game of logic, that is only half the story—the other half is a pure waiting game. Over thirty years, stocks can turn *any* patient pauper into a prince, but over thirty days, it can send impatient princes, in frayed cloth, to the poorhouse.

Let the tale of the *(ahem)* Long-Term Capital Management Hedge Fund serve as your guide. With $4.1 billion in assets marshaled by the top traders on Wall Street and two Nobel-laureate business professors, *and* underwritten by Merrill Lynch, this fund was an absolute shoe-in for success. But after leveraged bets on the short-term direction of interest rates in Europe, loans into Russia, and bond arbitrage, the fund had disintegrated by late September 1998, having lost more than 90 percent of its value. The *(ahem)* pros at the—*err*—*Short-Term and It'll Be Mismanaged Capital Hedge Fund* had set up computer models to race after hourly profit, which can be likened to a dog chasing flies up a railroad track.

The *New York Times* reported that the fund used its $2.2 billion equity to borrow $125 billion in securities, which were then leveraged into derivatives for a total market exposure of $1.25 trillion. Take a step back for perspective and you'll see that, in fact, all that those experts were doing was using other people's money to play keno. After a hot streak in the first couple rounds, they picked a few wrong numbers and, in less than sixty days, were annihilated. It was greed that forced them into a sorry reliance on a consortium of banks and the direction of the Federal Reserve to bail them out. As far as I can tell, though, you—a mere tiny Fool—don't have the luxury of a federally conducted bailout of bad investments in your discount brokerage account. But you won't need it, if you can remember that in investments, *long-term is the only term.*

The Everlasting Gobstopper

Not ironically, the same qualities that lead to wealth-building for investors in the public markets—reason and patience—are also what steer corporations into a position of name-brand leadership. In fact, most of the characteristics of masterful investing neatly double as those of superior business management. The everlasting-gobstopper investor builds a treasure house for her family using the labors of everlasting-gobstopper managers at everlasting-gobstopper companies. In every facet of the game, time and compounding are allies, not enemies. And while speedy growth is admirable, the brightest minds know that it should never come at the expense of stamina.

After all, let's remember that the stock market hosts a race run on an oval track that has no finish line. Thousands of competing public companies scamper round and round and round the ring—endlessly. This unusual style of racing actually rewards earnings acceleration in the upcoming quarter less than it does sustainable growth over the next decade. I don't need to ask you what happens to the registered businesses that are one-tank race cars, flakes, or flashes in an Indonesian gold pan.

But since I did, what *does* happen to them?

Often enough, the temporary wonder bursts out of the starting gate hollering for attention, and the traders jump aboard as it sprints down the track a few lengths before collapsing in a sweaty, distressed heap. Profitably placing your money on this sort of "company" demands the expertise of knowing just when its race will end, when the fervor will peter out, when its harrowing descent into failure will begin. If you stake your fortunes on the public runners that stir excitement but which you already *know* can't make every turn, bad timing of either the purchase or the sale will be your dismal end. The public markets are a race without a finish line, an unbroken string of turns and straightaways, and those who treat it otherwise may find that the fortunes of two o'clock are ruination by three (which, with the right connections, might be a federal bailout by four).

I don't recommend it to anyone.

Sadder still for traders of the latest hot whatever stock is that even when they appear to profit from timing their bets in our public markets, their approach racks up transaction costs and short-term capital-gains taxes that eat away at any real investment returns. On average, though, their investment style loses out even before accounting for such costs. Between 1991 and 1996, University of California–Davis Business School professors Brad Barber and Terrance Odean investigated the performance of actively traded portfolios among sixty thousand households. And they found that a passive approach to investing in the overall market via an index fund delivered returns 70 percent better *per year* than actively traded portfolios. Extend those separate rates of annual return out for decades, and it's like standing princes next to paupers. Off an initial investment of $10,000, we're talking about a difference measured in hundreds of thousands of dollars in the decades ahead.

The Davis professors concluded their report simply: "Frequent trading is hazardous to your wealth."

A NEW COMMITMENT TO TECHNICAL ANALYSIS

As much as the Barber-Odean report counseled *investors*, it could have been a consulting document for businesses, too—businesses like K-Tel International—for whom frequent trading, if only for a short period, can be a godsend. In late April 1998, the company announced its intent to sell its various and sundry greatest-hits albums and videos directly to you and me over the World Wide Web. In a microwave instant, K-Tel became an "Internet company." The trading volumes of its stock boomed and its shares ran from $3 to $40, an increase eerily resembling the early charge of the Long-Term Capital Management Hedge Fund. During the accelerated 1,230 percent rocket ride, K-Tel briefly experienced the phenomenal value of even a momentary brand, as traders played along and the markets shook for a few weeks with the retailer's name.

How much value did branding create for K-Tel? Well, during its dramatic springtime run, the value of the company ran from $20 million to $300 million. Then, before you could say "K-Tel executives are going to try to get out at the top!," company executives bailed on the majority of their positions at prices ranging from $30 to $35 per stub (count them among the *initiated*). All told, the insiders flipped out of 2.4 million shares, over 30 percent of the entire company, in the month of May alone. And they took away over $60 million in personal profits from their sales. True, it's not a shining illustration of why we have public markets. (Weren't they built to finance companies toward expansion, not executives toward their favorite Hawaiian island?) But let this example serve as a reminder that getting your name out there can be extremely valuable: The company that sells bottled air with a brand name and a great story can make a handful of corporate insiders (and a few investment bankers) an absolute fortune.

Lest you're considering *investing* in these sorts of businesses, though, I encourage you to return to the historical graph of K-Tel's stock performance today and as it is projected into the years ahead. Here's a look at its twelve-month stock performance, covering August 1997 to August 1998.

This graph displays what I affectionately call the Branding Bird-Flip. In addition to being my favorite form of technical analysis, it's also a highly proprietary theory (in fact, if you use this information by name in any forum whatsoever, you owe us a dime). Gaze at that graph and behold management extending its right middle finger to shareholders in May 1998. On the right of the chart, the pinky and ring finger are down, to the left, the thumb has tucked the index finger snugly into the palm. Down the center, the middle finger is raised, encapsulating management's primary message to long-term shareholders. I apologize for the vulgarism, but isn't it far more offensive to suffer the investment consequences of betting on a low-grade, self-promotional management team?

Here are a few more Branding Bird-Flip charts, from companies ded-

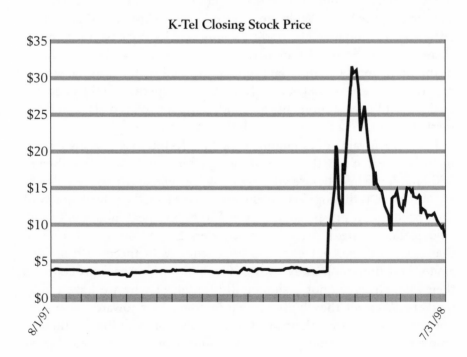

K-Tel Closing Stock Price

Ion Laser Technology Stock Price

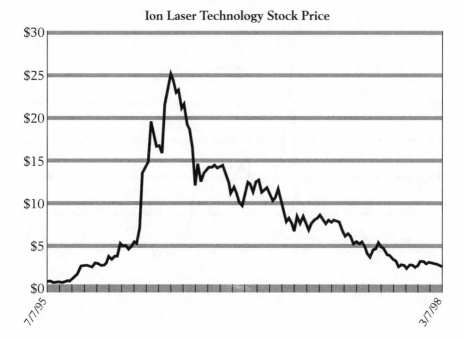

icated to winning in the short-term for executives and paper traders, to the abuse of their long-term shareholders.

A rising stock valuation, you see, does not always represent a rise in actual value. When the primary product to sell is stock, not service, executives turn their shares into South Pacific villas moments before the "business" they once owned takes on water, flails for a moment, then sinks heavily to the ocean floor.

Clearly, those are the companies we'll be trying to avoid in our quest for the brand-name builders that provide extraordinary gains for shareholders, when held for at least five years. As we search for these popular names that zing from border to border, we'll hold out for companies that can also sustain their momentum for a long time. That's because if a business is to reward you by ruling its industry—whether it be chocolate cookies or bicycle pumps, software tools or lightbulbs—yes, it has to start by getting its name out there. But it also has to keep its name out there.

Over a four-week period, the buzz over K-Tel drove the company's valuation thirteen times higher and $170 million richer than it had been at the beginning. Junk companies that make a name for themselves can send their shares skyward like this, sparking the little manias that reward the precious few. Whether our public markets should en-

Ancor Communications Stock Price

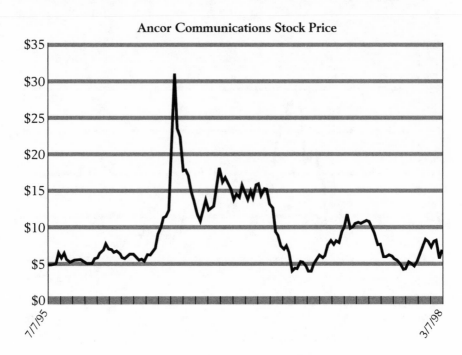

International Automated Systems Stock Price

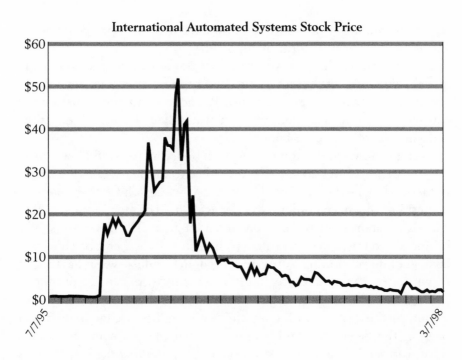

able this nonsense trading is a subject for another time and another book. For now, it's enough to know that companies that get their name out there derive substantial benefits.

Investors, though, need much more than just this: A name is only the first step on the road to Rule Maker status.

Are They Creating the Love?

The name is out. Now, the second challenge is to build off the early success and generate recognition with some staying power. How many businesses create the proverbial sizzle but lack ample proverbial steak? Far too many. They leave you, the share owner, holding a half-eaten hot dog, a tearstained hanky, and a bag of tax-deductible ticket stubs. If a business wants to survive and use the public marketplace for its proper purpose, by rewarding shareholders for many years, it has to get beyond faddishness. Like Johnson & Johnson selling Band-Aids, like Ocean Spray and its cranberry juice, a company has to leverage its brand to create sustainable love among the public.

Love is a strange quality to introduce into the world of business, with its harsh buzzing of cellular phones and its shouting matches over legal contracts. But to prosper for decades, it's critical for a public business to create and retain the love among a broadening base of customers. Which isn't easy.

Just ask Philip Morris, probably the greatest food business in the world's history, whose name has been held in the highest opprobrium, owing to the company's sale of tobacco to minors around the world. As a result, this historically superior stock has trailed the market over the past two years, hobbled by investors fleeing the enormous legal exposure it may carry and small groups of consumers boycotting the company's food products. The Philip Morris brand is certainly salvageable, but it'll take radical change inside that business to catapult its products, which include Altoids, Jell-O, Oscar Mayer, and Maxwell House coffee, to their maximum potentials. In our world of quick cuts and channel surfing, companies must earn and sustain their customers' respect and affection; they have to hold the love. And now, with networked computers through which people can talk in large groups spanning the globe, consumer companies must have and hold the love all the way down their product line, throughout their enterprise. Which, after all, is more valuable? The safety and satisfaction of a growing but small customer base, or the gradual disillusionment of a very large, but eroding, customer base. Your answer will tell you something about why Philip Morris, despite some great people and excellent financial management, has been underperforming.

Or ask Johnson & Johnson about fostering the love. For a century, the company had worked masterfully with a wide range of consumer products, yet it literally faced bankruptcy in 1982 when its Tylenol pills were being laced with cyanide. In a classic public-relations case study, rather than put its customers at risk, Johnson & Johnson pulled all of its Tylenol off the shelves while it developed safety tops. Johnson & Johnson chose safety over sales, the long-term defense of its business over the short-term churning of profit. And that has made all the difference.

Similarly, ask Nike, which began to regain *the love* only after upping its minimum working age to eighteen overseas. Ask the New York Jets, derided by fans and in the cellar of the AFC East until they hired Bill Parcells. Ask members of Aerosmith, who had to clean up their lives before they could restore the love, and are now selling more albums than ever before. Just ask America Online, which was rapidly losing the love until it dramatically improved network connections for its more than ten million subscribers.

Fostering and protecting "the love" is an extraordinary challenge for every leading business. Wal-Mart, even as it was attracting millions of new customers, was being picketed aggressively in small towns across the nation, mostly by the boutique stores it was ravaging. For the discount retailer to simultaneously promote their customers' benefit while deflecting public complaints from their competitors was a monumental task. But it wasn't even half as difficult as trying to reignite the name after it fizzled out, the task that faced Johnson & Johnson, Nike, and America Online. Pulling this off as a growing multinational corporation, given that such a business must also eat through its competition to survive, is nearly impossible. Yet the best companies endure, skating around the dark holes in the ice. They make it through the endless series of false starts and work stoppages and disappointed clients by relentlessly reengineering their businesses back to the people's choice. They win back public enthusiasm through service, corporate loyalty, and a steady spate of small innovations.

WAVE GOOD-BYE TO THE GREAT CORPORATE OZ

Being of service to society is the corporate aim. Our nation's best businesses have *the love*. Now, over a cup of Starbucks coffee, the anticommercial types will tell you that all corporations are the engines of exploitation and should be ignored on moral grounds. To respond, just point to their coffee. Every child, man, and woman in America benefits from a slew of corporate services every day. And rooting against the climbing popularity of democratic commercialism around the world is like trying to turn out the moon or push back a summer breeze. But that doesn't mean that, as mere common Fools, we can't have an effect on corporations by witholding the love from companies that disappoint; our consumption patterns act as a voting mechanism. Plus, very simply, corporations survive only as services to the people. If one person, and then another, and then five million more, then twice that, find the products or practices of a business to be repugnant, said business will change or it will die. As our platform for mass communications broadens, the businesses that talk down to customers rather than listening up—that dictate rather than taking notes—risk extinction. Investors, take note.

The twenty-first century is going to ring in new dangers for mass-market corporations that jeopardize the enthusiasm of their customers. The networked computer is already beginning to restore the connection between millions of individuals and the institutions (political, academic, medical, commercial, and so forth) designed to serve them. In the decades before the Internet explosion, that bond had been weakening. Institutions were growing overlarge for their britches. The giant-screen image of the Great Corporate Oz shouted commandments at the people ("You *will* wait at least four days for your regional Bell technician to fix our faulty line!"; "You *will* pay up even when your cable service goes down for a week!"), while the corporate man behind the curtain madly worked the profit levers. The individual was getting tinier, a lonely little schmo lost in a skyscraper maze or sitting on a customer service 800 line for an hour without response—or worse. Personalized services and any real connections between the individual customer and the corporation were waning.

The Rule Makers of today—and of the future—are aware of how unsatisfactory such a situation is and actually want to subvert it. They *want* to be scrutinized by the public. They know that their brands are the crown jewels of the operation, and, furthermore, that consumer love is the critical value driver. And they know that to maintain that affection in today's open forums, they'll have to treat their subjects like royalty, draping them in purple and following them from room to room, tunefully addressing them as "Your Majesty." Rule Makers know that gaining and holding that love is crucial, whether they're providing the convenience of dry cleaning delivered to your doorstep, trying to offer all the possibilities afforded by worldwide e-mail, or just making the hot chocolate consumed in a Minnesota snowstorm on Super Bowl Sunday. (Will the Vikings ever get back to it and win one?)

The powerhouse businesses of the future are developing a service-and-technology model in which standout customer relations can propel an enterprise into a lifetime of success, or poor service can drop it into a cold oblivion. The business that wants to make the rules in its industry will quickly learn that it has to have a name, then that it has to establish the love among a broadening base of customers.

And then one more thing.

Has It Become *the* Name?

Being known and being loved, sadly, are not enough on their own to crown a company king. The real leaders have to become *the world's default setting* in their industry or product sector—the leader in the market; the industry's representative to the world. The Ali of boxing, as it were. The Frost of poetry . . . the Doritos of chips . . . the Kleenex of Kleenex.

Let's try some word association:

Soda? Coca-Cola.
A television set? Sony.
Money? Fool.com(?) *(we wish!)*
Chewing gum? Wrigley.

You can't hope to survive for even a year as a consumer business if you haven't pressed palms and built a name for yourself. Then, to sustain that, you'll need to attract the love. But to nail down Rule Maker status, to convert the business model into a long-term earnings groove, you have to stake out a home in the collective unconscious—you've got to gradually and inevitably become *the name* in the category. Chocolate must continue finding its way back to Hershey's. Humor needs to land on *Seinfeld*. Heroism? Harrison Ford. Sleep when ailing? Nyquil. Long-distance services? AT&T. And bottled water? Evian.

It takes time and effort to become that default. Harrison Ford has now starred in six of the world's top thirty box-office films, but he had to struggle, fighting his way up through bit parts in *Ironside, Gunsmoke,* and *The Virginian*, then leaving the industry altogether to become a carpenter. It wasn't until he turned thirty-five years old, after an unremarkable return to acting, that he landed the role of Han Solo in *Star Wars*. A layman's understanding of how a guy like Harrison Ford then plowed ahead to capture leading roles in 20 percent of the world's most successful films is priceless for an investor. But for now, let's keep digging out the names that make the rules. Here's another round of the word-association brand game:

Ketchup? Heinz.
A diamond ring? Tiffany.
Online retailing? Amazon.com.
The national newspaper? *USA Today*.
Stomach pain? PepcidAC.

The patience, perseverance, and integrity required to create powerful brand associations have helped products like these and their companies create nearly unthinkable amounts of wealth for their share owners. The five companies in the last list—Amazon.com, Heinz, Tiffany, Gannett (*USA Today*), and Merck (PepcidAC)—have produced over $200 billion in wealth. I'd hazard the guess that their products are not only familiar to all of the readers of this book but that they also represent for readers the defining brand in their given categories.

I consider the following unsophisticated finding to be one of the three or four most noteworthy principles of investing. For generations, *wealth has been built out of what we all know*. It rarely comes from the unknown diamond miner in Zaire or the nameless distributor in China, or from any company that ever traded below $5 per share. For individual investors, on average, wealth certainly wasn't accumulated from the proprietary information on Wall Street, from buyout rumors, special deals, hot IPOs, or the cold-called stock tips from a commissioned salesman (*err*, financial consultant. Err, broker. Sigh, they keep changing the name!). Wealth for investors came from companies that we'd all heard of, companies with increasingly ubiquitous products or services and a long-term commitment to expansion of those products and services. For investors, it wasn't magic; it didn't take a Ph.D.—it was right in front of us. And it will always be.

We should also remember that the most satisfied shareholders of these five consumer companies weren't looking to triple their money in a fortnight; they've held or plan to hold their shares for many, many years. They understand the basic principle of compound interest. The greatest investors of this century, large and small, have accumulated financial security for generations by searching out name-brand familiarity and consumer demand, and then exercising turtle patience.

Now, one more round of association. You can decide whether to keep playing or not on your own.

Coffee? Starbucks.
Horror? Stephen King.
Software? Microsoft.
Snow skiing? Aspen.
The latest news? CNN.
Macaroni and cheese? Kraft.
  (In Canada, they actually call mac and cheese a "Kraft dinner.")

Let's restate it again: Like the great leaders in any field, a business has to build its name over time, then inspire the love of the people, and finally become *the* name in the industry before it can make the rules.

HERCULES COULDN'T SNARE POP ROCKS FROM THE GATES OF HELL

That battle to establish the automatic brand is an enormous undertaking, one that requires backbreaking expenses and Herculean efforts. (How many of Hercules' twelve labors can you name? I'll get you started with two: slaughtering the Hydra and snaring Cerberus from the gates of Hell.)

An automatic brand gets built only through trademark law, copy editing, deal making, creative genius, product development, manufacturing equipment, a lot of failure, product redesigns, multimedia marketing, more mistakes, mass distribution, human resource management, and supernatural perseverance. Every one of today's automatic brands has endured this process and much more: scorn from the mass media, petty lawsuits, initial losses, and stiff competition. Becoming a rule-making brand takes enormous investments of time, energy, and capital (not to mention a good dose of ego).

To remind myself that thousands of businesses are engaged in just this battle, I flipped on the television set for one hour (research purposes only, you understand) and scanned channels for advertisements. I watched, amazed, as commercials with top-quality production rolled past, offered by everyone from drug makers to discount brokers, travel services to dog-food mixers, pain relievers to automobile manufacturers. All of these advertisers were pushing their names out to the public. Turn on your television—it's a name-brand brawl out there. Hundreds of millions of dollars are spent building and defending names on television each month.

Given the major-league spending on and the potentially enormous rewards of a global brand name, we'd be idiots if we didn't try to figure out how exactly the best ones got made. As we do, let's keep in mind some pretenders to the throne that Hercules could not save from the Gates of Hell—K-Tel, Gloria Vanderbilt jeans, Arthur Treacher's Fish and Chips, Pop Rocks candy, Atari game systems, Tang, People's Express airlines, and others. Each of these flourished briefly, only to dissolve into sprays of dust blown off the major stock exchanges. Poof. There are plenty of branded companies trading on our stock exchanges today. But which are the good ones, the ones that will endure, and how do we spot them?

The Demi Moore Sizzle

If it now seems obvious that businesses that sell all the way through to the consumer and aspire to Rule Maker status should immediately embark on ambitious, worldwide promotional plans, stop. Stop right there. The expense of it all can be too terrific to stomach. And the rule-making brands of today will meanwhile shell out billions of dollars over the next ten years defending and extending their consumer names in numerous markets. It's estimated that in its seventy-nine-year history, for instance, Coca-Cola has spent more than $80 billion promoting its beverages, most of that money going to its primary three brands, Coke, Diet Coke, and Sprite. That's an overwhelming bet on branding.

In fact, the investments in brand development and advertising that drive names into the collective unconscious can eat right through a company's revenue base in the early years, and continue to gobble substantial portions as the business matures. Promotional expenses also represent a stiff opportunity cost, since they draw capital away from investments into the development of new products. And when mass-market branding fails, the morale at corporate headquarters can deteriorate: grumblings are heard at company meetings—"Why waste more money promoting when we should be *improving* our products!?" Sales volumes slacken; key employees take to the hills. The investing community vanishes, and shareholder value slants. Next thing you know, the *Routine for Roman Penny Stock Newsletter* (the angel of death) is recommending the shares. And the final stop? Tall grass, a wooden box, carved stone, rose petals, and a minister. It's over.

Submitted as evidence, consider Planet Hollywood's stock graph since its IPO:

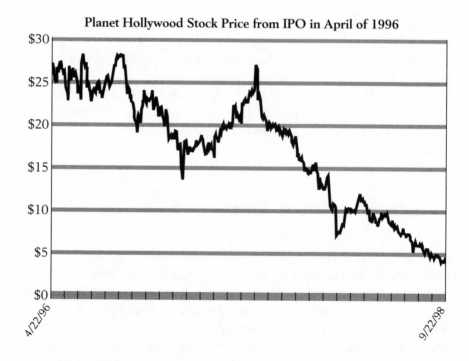

Planet Hollywood Stock Price from IPO in April of 1996

Promoting what will last but a short time, pursuing an ephemeral product line, stamping your name on a passing breeze can create wonderful upward momentum on a stock graph, but it ultimately leads to a prolonged descent as the whirring market machine rattles it, then stalls it, then it goes dark. *Tilt.* Game over.

HOLD, PLEASE

But now here's where the flip flops, the zag zigs, and the momentum shifts in this section. Because the reverse of heavy promotion—the absence of promotion—is deadlier than a cap and noose. Without promotion, a consumer business fills up with water—*glug, glug*—forthwith. An excess of attention to product development, reviews, and perfection in mass-market consumer industries can bring business to a grinding halt. Over time, it's become clear that in a broadening number of product categories, the general population prefers to get their stuff *now* at a lower price rather than to wait for absolute perfection at greater expense. The markets demand convenience and a brand.

I can make that point by intentionally going on and on in this sentence, holding you up from getting to the good stuff in the remaining hundred-some-odd pages of this book—pages that might bring your family untold sums of wealth in the decades to come, if only you could get to them, and didn't have to deal with this run-on sentence, much like standing in line—or sitting on a waiting list—for a product you wanted so much but whose delay has brought such frustration this past week, or even just today, or even for the past hour, or sometimes all it takes is a minute to annoy you, and—

Hold, please!

(Insert Musak here.)

Yes.

OK, sir.

OK, begin again.

Oops. Hold, please!

(Insert Musak again.)

That's enough to prove that our world's demand for immediacy, for convenience, is growing by the hour. It's as if we're putting the entire planet into a microwave, setting it on high, and walking around anxiously during the one-minute interval, whispering, "Let's go, let's go, let's go . . ."

If this sounds just dismal—human beings taut with anticipation and quality gone out the window, sacrificed for convenience—hey, perhaps it should. But this mass-market business model is what consumers demand. And the corporations who have listened have prospered.

The single most important quality of the superior consumer franchise is its ability to get stuff to us *today*. The Internet, for example, will blow away every other broadcast medium in existence, once it's as easy to access as one *(Where's the remote?)*, two *(Click! It's on)*, and three *(I want this channel)*.

Increased convenience and lower prices are prevailing over boutique-shop quality at every turn, whether we're talking about giant super-stores stamping out independent bookstores, Microsoft crushing small shops of software developers, or Wal-Mart driving locally owned businesses into bankruptcy. When it comes to commercial products and services, consumers want around-the-corner convenience or fast delivery—preferably both—far more than they want perfection.

Given that, you might expect that we'll be searching for the convenience brands as we go hunting Rule Makers. If so, you're right. Gone are the days when selection or high-end perfection or prestige drove mass markets. (In fact, it's doubtful that they ever did.) Instead, the battle is to promote total inclusivity, worldwide ubiquity, around-the-corner immediacy, and limited, though sufficient, selection. Naturally, in that game, new-product development plays second fiddle while promotion takes center stage.

Consider this. The epitome of a doomed commercial effort is a manufacturing floor full of cuckoo-clock makers, toiling over dials and springs and hundreds of new models, with no aggressive marketing department to champion their works. Now, what's the exact opposite of that? How does branding work exactly? What does Coca-Cola really get for its $80 billion investment? The answer was made clearer to the world back at the dawn of the twentieth century, in the offices of a Dr. Ivan Petrovich Pavlov.

The Craving and the Name

Dr. Pavlov was the first scientist to systematically study learned behavior in animals. Among other things, Pavlov examined secretions in animals, and his most renowned work measured a dog's salivation at the sight of food. His work proved that in front of a slice of beef, his dog

Mackie drooled. (Actually, I'm certain that Pavlov's dog was *not* named Mackie. That's our sister's name, and, unfortunately for her, she has yet to finish one of our investment books.) Of greater interest, Pavlov then began coupling other stimuli with his delivery of the food to the dogs. Each time that he laid the meat in front of the dogs, he rang a bell. Then, after a while, he stopped offering meat but kept ringing the bell. And what he found was that, with enough prior reinforcement, the dogs would actually salivate at the clanging of the bell. They had learned that its ringing *meant* food.

Ding!

Drool.

Mass-market branding is designed to stimulate just that sort of physical craving, not always as powerful as cuts of beef to a hungry dog, but sometimes more so. In commerce, by reinforcing a craving and associating it with a name, consumer franchises begin to actually dictate behavior. As that behavior turns into habit, and as that habit entrenches with age, lo and behold, a Rule Maker has created permanently recurring streams of revenue. The bell rings and the buyers line up, just as they always have, and the cash registers jingle—almost as if choreographed. "One, two, three! One, two, three! One, two, three!"

Ding!

For a company to embed itself in our unconscious, for it to generate thoughtless, repeat purchases of its products ("Honey, can you grab two bags of *Doritos* for the party?"), its promotions have to remind us of the ubiquity and the uniqueness of those products. They have to foster a need for their specific product while isolating their name as the ringing-bell stimulus. They need to persuade and reinforce the idea that there is no comparable offering in their category—no product that is so useful nor so easy to reach. For, as turn-of-the-century Harvard psychologist William James explained it, "Humans would prefer to conserve higher mental processes for more demanding tasks."

When it comes to staple convenience products, we don't really want to think much, nor should we have to. How many of us want to debate the merits of Fig Newtons over the number-two brand of chewy-fruit cookies? Just grab the Newtons. And when we need to shave? Gillette. Looking for sports coverage? ESPN. Searching for casual clothes? The Gap. The list goes on. Entire businesses, worth billions of dollars, have been built by designing a few low-cost convenience products, automating the manufacturing process, and then investing heavily to promote the spirit and ubiquity of the brand.

THE DYNASTY OF *DYNASTY*

Think about Aaron Spelling, whose magic programming formula of swimming pools, youthful energy, conflict, gossip, and beachwear has raked in hundreds of millions of dollars. It's a brand; it's a default setting for television viewers. Say what you will about *Melrose Place, Beverly Hills 90210,* and *Dynasty,* but the consistent associations that people make between them and mating rituals have created a mood that draws millions of viewers each week, and has earned hundreds of millions in advertising revenue over the lives of those products. That's enough to allow Spelling and his team to pay down their losers (see *Central Park West*) with plenty of cash to spare.

Let's go even cheesier. Rupert Murdoch and his company's mix-'n'-match formula of scandal, speed, danger, and destruction has pulled in hundreds of millions for News Corp. as well. Go ahead and mock Fox's *Cops, America's Most Wanted, World's Scariest Police Chases, When Animals Attack,* and *A Current Affair,* but their popularity more than funds Murdoch's losers (I can't think of any failures to this model—gasp!).

When the images and brands established by both Spelling and Murdoch take shape on the television screen, Pavlov's bell starts ringing. Viewers plan their evenings around the television schedule, a shining example of brands and experiences reinforcing each other.

That behavior permeates all mass-market products. Chances are that you've heard many or all of the following statements over the past decade. Each expresses a need, communicated through a name:

"Honey, where's my Right Guard?"
"I'll have a Coke."
"Where do you keep the Q-Tips?"
"Sarah wants Domino's for dinner."
"Ah-choo! Kleenex?"
"I'll have two Hershey bars and a bag of Doritos."

Take Coca-Cola as the greatest twentieth-century exemplar of a name-brand franchise—the company spends billions of dollars to market a can of soda that's remained essentially the same for decades. As we calculated in *The Motley Fool Investment Workbook,* a $4,000 investment in the Coca-Cola Company at its 1919 initial public offering is worth over $650 million today. Mark down Hershey's as the same sort of company—it also spends billions to promote a changeless slice of chocolate in brown wrapping paper. Starbucks is headed that way, too, as they cut back on the time and capital costs of searching for new merchandise to offer, and concentrate on driving their existing products into new markets and into position as a habitual buy.

At well-run consumer businesses, products not attracting a widening audience of repeat buyers are quickly eliminated, while the products that do curry the public's favor never change but instead benefit from increased investments in their promotion. Gradually, the whole enterprise focuses its operational machine on the repeated promotions of a few products sold through to hundreds of millions of consumers each week. (Please reread that last line, if it was lost on you. Its idea is critical to rule-making manufacturers.) Here, I'm talking about stuff like razor blades, chocolate bars, tomato soup, soda pop, syndicatable television programs, chewing gum, bottled water, ballpoint pens, blue jeans, hamburgers and french fries—staple items that intentionally are very seldom, if ever, altered. They don't need to be. In most cases, changing them would create confusion in the marketplace, resetting their brands to ground zero—a very bad thing. The far superior model is to mass-produce and then to mass-promote these items. By doing so, a company can create the manufacturing efficiencies that come with volume sales while heavily paying expert marketers to infuse their few items with some soul, with an identifiable attitude.

It's the spirit, the soul, the attitude that will persuade people to buy products in volume from a single source, to purchase the same item many times over, and to do so without giving it a moment's thought. As William James said, we'd prefer to conserve our mental processes for more demanding tasks. And as we grow more conditioned to a product like Campbell's tomato soup, a true monopoly brand, the brand and product become virtually synonymous and we pull it down off the supermarket shelf automatically. We do so overlooking the small premium in price that we have to pay for the name-brand leader. Campbell's is priced at 95 cents per can, while its unbranded competitor charges 60 cents. But when it comes to convenience brands, who's counting?

As we grow familiar with the look and taste of Campbell's, the last thing we're going to do is to quibble over the extra nickel or two and decide to switch brands because of it. There are mountains of evidence to suggest that, over time, the most powerful convenience-product brands actually increase their pricing authority well beyond inflation. That means that someday we may even pay 50 cents for a can of Coke when we could get a generic-label soft drink for 35 cents. . . . Whoops, we already do. The taste, the look, the experience—*ding!* Pavlov's bell goes off, and we crack open another brown bubbly from Big Red in Atlanta.

So what does Coca-Cola get for its $80 billion investment in branding? Plenty, if the branding is effective. The constant promotion helps to initiate new behaviors, which then turn into habits, which then harden with age. The same habits of Pavlov's conditioned dogs are what bring customers back to a product, again and again. Today, the average U.S. citizen drinks more than one eight-ounce serving of a Coca-Cola product each day. That means that tens of millions of Americans think "Coke" at least once per day.

These nearly or totally unconscious acts form the bonds that foster repeated purchasing, and that translates into pricing power for Coca-Cola. Will most of us notice, when pushing our metal carts past refreshments in the supermarket, that a twelve-pack of Coca-Cola now costs $3.99 instead of $3.79? 1 doubt it. But that adds up to a 5 percent increase in Coke's pricing, which, played out in large volumes, can dramatically increase the company's profitability. And steadily rising profits result in steadily higher stock valuations, making for steadily happier long-term share owners. How are those achieved? In part, through first-rate branding.

Superior branding can earn hundreds of millions of dollars for a corporation and its shareholders each year—even each quarter. On average, Coca-Cola in 1998 earned more than $1 billion in after-tax profit per quarter. And for selling what? Changeless colored and flavored water. Those profits came largely through the heavy promotion of a single product to a broadening worldwide audience.

Mick Jagger vs. The Beatles

OK, so a brand name is important—it can generate billions of dollars in value. But what *specific* actions do the winners take to drop their names into the minds of women, men, and children across the globe?

First of all, let's recognize that there are as many ways to build a great consumer name as there are brand names. Mick Jagger attracted worldwide audiences by strutting from stage to stage and flouting authority—and then destroying his hotel room in the small of the night.

On the other hand the Beatles drew even *more* adoration, shaking their mops and grinning as they tried to outsing their shrieking fans. Other popular names have been built out of other pure opposites, like Dean Martin and Jerry Lewis or George Foreman and Muhammad Ali. Just as there's a salt and a pepper shaker on every dining table, just as we squirt both sugar-sweet ketchup and tangy-hot mustard on a bacon double cheeseburger (who's got the heart paddles?), there's never just one experience to be had, never just one name to be built, and never just one way to build it.

However, be that as it may, when it comes to corporations spinning *maintainable* mass-market appeal, something that stays for a generation, or a century, there *are* a number of elements common to superior brands. I've narrowed it down to seven critical features that help explain how names get taken across the nation, over oceans, and into the living rooms, kitchens, dens, and bathrooms of the world. I've also instituted a simple rating system by which we can track a company's progress. For everything from passable to excellent in a given category, we'll assign a score of one point; for failure, a score of zero. Under this straightforward Foolish system, the greatest of all consumer brands rates a seven—one point for each of seven qualities (7 x 1 = 7)—and the weakest scores a zero.

Let's take a look at the Foolish characteristics of a powerhouse brand.

Because I will be listing seven criteria with rankings, I suggest that you read straight through to the end without trying to record all the information. A full restatement of the ranking system sits at the back of the book. Okay, onward!

1. FAMILIARITY

To make the rules in an industry, a company has to thrust its name on the world, from corner to corner, house to house, one mind at a time. The only way to gain the status of an automatic brand for hundreds of millions of people is to get your product or service in front of their eyes at the point of purchase—and then to move it even closer by dropping it into view whenever a person so much as *thinks* of buying.

That's why America Online sent out hundreds of millions of free sign-on disks this decade; it's why McDonald's throws its golden arches into the sky from one highway exit to the next. It's why Heinz ketchup pays for eye-level shelf space in supermarkets across the world, and it's why local and national newspapers alike rent street corners for their boxes. A furious battle is being waged every day by restaurant chains, food makers, drink mixers, newspapers, booksellers, banks, and other businesses of every stripe. The fight is to win the game of familiarity by moving their name into your line of vision, just when you're thinking of buying. And then closer, then closer still.

Let's look at winning and losing examples of branding for familiarity.

A One: Coca-Cola is better than any company in the world at promoting the ubiquity of its brand. Of course, it's easier for them than most, since, on average, humans are supposed to drink sixty-four ounces of fluid each day. Because we don't buy books, automobiles, or magazines with the same frequency, it's dollar-for-dollar more difficult and less rewarding for those companies to addict you to their brand every day. In that way, beverages have a tremendous advantage over other industries.

But Coca-Cola has no inherent brand advantage over any of its direct beverage competitors, so how has it won the battle? There are plenty of reasons for it, but from the perspective of branding, the company has extended its lead by plastering Coca-Cola cursive on billboards and barroom walls across the world. And what word stands out on the red can? "Always." Coke doesn't aspire to please the *next* generation, but rather the *always* generation. The result? While Pepsi, a fine corporation, is now worth $60 billion, Coca-Cola is a $215 billion enterprise.

A Zero: You might think that Ben & Jerry's has done a bang-up job of raising awareness of their many irresistible ice-cream flavors—Chunky Monkey, Cherry Garcia, Wavy Gravy, Chubby Hubby, and Cool Britannia, to name a few—but I'd encourage you to think otherwise. Ben & Jerry's has never run consistent national advertisements to solidify and expand its image. Its grassroots promotional approach was extremely successful in its early years, but to become *the* worldwide brand for ice cream, Ben & Jerry's now must advertise with regularity. Unless that happens, the company will see its brands decrease in familiarity as competitors crowd them from every side. Häagen-Dazs, Breyer's, and even Starbucks are knocking on the door.

2. OPENNESS

No rule-making manufacturer serves anything less than a mass market. And no company can rule a mass-market industry without recognizing that inclusivity, harmony, outreach, and acceptance are the only ways to welcome in buyers from every age group, race, gender, and economic status—every walk of life. The truest worldwide brands simply cannot afford to be discriminating about their customer base. Their sincere, open-armed hospitality is crucial to creating new markets, driving profits higher, and benefiting from the imagination of individuals in every country. The notion of Open Brands takes me back to a statement made by Margaret Edwards, a professor at the University of Vermont as well as a good friend: "Capitalism is spreading across the planet because commercial success and freedom rely on our not killing each other—something that most of the world's population finds preferable. You can't go on killing your future customers; it violates the mathematics of commerce." Well said.

In light of this inclusivity, think about the achievements of a brand like *USA Today*. Debates about its quality as a newspaper aside—it's often charged with dumbing down news for the nation—look at its success as a brand. The newspaper's price is within everyone's range. And Gannett, its parent, has made it convenient to purchase on street corners, in airports, in magazine shops, or at your hotel door. *USA Today* dooen't put on airs, its publisher recognizing that millions of people are just looking for bright and bite-sized news briefs. As a result, Gannett is valued at over $19 billion today, while the New York Times Company stands at just $7 billion. Inviting in all potential customers, becoming the paper of the people by building an Open Brand, this has turned *USA Today* from a newspaper that didn't exist in 1982 into the one with the nation's largest subscriber base today.

A One: Nike is an excellent example of a company that has reached out in one way or another to every type of athlete in America. Using humor and inspiration, and maybe a few too many swooshes, Nike's branding campaign has blanketed the planet and associated itself with athletic achievement at all levels.

A Zero: American Express has changed a lot in the last decade. Under the leadership of Harvey Golub, the company has snapped back to take market share from Visa and MasterCard. Before Golub's reign, though, AmEx had chosen to market its classic green American Express card as a symbol of wealth, exclusive club membership, and privilege. In doing so, the company limited its audience, and, inevitably, eventually ran out of wealthy Americans in need of ego boosts. Business stagnated. Visa and MasterCard turned American Express's stumble into an opportunity, finding fertile commercial ground by bringing their plastic to everyone's wallet.

The investing community demands continuous expansion, which gets increasingly difficult with every limitation placed on the customer base.

3. OPTIMISM

This third quality will probably be the most controversial of the group, but what's Foolishness without a little debate? In my estimation, rule-making brands rely on a positive message brimming with energy, alive with a sense of limitless opportunity. Optimism is their animating force. How can a company inspire repeat purchases by billions of people without offering a realistic promise of at least a slightly better world? A great example from this decade is Nike's "I'm Tiger Woods" advertising campaign—a television commercial that should be studied in business schools around the country. The sneaker company attacked the small-minded cynicism of country-club exclusivity, yet did it with a joyful, youthful vigor.

Any number of corporations have created short-term business momentum through images of sloth or pessimism or isolation, even despair. But sustainable, rule-making brands rely on optimism. A look now at a winner and a loser.

A One: General Mills has thrived at creating cereal brands for decades, but none was ever so notable as Wheaties, the Breakfast of Champions. On the market since 1933, Wheaties has featured athletic achievement on its boxes for generations. Take a look at just four of the successes featured there: Babe Ruth, the United States Women's Olympic Hockey Team, Michael Jordan, and the world-champion Minnesota Twins. Optimism and achievement are what define the Wheaties brand ("Eat your Wheaties!") and what have made it a staple in the American diet for over sixty years.

A Zero: Flip over the optimism card this decade and you'll find an ad picturing a spindly, half-dressed young woman with sunken eyes. The look has been called a number of things, from CK Mystique to the less-flattering Heroin Chic. Calvin Klein's promotions provoked controversy throughout the 1990s, drawing harsh written reprimands from organizations like African American Parents for Drug Prevention, the National Asian Pacific American Families Against Substance Abuse, and the National Hispano/Latino Community Prevention Network. However, far more commercially harmful than any protest (which, at times, can be commercially helpful), Calvin Klein's strategy of marketing narrow, smileless adolescents putting on exclusive airs could never reach and sustain a mass-market audience. The approach has created a successful short-term run in a niche market, but that popularity has—at least temporarily—come at the expense of being closed out of the broader market.

4. LEGITIMACY

The fourth primary charge for a marketing department is to legitimize its line of products and services: To take "Our Brand" licorice, for example, and believably advance the notion that it is substantially better than the competing brands. To take a software application and make it critical to computing. To convince us that one watery beer is better than another. This sort of legitimacy relies on stating the actual value of a product and then drawing as many positive associations to that value as possible. Gatorade is a thirst quencher—which then means that it can improve your tennis game, which can make you a happier person, which can lead to a wonderfully loving relationship, which led to that courtside kiss from your sweetheart. The advertisement began and ended with a gulp of Gatorade.

The message has to reflect the core realities of the product, but it must also be burnished with positive exaggeration. Can rubbing Zest soap on your shoulders really wake you up in the morning? No—but is it beyond the realm of possibility?

The key factor in building a legitimate brand is locking in the one or two most positive benefits of the product, then surrounding those with smiling success on the faces of every participant or user (Voltaire's hell!). Who's our one and zero? Philip Morris!

A One: Philip Morris's food business does a phenomenal job of building legitimate brands. Among the very best examples over the past quarter-century is the advertising campaign featuring a dozen kids eating Jell-O with Bill Cosby. The Coz, parent to the world, spooned mouthfuls of jiggly cherry Jell-O, making the product fun for kids while legitimizing the brand for parents.

A Zero: At the other end of Philip Morris's corporate operations is their tobacco business. Whether or not you favor this component of the company, likely you'll agree that Philip Morris has done a poor job of earning legitimacy for its tobacco products in the marketplace. All hot regulatory issues aside, in an open society with technology enabling mass communication, the company can no longer associate cigarettes with youthful vigor and good health (as it has for decades). To legitimize its tobacco products, Philip Morris will have to extol their real benefits to smokers, then build off these qualities toward believable extremes. This is no easy task, but they must perform to survive. Brands that fail to gain or maintain legitimacy dissolve into an ashen heap with time.

5. INEVITABILITY

Rule Makers also have to establish the power and purpose behind their merchandise, the aim being to make their stuff increasingly relevant in our daily lives. There may be no better negative example of this than the computer industry, where over the past decade an entire line of products has allowed itself to be labeled "peripherals." Modems, adapters, sound cards, disk drives—these and more are considered peripheral products. It's no wonder that the group has seen the value of its businesses wobble even as technology has been driving the public markets forward in the 1990s.

No Rule Maker would *ever* allow itself to be positioned outside the core of its industry. Branding campaigns should clearly state the purpose and *necessity* of the product—the inevitability of it. As the years pass by, those products and services that become more integral to our lives, those for which we pay every month, week, or day of our lives, have a strong chance of earning Rule Maker status. And those that grow increasingly irrelevant, of course, do not.

A One: Gillette CEO Alfred M. Zeien is quoted as saying, "At sunrise, I'm the happiest man in the world because I think about all the hair that has to be shaved off the bodies of men and women around the planet." Gillette's shaving products are important brands, relevant brands, necessities in the lives of over a billion people each week. The company's Sensor family of products literally outsells all of its competition combined. Simply put, Gillette has thrived by concentrating its attention on building and promoting a few great, inevitable products.

A Zero: The Italian fashion house Gucci Group has built a $3 billion business selling leather goods, handbags, scarves, and other luxury items. But Gucci Group is also the public company whose stock fell from $70 to $40 in 1997, not long after it entered the public markets. That 40 percent decline for shareholders came while the general market was up 33 percent. One problem (among a few others) for Gucci is that it has positioned its merchandise as a collection of fashionable luxuries. Take a look at how the company's press corps describes it at the close of each of its announcements:

> Gucci Group is one of the world's leading designers, producers, and distributors of high-quality personal luxury accessories.

I don't believe that an expanding worldwide brand could ever succeed by selling "luxury accessories." These sound too much like expensive, unnecessary peripherals. To gain mindshare, Gucci needs its products to become more essential to daily life. For example, I believe that Gucci could easily begin to strengthen its message, without risking its existing audience, by referring to its merchandise as "high-quality *personal necessities.*"

6. SOLITARINESS

As a brand gains momentum and begins to explore and expand its niche in the world, it must define itself as the single solution, the only alternative to nothing. Whether it gets there or not—and frequently brands can't—the *aim* is the thing. The direction is what matters. The hope is that someday the majority of consumers the world over will automatically go to your company's brand, whether you're a maker of pharmaceuticals, fruit juices, blue jeans, or shampoos.

Business franchises that create *the* monopoly name in their industry by inspiring the people's enthusiasm can drive extraordinary long-term rewards for their shareholders. Try this one out: Can you think of a true national competitor to Starbucks? I can't. Since going public in the spring of 1992, Starbucks stock has risen 950 percent versus S&P 500 gains of 250 percent. The company entered, fought for, and has been dominating a market with worldwide potential. Today, Starbucks is really the only storefront brand from which you can buy the same coffee across America. They've created the coveted monopoly tollbooth, with one critical and attractive distinction: unlike the $2.00 toll on I-95, Starbucks's toll isn't mandatory. We choose to pay. That marks the success of an Obligation Brand.

How about a winner and a loser?

A One: American Home Products, the creator of Chapstick, Robitussin, Centrum, and Preparation H, is also the maker of one our nation's greatest Obligation Brands: Advil. You can't really get ibuprofen relief without it, which is why tens of millions of Americans use it every year. Advil was the first nonprescription ibuprofen product available. By getting to market first and following it along with very heavy and very constant promotion, Advil earned Rule Maker status as an Obligation Brand and created substantial shareholder value for AHP investors. It also gets the country working again after New Year's Eve.

A Zero: It is a radical—and perhaps very imprudent—point to make, but the publisher of this Foolish book has failed to create much measurable brand awareness among consumers. In all likelihood, nine out of ten readers of *The Motley Fool's Rule Breakers, Rule Makers* don't know whether we're being printed, bound, and delivered by Random House, Penguin, Warner, Hyperion, Simon & Schuster, HarperCollins, Oxford, or McGillicutty—proving that our beloved publisher does not yet have an Obligation Brand. While industry insiders may know the names, outside of the publishing world, there is no compelling reason today for consumers to track which books come from which house. Though the publishers consciously make the decision to promote their authors, first and forever, by doing so they *are* losing out on the many wonderful advantages of consumer branding.

Oh, and, as far as I know, there's no such animal as McGillicutty Publishing—but would you have known?

7. HUMOR

The last of our seven qualities of superior brands is simple—*kapow!*— humor and surprise. In branding, creating a memorable name can be made far easier by elegantly spinning in a little magic and chance. Like the flea-flicker in football, the occasional razzmatazz can get the crowd up on its feet, grinning, and catch the competition off guard. No consumer brand can survive on humor and surprise, but companies that plod along cautiously—like a mathematics teacher without a story—miss a great opportunity to build and expand the love for their services.

A fine example of humor branding exists in the ongoing series of ads *for* ESPN *on* the ESPN Network. Featuring sports anchors interacting with athletes and often acting like fools, ESPN has capitalized on surprise and humor to build loyalty among its regular viewers. It's an ad campaign that has proved successful at a crucial time; ESPN is being crowded in by both CNN/*Sports Illustrated* and the Fox Sports Network. The battle for loyalty is growing furious, and ESPN has proven that a smidgen of cleverness can go a long way.

A One: You're watching television. It's the eighth inning of a major-league baseball game, and the home team's pitcher just gave up a game-tying home run. The manager walks to the mound, signals to the bullpen to bring in the righty, and before the announcer can walk through the reliever's statistics, a banner pops up in the top left of your television screen: "Rolaids Spells Relief." Simple, surprising, and clever. 'Nuff said.

A Zero: Can anyone think of a single political advertisement, beyond the smashing success of Jesse "The Mind" Ventura, that wasn't overly idealistic or unduly fierce? The convention of political advertising, as far as I can tell, lacks any hint of surprise, humor, or self-deprecation (to say nothing of the remainder of most campaigns). In the struggle for mainstream interest, politicians would do well to inject a little unpredictable wit into their promotions. The world even might be a slightly better place for it!

THE SIMPLE, BRANDED MNEMONIC

Before applying the formulaic branding test to our model company this chapter, it behooves me to mention the little mnemonic I've created for your consumption. In searching for brand names that are Familiar, Open, Optimistic, Legitimate, Important, Solitary, and Humorous, I seem to have assembled qualities whose first letters spell . . . FOOL-

ISH. How fitting. The FOOLISH brand is one that hits forward on all cylinders; it rallies together millions of new buyers each year by promoting the spirit, integrity, convenience, and necessity of its products. Ranking these qualities for companies that you are considering investing in can put your savings on firmer ground.

And, because branding is so important to rule making, I'd like to walk through a single example of one of America's great masters of it: Gap Inc.

Gap Inc.

With a very broad sense of what's in a name and the value of that name, but without a specific example to ground us, no dirt to dig our hands into, it's time to trot out San Francisco's Gap Inc. to center stage. Under the golden shaft of light, Gap makes for a perfect study: The company has a handful of leading consumer brands—Gap, babyGap, Gap Kids, Gap Body, Old Navy, and Banana Republic—and alongside privately held Levi Strauss, it's one of the two leading retailers of casual clothing in America.

I'll put the disclaimer up front: The Fool purchased thirty-seven Gap shares on May 1, 1998, for the Rule Maker Portfolio (view it at www.fool.com/rulemaker). Within three months, the stock had risen 30 percent. We might've congratulated ourselves loudly for our good fortune had it not been for an acute awareness of the company's superior *historical* performance. During the three years prior to our purchase, Gap's stock went on a rampage, rising from a low of $11 to $62 per share. A $20,000 investment in Gap, then, would have grown to more than $110,000, marking a 460 percent return in just thirty-six months. Those gains dramatically outpaced the stock market's average growth of 112 percent over the same period.

But even that view was too narrow.

Looking across the company's entire horizon line, back through its twenty-two years in the public markets, Gap stock has averaged more than 26 percent annual growth for its share owners. That's almost unthinkable. A $20,000 investment in Gap in 1976 has grown to more than $3.2 million today. For comparison, in a passbook savings account for twenty-two years, that same $20,000 would've turned into just $47,000, reminding me of an important line in *The Motley Fool Invest-*

ment Guide: "The least mentioned, biggest financial risk of all is not taking enough risk." Because, as you probably guessed, that $47,000 in a
savings account today buys you just about exactly what $20,000 did
back in 1976. Match the returns from your savings account up against
inflation, and neither can much outrun the other over time. By investing in true Rule Making brands, though, you stand to consistently preserve and extend wealth to dramatic ends.

Now, Gap *has* been a fairly volatile stock over the past twenty-two
years. To have earned the 26 percent annualized returns over that time,
you had to be patient and you had to be an investor more interested in
business than in stock. And at the same time, how fitting is it that one of
the dozen best investments on the U.S. market over the past twenty-
five years has been a company specializing in the sale of jeans, T-shirts,
button-downs, and spring dresses—products right in front of our eyes.
The investor using fifth-grade mathematics to sort through the financials, and taking the time to assess the expansion of the brand, could
have seen Gap's position strengthening, at least over the past decade.
Over the last ten years, Gap shares have increased 2,400 percent against
a market rise of 330 percent. Look at this split-adjusted graph:

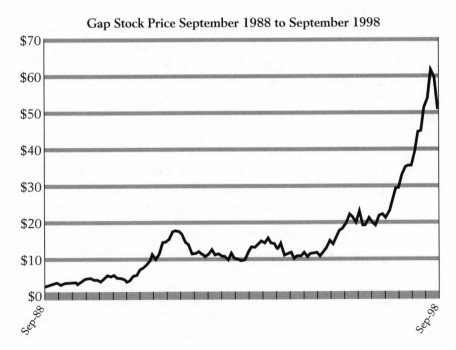

Gap Stock Price September 1988 to September 1998

The future for Gap looks just as bright, frankly. Why? The company is in the middle of a methodical transition from being a pure retailer of casual clothing to being a name-brand business. That's the flip-flop that we mentioned earlier in this section, whereby a company evolves out of heavy investments in product creation into a world where it drives more capital to the marketing and delivery of a few fixed products. As of late 1998, Gap has $7 billion in annual sales and is valued at $25 billion. If Gap continues its rule-making ways, you can expect it to limit its exposure to fashion trends, instead promoting and pounding away at the sales of staple products: T-shirts, shorts, denim, and khakis. It will need to infuse denim with spirit, give energy to a colored shirt, and broadcast—as it has—roomfuls of young Americans shaking and grooving in Gap khakis.

Those are some of the promotional actions of a company realizing that it is now more of a mass-market franchise than a niche designer. If it can become our casual-clothing default, Gap will no longer have to compete on the trends—it will only need to reinforce awareness of its staples while making its purchasing points as convenient as possible (from block to block, in malls and superstore chains, and via the Internet). The triumvirate of brand, convenience, and volume pricing today puts Gap in a mightily powerful position.

To better understand Gap's strategy, again draw up a mental image of that changeless brown bubbly that Coca-Cola has promoted for decades and turned into a company that is now worth more than $215 billion. Gap appears headed in the same direction. And if the company succeeds at becoming a worldwide brand, it can eventually begin implementing slight, systematic price hikes. Because as buyers return to the name brand time and again, at each purchase point, the majority of them will temporarily (and then permanently) lose their focus on the price. So long as its price escalation is carried out in small increments, Gap will have consumers looking past the cost to the comfort of a brand.

Let's try to determine if Gap is the sort of brand with staying power.

GAP'S FOOLISH RATING

Familiarity: Is it everywhere? Gap has made enormous investments to put its various stores on the street corners of every major city in America. It has then supplemented those investments by attacking and never letting up. During the week leading up to Independence Day 1998, Old Navy began selling T-shirts featuring an American flag under the Old

Navy banner, for $5. If you were out for a parade or gathering at an out-door party, you probably saw a *ton* of Old Navy T-shirts. For five bucks! **Score: 1** on familiarity.

Openness: Does it welcome everyone? Few consumer brands have reached out to every demographic in the way that Gap has. The company has concentrated its attention on the thirtysomething employee of a growing firm, but its message has been inclusive, far-reaching, and alive. You almost can't walk through urban areas of America without seeing an old woman, young man, tall girl, or chubby kid with a stuffed blue-plastic bag lettered white GAP. Any company with spokespeople that have ranged from Miles Davis to Kim Basinger, from Warhol to Whoopi, is bound to attract an expanding audience. **Score: 1** on openness.

Optimism: Can it promise a slightly better world? The Gap's three 1998 advertising spots for khaki pants were entitled "Khakis Swing," "Khakis Groove," and "Khakis Rock." If you ever see advertisements for Gap, babyGap, Gap Kids, Old Navy, or Banana Republic featuring models that look emaciated, unhappy, or self-absorbed, beware. Drop by www.fool.com and see what others are saying. It may be time to sell. **Score: 1** on optimism.

Legitimacy: Is it accepted by the people? Almost no better example of legitimacy branding exists than Gap's ability to take advantage of dress-down Fridays. In 1993, Gap sent a free pair of khakis and a white button-down shirt to every trader on Wall Street. More important, Gap went on an advertising campaign which featured celebrity corporate executives in informal attire. All of a sudden, it was okay to go to work in casual dress—and America's young technology companies set it as policy. **Score: 1** on legitimacy.

Inevitability: Is it becoming a necessary purchase? The Gap has gone to great lengths to establish a presence at every price point for potential consumers, buying up Banana Republic for the fashion conscious while launching Old Navy to include blokes like me who'd prefer not to spend more than $200 on clothing each year! The result is that Gap has become a more relevant and more necessary brand to our daily lives than any clothing retailer today. **Score: 1** on inevitability.

Solitariness: Is it the standout category king? Achieving status as the Stand-alone Brand is no small feat. Advil has had no meaningful competition. Same with Starbucks. It took Coca-Cola seven decades of work before it became the automatic brand for the world's sugar-water drinkers. Gap is certainly headed in the right direction, but it'll be another decade before the company becomes America's automatic brand for casual apparel, and longer still before it conquers the globe. I wouldn't call it failure. I'd just note that there's room for improvement. **Score: 0** on solitariness.

Humor: Has it surprised you in the last five years? Unanticipated cleverness has been a staple of Gap's branding strategy, and it's scored rich rewards over the past decade. For example—*kapow!*—they placed their company logo on the outfield walls of baseball stadiums across the U.S. For the uninitiated, right and left center field, the areas between the outfielders, are called the alleys, or "gaps," in baseball terminology. On the left-centerfield and right-centerfield fences in baseball stadiums around the country, look for the simple signs that read GAP—pretty clever. **Score: 1** on humor.

Gap's Total Score: Six out of seven reflects the strength of Gap's three primary brands, each of them distinctive: Old Navy, the warehouse, offers low-priced casual clothing. The Gap, the main brand, sells casual clothing at convenience prices. And Banana Republic, more of a boutique shop (and less important overall to Gap Inc.), stocks higher-quality duds at higher-quality prices. Today, rather than pay steep prices to offer a flurry of unique looks every season, Gap has concentrated on the heavy promotion of its old reliables (jeans, khakis, shorts, T-shirts), and worked to infuse its threads with a soul.

It's a mass-production and branding model for every consumer company to abide. Gap is one of a handful of operations that truly make the branding rules in its industry.

Concluding Thoughts

It's a simple but extremely consequential question for investors and business leaders alike. Where does an automatic brand come from and what sustains it? Yet it's amazing how many companies dive headlong into their industry without asking the question aloud, without articulating it and pondering it. And it's just as startling how many investors drop money into the markets without recognizing the value of a brand. Companies that don't recognize that every product and service is ultimately nothing more than a commodity until it is branded will suffer the slings and arrows of outrageous competition until their labors fall into nothingness and loss.

It's equally striking how few companies have a careful game plan for following up on early success. Making a name is just the first step down the red carpet. Surrounding it with admiration is the second, and locking it down as the default brand is the third. All of these are critical to becoming a rule-making brand, to wearing the ermine-fringed robes and sitting under a gleaming crown. Rule Makers need to fashion themselves into the people's old friends, a brand we know and trust.

But even these three branding qualities—a name, the love, and *the* name—on their own are not enough, else our book would end on the very next page. In the oncoming section, we'll focus on how a Rule Maker funds and manages its commercial expansion. Expanding a brand through different generations, across income levels, and into foreign lands is like a marathon steeplechase. Over the hedge, across the brook, around the turn, lift to get across the water jump, down for the sprint to the next hedge oncoming. It's a puzzle, a maze, and a marathon that demands a lot of reflection and continuous measurement of progress (or regress).

And it demands capital and smart management.

Which takes us to the very next page.

Chapter 12

A Measure
of Excellence

What! We have seen the seven stars.

—WILLIAM SHAKESPEARE,
HENRY IV, PART 2 (II, iv)

In the preceding chapter, I drawled on endlessly, like an old man in a fishing boat, about the power that branding holds for consumer franchises. Masterfully executed, branding can reward investors for generations. But throughout, there was such an emphasis on endurance, on the long-term, on generations of time, that I have to set something straight: Success in commerce doesn't require a century of excellence. I don't fault the makers of Tiddlywinks, Beech-Nut gum, Silly String, mood rings, and Izod shirts for not developing brands that could span the ages and gain popularity from generation to generation. If you manage a business that makes trendy furniture or stitches pajamas, you don't lose if your work generates tens or hundreds of thousands or millions in profits for managers and employees before disappearing first into legend and then silence.

Commercial success wears many costumes. It knows many routes.

But once a company goes public, it *does* change its clothes forever and walks a narrower road. Some of its color, the panache, the uncalculated daring that's permissible in private business, has to fade. The renowned British entrepreneur and playful mad hatter Richard Branson learned this lesson the hard way. Less than two years into his foray in the public markets, Branson felt compelled to buy back his unorthodox company, Virgin Inc., from the grip of investment bankers and anxious shareholders. He realized that rescuing the company from the public markets was the only way to restore some of Virgin's earlier genius and to protect the company's real charter: to stamp its brand on as many seemingly unrelated markets as imaginable, from air travel to mutual funds to soft drinks to perfume.

Public companies can't be so whimsical. They have a responsibility to their share owners across the world to conduct their enterprise in careful pursuit of maximal success. After all, they are using shareholders' money to expand their operations, and thus have a fiduciary obligation to shareholders not to engage in some sort of timing lottery where, say (perhaps not coincident with the sale of executive stock options), holders of stock between February and August 1993 made a fortune, while the rest perished. This isn't to say that stocks shouldn't or won't fluctuate, doubling or getting halved in a single year. And it isn't to suggest that, because public companies are obligated to serve their shareholders, all of our investments will eventually reward us. But it does mean that executives and managers of publicly held businesses have a duty to run their enterprises with an eye toward extending shareholder value for more than a fortnight, or a year, or even a decade.

A private company is a very different thing—it's an acting troupe, a street performer, an independent bookstore, a boutique shop. Its corporate mission can sleep until noon, then step into its walking shoes to wander whistlingly down a country road. A privately held business isn't charged with spending its dollars in the calculated and somewhat maniacal pursuit of profit. If she wanted, the CEO of a private business could distribute all of the company's cash to her nineteen-year-old lover. She could. Or she could choose to give away half of the profit to the local homeless shelter. But once her enterprise heads toward the public markets, it is using other people's money to grow.

At that point, the business needs to metamorphose from circus act to standing militia. It has to revert from the orange-tip butterfly, heedlessly darting through a meadow, back to its larval form, the army worm scooting forward one pair of legs at a time. A public company cannot ape the spirited noodlings of a Grateful Dead jam; it's on John Philip Sousa time. It has to be predictable, move with steely resolve, stand at attention. It has to focus on *pacing.* The transition into the public markets enters a business in that unending race to serve its owners, where today's acceleration is meaningless if it leads to an organizational nervous breakdown tomorrow—where this hour's profits are actually harmful if they leave little room for more in the next.

Strangely enough, in certain circles of the Wise, executives who launch their company's initial public offering into the marketplace regard the process as their exit strategy, and feel not a whit of an obligation to ensure the long-term viability of their corporation. *Hock-tooey! (Stage note: Fool clears throat into the kerchief he waved open.)*

Going public marks a company's *entrance* into obligations to the thousands of individual and institutional investors who fund its forward motion. And those obligations mean that a public company must transcend short-term ambition. Publicly held entities that don't aspire to an endless success are really engaged in a sort of pocket picking—the theft of shareholder monies for executive prosperity, say, beneath the shingled rooves of Nantucket.

The way to spot this behavior is to watch for heavily promoted product launches that, in your estimation, provide little foundation for future growth. A number of industries offer business models reliant on that short-term mentality—industries like filmmaking and software-game development. The up-front investment costs in those businesses are fairly considerable, but then the life of their products is brief. Such a business model is a death trap for public companies. In software, rare is the dragon-slaying game that can be upgraded for repeat revenue. Computer-game brands are typically short-lived.

Hollywood doesn't have it much easier, forced as it is to come up with new hits every year. One year it's *Passage to India*, then *Fletch*, then *Top Gun*, then . . . *Ishtar* (timber!). Valiant attempts to alter the business of filmmaking—such as going back to blockbuster stars, creating sequels, rereleasing the classics, and elbowing in on video-store profits—have helped, but not significantly enough to earn them Rule Maker status.

In our search for companies worthy of our decade-long ownership, we'll be avoiding both the consummate Hollywood studios and the software-game shops, at least in their present incarnations. Their models demand substantial up-front investments to chase a short-lived sale period. We prefer just the reverse—businesses that require relatively little financing to generate recurring, long-term revenues. This approach to public business has reaped untold sums of wealth for individual investors this century. And that brings us back to an important clarification: Certain industries don't yet (and may never) offer the sort of company that would attract my investment money. For instance, as an investor, the leading maker of sewing machines is far less attractive to me than is America's third-best pharmaceutical business. Some industries will create zero Rule Makers, while others may house a half-dozen. Finding Rule Makers is more about finding the appropriate business model for long-term investment than it is about picking the leaders in each category.

And as we go in search of these Rule Makers, bushwhacking through the knotty bracken of mediocrity and short-term thinking, we'll be asking ourselves questions and quantifying our answers. We'll ask questions like: How expensive is this business to run? How will the company's existing product line be expanded? From where will the repeat earnings flow? Does management have a plan to eventually sell their merchandise in every corner of the globe? And do they have the capital structure and business ingenuity to turn their enterprise into a sovereign power?

SILLY PUTTY DOES

Let's start with the successful model already implemented at Binney & Smith, a private business in Easton, Pennsylvania. Founded by two cousins over a century ago, the company mixed and sold the red-oxide pigment used in the paint covering the archetypal farmyard barn. Later, it moved into blending and selling waxy coloring sticks to schools. Today, Binney & Smith has made and sold over a hundred billion Crayola crayons, in colors from peach to midnight blue. In over sixty countries around the world, kids use crayons to bring us two-legged dogs and stick-figured parents taller than three-story houses. Crayola has provided their crayons for over ninety years.

Even though Binney & Smith invented the product, there was no guarantee that the company would own the twentieth century's leading crayon brand. Any number of turns could've taken the company down the wrong dark alley. Who knows—some larger entity could've stepped on its business early on, taking the "crayon idea" and running with it. Because in the business world—unlike on college term papers or final exams—copying someone else's unpatented work isn't punishable. Perhaps shockingly to the contrary, using the work of others without attribution often wins the richest reward (feel free to phone your elementary school teacher and blast her for not teaching you how to cheat).

Fortunately or unfortunately, in commerce, getting there first doesn't mean owning the place forever. In fact, the company with a settler's mentality—the one that sits back and studies the pioneers in its industry, then works to supplant them—will often assert dominance in its category, as it employs one of the greatest competitive weapons available to all businesses: duplication. Duplication happens everywhere; we see it in medical technology and mystery writing, in insurance sales and automobiles. However unsatisfying it may seem to the individual, every superior publicly owned institution mirrors its competition. It replicates the best ideas, marginally improves on them, and then storms ahead with greater efficiency and ambition. So, although Crayola crayons could've been slain, could have, like so many other useful ideas, been copied, renamed, and mass-produced by a competitor, that didn't happen. And to reveal how a company like Binney & Smith defended its markets, while creating substantial wealth for its private shareholders, is part of the mission of this chapter.

A tale similar to Crayola crayons' can be told of a thing as wacky as elastic in a blue plastic egg: Silly Putty. Developed in 1950 by Peter Hodgson, who purchased the patent from General Electric when he was a hurtful $12,000 in debt, Silly Putty is today available across the world. It's a trifle that is approaching its fiftieth birthday. And over the past decade, the business has tripled to more than six million eggs sold per year. Silly Putty—who'd have thought?! Hodgson did. When he died in 1976, he left a Putty estate valued at over $140 million. Oh, and Silly Putty is also a Binney & Smith product, bought by the Pennsylvania firm in 1977.

It's kooky, but Binney & Smith has built sustainable models for two highly frivolous products. Decades old now, both Silly Putty and Crayola crayons could have vanished, sunk without a peep into the eternal failed-consumer-product swamp. Would you have missed elastic in a plastic egg if its production had been halted in 1983? Probably not. Would the world have kept on at its feverish pace, even if Crayola-brand crayons were no more? We hope so. Neither the survival nor success of these products was divinely ordained (as far as we know). Rather, Silly Putty and Crayola crayons are here on account of patient commitment, the company's love of its business, and a sound use of capital throughout the organization.

Find these qualities in a public company and gold ingots are sure to follow. And they are there. The long-term mentality of Binney & Smith, a private company, produced the best of what can come out of a *public* company, too: products (1) with staying power that (2) gain in popularity each year, (3) grow more profitable over time, and (4) reward shareholders with market-beating results for many, many years.

This entire chapter is devoted to locating exactly those business models, because the longer you, the investor, can surf a single phenomenal wave, the better. Again, buying a successful company and holding it for decades lowers your trading costs, defers your capital-gains tax payments, and reduces the amount of time you'll have to commit to finding the next great dynasty. A collection of these superior companies will far outpace the total returns of the majority of mutual funds, before *and* after the deduction of annual fees and taxes. In fact, an investment portfolio of ten to fifteen companies that finds and holds even just one or two Rule Maker giants for decades can generate enough wealth to feed a family tree for a century.

Need an example?

A $10,000 investment in Pfizer in 1950 is worth what today?

	Invested Capital	Annual Growth Rate Since 1950	Present Value (September 1998)
Pfizer	$10,000	17%	$18.7 million

This investment required no tax payments along the way, beyond those on the relatively minimal cash dividend, and the investment racked up just one commission payment—back in 1950. *(Stage note: Insert the sound of an old shoe thrown at Foolish actors by a broker in the crowd.)* Yep, no regular flow of fees to a conflicted broker on Wall Street, no annual management fee to a mutual-fund manager, and no ongoing tax payments. In honor of and deference to Gertrude Stein, I'll repeat from the last paragraph: Even just one or two Rule Maker giants held for decades can generate enough wealth to feed a family tree for a century.

A TECHNOLOGY DISASTER

But let's turn over this table at which we've been seated, stand on our hands, count backwards from a thousand, and, rather than look at enduring greatness, study instead an example of short-term thinking by a public company. It's the story of Cybermedia Incorporated (the name almost gives its demise away), whose two years in the public markets included a mercurial rise to $33 in late 1997 and an equally hasty subsequent descent to a mere $3 per share six months later. Yep, from $33 to $3 in half a year.

Cybermedia came public to accolades toward the end of 1996, and why not? The company had a promising story: It was the consummate small software shop, writing security and support applications for a world full of computer users who want to monitor the performance of their machines and protect them from viruses. Perfect. It was the age of the Internet, the dewy dawn of a new day. Cybermedia's troubleshooting software—First Aid, Oil Change, Guard Dog Deluxe, and Un-Installer—was flying off the shelves of computer retailers across the country, while its applications were winning technology awards from *PC World* and *PC Magazine*. And its five-year rate of sales growth had hit 566 percent per annum. *Kapow!* It had the stance and strut and swing of a champion.

Why not invest in it? After all, at the end of 1996, not long after its public offering, the company had trailing sales of $39 million, up from $240,000 just two years previous. Then, over the next four quarters, Cybermedia went ballistic—it closed out fiscal 1997 with more than $71 million in trailing revenues. Wow. Look at those numbers again:

Sales Growth at Cybermedia, 1994–97

1994	1995	1996	1997
$240,000	$5 million	$39 million	$71 million

That's just enormous growth. The stock bounded about, as any small-cap is wont to do, before climbing the hill to $33 per share in November 1997.

But then everything stopped.

It was a bit like the last click of knotting bicycle gears the instant before an ugly forward tumble. Cybermedia posted third-quarter 1997 sales that were up, but shortly after that, the vice president of international sales stepped down. Then, in February, its chief financial officer bailed, followed closely by the CEO in March. And the company ship sailed off and away, rudderless in choppy waters, with no skipper or second officer to guide it. Its stock plummeted from $33 in late 1997 to $4 by the summer of 1998, slashing the value of the company from $425 million to $50 million in less than a year. The investor with $40,000 invested in Cybermedia in November was, by summer, left with less than $5,000, a wet hanky, and a single recurring nightmare.

What the heck had happened at Cybermedia? Product sales looked so strong; the company was in an expanding industry; the stock had risen sharply—to some, everything looked just perfect, like a peach, a ray of sunshine, like Michael Jordan on the outdoor courts. What the heck happened? Let's not answer that now, because by the end of this chapter, you should be able to solve the mystery for yourself. To get there, though, we'll need to explore the financial characteristics of businesses that successfully expand operations with an eye toward the forever. We'll start with the obvious.

THE OBVIOUS

For a public company to expand its business year after year, even for decades, it has to master an efficient process for designing and delivering its products. It also has to exhibit superior financial management by tending carefully to the flow of money into and out of its business, one dollar at a time. Sometimes the financial media forget that managing the flow of cash and products is critical to winning in business.

Take Microsoft, for example. Oddly enough, in this decade's ongoing media debate over whether Microsoft products warrant the company's great prosperity, what gets left out of the discussion is the single most important element for a public company—the sophistication and the durability of its business model. The business pages sometimes forget that the primary directive at public companies is commerce. Winning product awards, getting on the cover of *Time* magazine, spinning an inspiring advertising campaign—these are valuable developments at any business. But until a company can show repeated sales to customers and consistently expand its profits, it hasn't mastered the art or game of public-market enterprise. Take Microsoft.

Before Microsoft came public in 1986, it practiced as a private company for eleven years. When it stepped onto Wall Street's playboard, it was performing like a grand master, turning product into pure profit with alarming frequency. Ten years later, Bill Gates's company controlled the most valuable industry on the planet. During its public history, the software giant has turned the individual investor's 1986 investment of $10,000 into over $3 million today.

In the 1990s, Microsoft stands as the premier Rule Maker in the public markets, topped with a platinum crown, earned through its widening base of customers and polished by shareholders time and again. There are many other kings awaiting your long-term investment, and in the pages ahead, I'd like to outline seven criteria for finding companies bound toward Rule Maker status. By matching these up with the branding approaches covered in the preceding chapter, you'll be a giant step closer to your own Foolish domination of the public markets.

Because there are seven different measurements to make, and small doses of mathematics throughout, it may seem that a common Fool can't pull off this approach. Not so. Fear not. Steeped in grade-school math, the Rule Maker model will actually take you less than one hour per company, per year, once you've mastered it. With a spreadsheet at your disposal, it could take less than fifteen minutes. When reading this section, again I recommend that you read straight through to the end, without feeling the need to commit each item to memory this instant.

So, let's begin with the first standard.

1. The Mass Market, Repeated Purchase of Low-Priced Products

Our brand of Rule Makers relies heavily on the sale of goods and services to an enormous audience of buyers who automatically return every month, week, or day with open wallets. Soft drinks and bottled water, razor blades and toothpaste, chocolate bars and aspirin, toll booths and taxes—they're all necessary and regular cash outlays for hundreds of millions of people around the world. A business model designed around that repeated purchasing, and linked with a focus on building automatic brands discussed last chapter, can turn consumers into zombies. It's *Night of the Living Dead* down at your local Starbucks, as the crowds roam in with their arms outstretched, hair sticking up, sometimes decked out in pajamas, buying their coffee without hesitation.

Like Starbucks, Gillette is another great example of an automatic repeat-purchase model. In many parts of the world, the word Gillette *means* razor, even the entire shaving experience from razor to blade to shaving cream. Buyers make repeat visits to pharmacies and supermarkets every month to get their blades, illustrating that zombie-style automatic purchasing of an automatic brand. When a business has built this model, it can jam down the accelerator in the unending race to capture the public markets and worry little about running out of fuel. Most other businesses can't, but automatic brands can because the inflow of money from their customers grows more visible each year. After selling billions of the same razors, or Band-Aids, or juice cartons, a company can spend its time tracking consumer patterns and making educated guesses about the direction of its markets. The business becomes thus increasingly predictable, allowing management to invest more aggressively in reaching new markets. Contrast this with Hollywood's battle to launch another great movie next year, created nearly from scratch, and you can't miss the power of mass-market repeated purchasing of the same product, time and again.

Naturally, the perfect illustrations of this business model are those companies that sell low-priced goods. Can we really return once a week to buy diamond trinkets, silk kimonos, or ruby-studded slippers? Maybe once, yes, but not every week! The true repeat-purchase brands are inexpensive enough that all Americans (and one day, all earthlings) can return to them again and again. Here are a few examples, along with some stuff that doesn't meet our criteria, included for contrast:

Repeat-Purchase Products

Razor blades? Yes.	Bathroom sinks? No.
Paper? Yes.	Furniture? No.
Oil? Yes.	Automobiles? No.
Lemonade? Yes.	Refrigerators? No
$25 blue jeans? Yes.	$250 shoes? No.

Only Imelda Marcos and her ilk can repeatedly purchase pairs of $250 shoes, through good economic times and bad. The rest of the world would need an extremely healthy (or overheated) economy to ceaselessly buy expensive boots. And as the economic environment worsened (which is its habit from time to time), consumers would price shop when buying shoes. While Imelda was continuing to funnel foreign aid into her bank account for the purchase of more shoes, the rest of us would track down the bargains. And then, in the darkest economic hours, beset by high unemployment and high inflation, we'd place a halt on all of our frivolous spending. Thus is it clear that *expensive* products cannot be repeatedly purchased, month after month, day after day, by a mass audience. But for inexpensive products, the reverse is true. Would we stop buying razor blades in a recession? That's unlikely. And, even in the worst of times, are the masses of men and women likely to shop on price rather than familiarity when buying razors? I doubt it.

That's the other interesting benefit to this business model: Because the prices on repeat-purchase products are relatively low, over time their providers face fewer real competitive threats. The reverse is also true, too: The higher the price of a product, the greater the competition. That's because expensive tennis shoes or personal computers or entertainment centers have buyers thinking about price and begging for competitive relief. Consider and contrast the enormous used-car market with the nearly absent market for used software, used razor blades, and used clothing. In the automobile market, where one might spend $15,000 on a new vehicle next year, the average consumer researches a number of different options, including the possibility of buying a used car.

Research, choice, price shopping, competition . . . these concepts and words don't buzz around the crown of a Rule Maker. Their antonyms (habit, necessity, inattention to pricing, and monopoly) do. And those rule-making words are most suited to the products that you pay less than $10 apiece to have, because when consumers wander into stores like zombies and have to plink down an extra dollar or two (who's counting?) to buy the leading brand, it doesn't threaten the short- or long-term condition of their savings accounts.

In low-priced daily items, we buy familiarity. But imagine roaming into a financial adviser's office and just buying investment products at any cost ($1,000 here, $25,000 there). Through ignorance and impatience, someone could blow hundreds of thousands of dollars on financial services over a lifetime. Most of us have learned that we can't afford that luxury. And that's why your truest Rule Makers avoid high-priced categories, tending instead to sell small inexpensive necessity items that are easy to store and transport: Pill bottles. Drink concentrates. Information. Shaving cream. Soup. Candy bars. Internet services.

To nail home the point, let's reflect again on how buying an automobile differs from buying a razor blade. Let's contrast General Motors and Gillette—so close alphabetically, so distant commercially. On average, people buy a new car every five years, not every five days. And because they'll likely be laying out between $10,000 and $30,000 for a new car, consumers are unlikely to ever en masse act like the living dead, picking up the brand-name automobile at its sticker price *(gasp!)*.

If they did, they'd lose out on thousands of dollars in savings. Most don't. Instead, today, new-car buyers get copies of *Consumer Reports* magazine, talk to friends, and sign on to www.fool.com/car to listen to other buyers—and even disgruntled former car salesmen—explain how to whittle away at the price. An hour of research online can save a car buyer a few thousand dollars. And five long years later, when the buyer has to repeat the same (dare I say gloomy?) process, she'll work through the same considerations and negotiation carefully once again.

That's all tough news for car dealers *and* car manufacturers, because it means that the auto business is built upon the informed, infrequent purchasing of high-priced products—a rickety model, indeed. If that doesn't scare you as an investor, add to it that when the U.S. economy is shadowed by dark thunderclouds, car sales will sputter and wheeze to a halt. In grim economic times, most of us will stick it out with our current cars, so long as they're roadworthy, or head to the used-car lot, or, if we do choose to buy new, battle even more relentlessly on price.

These are very bad signs for the makers and retailers of automobiles, and for their investors.

There now. The point has been made. But, to use our knowledge to maximum potential, we need to quantify. So we're going back to the rating system of the last chapter, this time awarding two points for the leaders, one point for the followers, and zero points for the laggards. In this category, the truest Rule Makers are businesses that get us to return for purchase at least once a month or more. That earns two points. The next best are those that draw us back to them between once a month and once a year, for one point. And the least likely to rule an industry that can create substantially increasing value for shareholders are those businesses that have customers returning less than once per year. Hence zero points for them.

A Two: Exxon, a former Standard Oil company, is repeatedly purchased by tens of millions of automobile drivers across the world, from one week to the next. The company's petroleum products fuel cars, airplanes, boats; lubricate heavy machinery; and appear in fertilizers, paints, plastics, rubber, and various fibers. Even without knowing it, you're probably a weekly repeat purchaser of many Exxon products.

A Zero: Chances are, you don't go out and buy a sewing machine every week. That's to the great dismay of Singer, whose sewing-machine business has been drying up in the 1990s. Never a repeat-purchase operation to begin with, Singer is now in a tangle of trouble, as their ma-chines are even less of a necessity in the average household than they once were. Thus, Singer gets stuck with zero points here: Most of us buy a new sewing machine less than once a year.

2. Gross Margins

Ah, now for something a little more numerical. Something we can sink our sharp teeth into. Something to view on our calculator screen. Gross margins, huzzah! (Did you ever think you'd be clamoring for *gross margins*?) A company's gross margins, appearing on its income statement, are toted up using one of the following equations:

a. $\dfrac{\text{Total Sales} - \text{Cost of Goods Sold}}{\text{Total Sales}}$

or

b. $\dfrac{\text{Gross Profit}}{\text{Total Sales}}$

Gross margins are a reflection of how expensive it is to manufacture a product relative to the price at which it can be sold. That's a critical concept for rule-making businesses: A product that costs a lot of money to manufacture, but that can be sold for relatively little, is extremely unattractive. If it costs you twenty dollars to make a broomstick that you can't sell for any more than fifteen, you don't want to be selling broomsticks. On the flip side, a product that costs very little to make, but that can be sold dearly, is fetching. The gross-margin calculation helps us make sense of the relationship between the manufacturing cost of a product and its sale price.

If you think about it, that makes the state lottery one of the truly great businesses on the planet. *(Stage Note: Insert sound of Fool vomiting in bushes.)* The manufacturing costs of printing and distributing those tick-ets are very low. Plus, there's no pricing competition. None. State-run lotteries are a monopoly. So, as millions of players return day after day, week after week, to drop their hard-earned savings on a hopeless dream, state lotteries mass-produce tickets for much less than the one-dollar cost per stub. A great business, your average state lottery brings together a host of rule-making qualities—great branding matched with a repeat-purchase model that sports very high gross margins. While you may sympathize with the Fool hunched in the bushes and retching, as well as entertain not a lick of respect for your state representatives, you've got to give them credit for building a brilliant commercial model at the expense of their citizenry. The lottery is *their* dream; they win every day.

Contrast the Lottobucks business model with that of, say, making and selling television sets. First of all, it isn't cheap or easy to make TVs—with wiring, glass, plastic, tubes, antennae, filters, input jacks, decoders, converters, packaging, and the rest. The cost of making a TV is prohibitive relative to that single slip of state-promoted gambling paper. And not only are the manufacturing costs high, but the pricing of television sets is subject to natural and rapid erosion. Because people pay upward of $500 per set, they welcome new blood in the world of television makers. They won't allow a monopoly. They want prices to come down. Put those two—high manufacturing costs and consumer price awareness—together, and you have a lot of bad news for investors. I would tell you to ask television manufacturer Zenith to talk to you about it, but I can't. They're not in business anymore.

Let's go back to the well for another example from the world of automobiles. The underlying cost of manufacturing a car is very, very high, what with window glass, knobs, seats, rubber mats, pipes, headlights, valve cover grommets, fuel pumps, cylinder-head gaskets, caps, filters, a gleaming Elvis Presley hood ornament, and much more. The expenses are much higher than, say, the costs of mixing and baking a single peanut-butter cookie. At the same time, a Lexus Sweep (shouldn't they create that brand?) can be sold for about $45,000 more than that cookie. So which is the better business? In part, the answer relies on what margin of gross profit the two can create on a dollar of sales. If a cookie turns higher gross margins than does an automobile, then, through the ages, it could be, and I propose that on average it will be, a better business to bake cookies than to make cars.

How about one more illustration? The manufacturing costs of running an airline are obviously much higher than the manufacturing costs of the Planter's peanuts that you nibble back there in Row 26 (or are you flying first class these days?). But, more important, the gross margins on Planter's peanuts are miles higher than those at Delta Airlines. The lower manufacturing costs and the greater pricing power make the little peanut our sort of Rule Maker (all hail Jimmy Carter?). To take this one step further, consider this wonderful point made by Howard Anderson in an article entitled "Technology Goes Mainstream" featured in *Upside* magazine in the spring of 1998:

> Take this interesting fact: OAG—a division of Reed Travel Group that sells travel information—has, during the past 10 years, had bigger profits than the entire airline industry. In other words, information about airline flights is more valuable—to someone—than the flights are.
>
> Think about this a minute: The airlines willingly supply data about their flights to OAG, which then sells this data—combined with other airlines' data—to clients, who pay hard cash for it.
>
> Another data point: Over a period of 10 years, *TV Guide* made more money than the top three networks by doing exactly the same thing—taking information that it did not create and packaging it for consumers.

So which do you think has higher gross margins—the company gathering and transferring light information, or the company managing a fleet of heavy airplanes? Which has higher gross margins: *TV Guide* or CBS? The lighter the manufacturing costs and the higher the sale prices relative to those costs, the higher a company's gross margins will be. And the happier is the Foolish investor. Then, as those gross margins rise, a company can afford to squirrel away more money to spend on marketing and promotion, even as it allows more cash to spill down to the bottom line. Now I don't mean to pick on the automakers too much, but compare General Motors to Microsoft. GM's gross margins are 22 percent. Microsoft's are 92 percent. In your quest to master the valuation of businesses, consider that as of this writing, General Motors has $171 billion in sales and is valued at just $46 billion. Meanwhile, Microsoft has $15 billion in sales and is valued at $260 billion. Let's put all those numbers together in a box to make it starkly clear:

	Sales	Gross Margins	Market Value
Microsoft	$ 15 billion	92%	$260 billion
General Motors	$171 billion	22%	$ 46 billion

The company with twelve times less in sales is worth five times more. Gross margins aren't the only reason for this, but they're a primary one. And the many market watchers that think this difference in valuation is ludicrous are overlooking both the benefits of a highly profitable business that is light on material costs and the drawbacks of a barely profitable business that is into heavy manufacturing. Microsoft's manufacturing costs (eighteen-year-old programmers compensated with stock options and a whole lot of pizza) are so low that it can punch enormous investments into marketing and development, yet still leave a fortune in earnings for their shareholders. The same cannot be said at the headquarters of our nation's leading automakers, who must spend large fortunes on factories, then small fortunes on dozens of parts and accessories per automobile, before ever getting down to promotional spending and profit.

That said, there is one legitimate complaint about companies that carry high gross margins—namely, that they can bring with them uninspiring, and even declining, sales volumes. Recognize that pushing gross margins higher relies on a one-two punch. First, the company has to establish pricing power. Second, it has to generate manufacturing efficiencies. Steadily rising gross margins over time rely on lower material costs *and* higher prices. And those higher prices may scare off potential customers, hindering sales growth. After all, I can make ten cups of cranberry lemonade for a nickel each, sit at my plastic table on the sidewalk, charge ten dollars per cup, and bask in the smug satisfaction that comes from knowing that I'm generating gross margins above 99 percent on each sale. But if I only sell one serving every decade, my business is uglier than a squashed Dixie cup in a mud puddle.

Pricing balance is a challenge for every company.

Thankfully, the truest Rule Makers, engaged in the business of encouraging *zombie automatic buying of inexpensive products*, don't much sweat the balance of pricing and sales volume. There's such buying demand for their stuff that consumers wouldn't balk at a ten-cent price hike. For instance, if Heinz raised the price for its ketchup from $2.00 to $2.40 per bottle, would you stop buying? Doubtful. Yet that toss-off extra 40 cents from consumers would amount to a 20 percent price increase and a strong gain in gross margins for Heinz. Not every company has this luxury. Large companies with Faker-Maker business models might have to raise their price $2,000 to notch a 20 percent increase per sale. Not good.

Returning to our simple rating system, Rule Makers have gross margins above 60 percent (2 points). Those next in line to the throne have gross margins between 40 and 60 percent (1 point). And least attractive to us are companies whose gross margins are below 40 percent (0 points).

A Two: Drugmaker Schering Plough, the maker of Claritin antihistamine, has gross margins of 80 percent, meaning that on average their products sell for five times more than they cost to manufacture. Working off an inexpensive operational model, Schering Plough can commit heavily to promoting existing drugs and researching new ones, while sending healthy rewards to their stakeholders. Credit Schering Plough with two points.

A Zero: Supermarkets are notorious for having razor-thin margins. The task of managing food inventories, the high expense of leasing or owning conveniently located warehouse space, and the pricing competition throughout its sector all contribute to a relentless downward pressure on gross margins. Safeway Corporation, with gross margins of just 29 percent, is not alone in its industry. Score it with zero points here.

3. Net Margins

The reward of high gross margins is surpassed only by the treasures of high net margins. Net profit margins are calculated by the following simple equation:

$$\frac{\text{Net Income}}{\text{Total Sales}}$$

This equation tells how much profit a company is making after every cost has been subtracted from sales revenues. If Sunshine Brew Inc. has 12 percent profit margins, it's making twelve cents on every dollar of sales. Similarly, if Midnight Pub Inc. has 6 percent profit margins, it is making just six cents in profit on every dollar of sales. You guessed it: To equal the total profits of the beer, the pub will have to do twice as much in sales.

To make it very clear, if Sunshine Brew has $100 million in sales and net margins of 12 percent, it has posted $12 million in profit. If Midnight Pub also has $100 million in sales but net margins of just 6 percent, it made $6 million in profit. In other words, though Midnight Pub has racked up the same total sales, it has secured merely half the profit. In nonfinancial terms, they've put in the same amount of effort, but earned just half the reward.

When looking for Rule Makers, I concentrate my attention on businesses with heightened levels of profitability. It's nice to know that a company can sell its wares for more than double its cost of manufacturing them—earning *gross* margins above 50 percent—but that would be of little positive consequence if the promotion, sale, and interest expenses associated with that product ended up thinning profits to near nothingness. Businesses have much more than just manufacturing costs to manage; they have to pay out $1 million for the halftime advertisement on the Super Bowl. They have to cover legal fees, provide customer service, pay phone bills, and chip in for that company pizza every Friday. Then they have to meet state and federal taxes on every remaining dollar of profit. Yep, there are costs well beyond the making of merchandise, and they're all reflected in the calculation of net margins.

The public companies that we'll target are those which, after subtracting out all costs associated with the business, earn more than ten cents off each dollar of sales, or return net margins above 10 percent. For illustration, let's again compare the two corporate giants, Microsoft and General Motors:

	Sales	**Net Margins**	**Market Value**
Microsoft	$ 15 billion	30%	$260 billion
General Motors	$171 billion	3%	$ 46 billion

GM today only takes three cents in profit for each dollar in sales of automobiles and services. Microsoft secures ten times that. Here again, though the automaker has nearly twelve times more sales than the software house, it is Microsoft with its far higher margins that's valued five times richer. Despite the sales discrepancy, Microsoft almost earns more total profit than GM.

Our second rule-making directive is to find companies with net-profit margins above 10 percent (2 points). The next best things are net margins running from 7 percent to 10 percent (1 point). And uninspiring for us are those larger businesses with net margins below 7 percent (0 points).

A Two: With each passing day, the world becomes more aware of the leading builder of the Internet, Cisco Systems. The company's routers and switches open the interactive digital world to tens of millions of computer users around the planet—a figure that will, no doubt, climb to over a billion in the next decade. All the while, Cisco Systems has maintained superior net margins, settling in at 16 percent today. It's no wonder that this company, which had less than $10 million in sales in 1988, is now worth over $100 billion. Customer growth and a steady growth in profitability have traveled arm in arm.

A Zero: Dayton Hudson has turned out one of the truly great retailing performances of the decade. Driven now primarily by its wildly popular Target stores, Dayton Hudson is building a nationwide infrastructure of retailing convenience and service that is largely unmatched. The problem is Dayton Hudson today turns just three cents of profit on every dollar of sales, for 3 percent net margins. The company needs to rigorously focus on inching its margins higher, one merchandise shelf at a time, or else it risks being so much long-term roadkill en route to the throne. Dayton is a potential Merchant King, not a rule-making manufacturer.

4. Sales Growth

Like every living thing, large companies see their rate of total growth naturally slow with age. The average eighty-five-year-old man will not, in percentage terms, outgrow the average eighty-five-week-old infant. And decades-old companies with $50 billion in sales won't expand business or their customer base as quickly, in percentage terms, as the next great Internet company to accelerate into American living rooms. What matters for larger companies is not how quickly they grow from here, but how well they take advantage of what they've got.

So, on the face of things, total sales growth appears to be a less important metric for veteran companies, with their success relying instead on increased efficiency and earnings growth. But don't forget that, however relatively meager in percentage terms the sales growth is, it's still a driver of business momentum. No public company, small or large, can rest on its laurels, comfortable that they've pursued *enough* growth and reached *enough* customers. The commercial charter of a public company is to aggressively pursue new markets and to fuel rising demand for their stuff, whether it's bananas or mainframe computers, back massages or construction equipment. Consequently, the large-growth company that cannot expand its customer base or experiences flat-line sales for an extended period is a business that should trouble its shareholders.

Tracking sales growth from year to year, I prize those larger companies that grow sales by more than 10 percent per year (2 points). Score 1 point for any billion-dollar company with from 5 to 10 percent sales growth. And any potential Rule Maker with less than 5 percent top-line growth is a disappointment (0 points).

A Two: Over the past five years, Schering Plough has grown its sales at an annual rate of 11 percent. And its sales growth has been accelerating with each passing quarter. In its most recent reporting period, the maker of Claritin antihistamine posted $1.99 billion in sales, a 16 percent climb over the previous period. When sales growth at larger companies exceeds 10 percent per year, Fools sit up and take notice. And when that rate of growth increases, Fools stand and cheer.

A Zero: For years now, AT&T's business has been stagnating as smaller telephone companies have pecked away at its stranglehold on long-distance communication. With an unfocused management team, Ma Bell floundered in the 1990s. Accordingly, over the past five years, revenues have actually declined, only lately returning to growth. (AT&T sales rose 1.5 percent this past year.) That performance earns AT&T a zero in sales growth. Things may be changing at the telecommunications company, though, with CEO Michael Armstrong now in charge. Shareholders certainly hope so; Ma Bell has lost to the market over the past ten years.

5. Cash-to-Debt Ratio

Since inception, The Motley Fool has always said it of your personal finances, and we'll say it of rule-making companies: We prefer that the financial statements show little or no debt. Who wants to own a business that wins a rich valuation today after announcing phenomenal earnings, but only because they borrowed heavily from their tomorrow? We want to own companies that will thrive for ten to twenty years or more, so we're naturally repelled by any short-term profits that come at the expense of the long-term survival and success of the enterprise.

It's that kind of patience that will be your greatest strength in all financial matters. Patience alone can lead to investments in Rule Makers that will put you on the beach in your retirement (with sunscreen, a mai tai, your children, your grandchildren, your dog Haley, and a big blue frisbee), or anywhere you choose to be. And that patience should be doubled by the managers of your company, who should prefer to grow their mature business methodically out of operational profit rather than through external financing. Our Rule Makers don't need debt, or very much debt, to gain and maintain control in their industry—to the dismay of some investment banks. They do not trade away a life without interest payments in exchange for short-term gains.

Now, because most companies will, and must, borrow money at some point—just as you might take out a mortgage—I don't want to cross off our list every organization with some debt on their balance sheet. We can stomach a little bit of it, particularly debt incurred from smart acquisitions and international expansion. But I'm not an apologist for businesses that shoulder enormous amounts of debt, even when it's used to acquire a first-rate company.

Instead, my favor is with those businesses whose cash savings are at least 1.5 times greater than their long-term debt. This ensures that when business difficulties arise (and they will, for any company), when something goes bump in the night, when the industry's wind blows the other way, the enterprise will have ample and immediate cash resources to deal with the problem. Make no mistake about it—over the course of a decade or two, or three, bad things *will* happen to every company, even the greatest of them. Do you remember New Coke? How about Microsoft's MSN Online, version 2.0? And what about the infamous McDLT at McDonald's? Or who remembers their McLean Deluxe sandwich? Things can go wrong; things will go wrong. We want companies with the cash to buy themselves out of trouble when, unwelcome and unbidden, it knocks on their midnight door.

Let's run one more comparison between Microsoft and General Motors, digging into their balance sheets for the necessary information:

	Cash	Long-Term Debt	Market Value
Microsoft	$ 14 billion	$ 0	$260 billion
General Motors	$1.1 billion	$8.7 billion	$ 46 billion

Here again, software development wins, racking up significantly more cash than the heavy business of assembling and delivering automobiles. And the market has responded in kind, richly rewarding the lighter and more profitable of the two.

The greatest Rule Makers have cash and equivalents (which include short-term investments and marketable securities) equal to or greater than 1.5 times their long-term debt (2 points). The next best things are companies with between 1.5 times more cash than debt and equal amounts of debt and cash (1 point). And out of our favor are those with more long-term debt than cash in the bank (0 points).

A Two: Pharmaceutical company Pfizer has $2 billion in cash and $742 million in long-term debt, making for 2.7 times more cash than debt. The company's financial standing is not unusual in the world of drug making, which historically has been an extremely high-margin business. Today, if Pfizer wanted to, it could pay down its $742 million debt overnight. It is, in my opinion, in a position of considerable strength, in part because of its substantial cash reserves relative to its borrowings.

A Zero: Though operating off a strong consumer-brand business model, Gillette doesn't meet our cash-to-debt criteria in the wake of its Duracell acquisition. Gillette ponied up $7.3 billion to acquire the battery maker, leaving it today with $76 million in cash and $1.8 billion in long-term debt. And now, as of this writing, its stock is getting battered on news of continued commercial weakness in international markets. So, while other companies are withstanding the pressure, Gillette is taking a hit because of its heavy debt load and the accompanying interest payments. Although it's a great company, Gillette might have benefited from delaying its Duracell purchase.

6. The Foolish Flow Ratio

Well, we've made it through five of the seven Rule Makers' criteria, and we've unwittingly narrowed down the nine thousand public companies in America to a few dozen. All of them are companies with automatic sales into a mass market, superior gross and net margins, healthy sales growth, and plenty of cash to expand. Those five criteria alone put us well ahead of the rabble of mediocre businesses. Concentrate on just those and you'll find some excellent large companies to invest in. But let's take another giant step forward, tighten our filter even more, and move to the most important numerical, the Flow Ratio, which is used to measure the efficiency with which a company manages its product deliveries and cash flow.

Naturally, when we search for rule-making companies, we'd like them to make the best use of the money that flows through their business. In the daily management of operations, money is going to rush through the front door from product sales, but it's also going to fly out the back in expenses. As investors, we need to monitor those tides coming in and going out, because businesses survive on their cash. It's their oxygen. Without new dollars arriving, they can't pay for employees, equipment, insurance, holiday parties, new technology, or anything. So, how a company manages the dollars that move through its business is of critical importance to us. In ideal circumstances, a business will bring money in quickly, like the continuous rush of a waterfall, but pay it out slowly, like water drops from an old sink. More cash coming in today, less cash going out today. If that makes sense, then you've mastered the most complex concept I have to offer about rule-making businesses.

Here's how we'll measure it.

On the balance sheet, the listing of current assets includes three primary groupings: cash, inventories, and accounts receivable. Our nation's general accounting standards have made a small mess of things by classifying all of these as "assets." In fact, inventories are definitely a *liability*. Is it a good thing to have $25 million worth of unsold Wonka Bars sitting in a warehouse in Covington, Virginia? Definitely not. Those unsold chocolate bars represent an investment by the company that to date has offered a 0 percent return. That's a liability—that's $25 million in value to which the company has no access. You'd much rather that the Wonka Bars had already been sold, that the $25 million had been collected, and that the cash was parked at the ready for management's direction. Dear Fools, don't let the accounting misguide you. Inventories are a *liability*.

So are accounts receivable. Accounts receivable simply reflect bills that Wonka Bars Incorporated hasn't yet collected—money *owed* to them. If Wonka lists $35 million in receivables, it means that they've announced the sale of $35 million worth of chocolate (posted on their income statement), but it also means that Wonka hasn't yet been paid for that sale. Not good. Here, again, we have value that our company cannot yet access, and that's a liability. Interestingly, a precipitous rise in accounts receivable can possibly signify that Wonka Bars is padding its sales. Its report of $35 million in accounts receivable this quarter, $50 million by the end of next quarter, maybe $100 million by the end of the year can reflect contract provisions that allow the stores that carry Wonka's magic chocolate bars to return any unsold product for a full refund. The line item of accounts receivable causes a Fool to ask, "What exactly *are* sales, if the products can be returned for a full refund?" *(Author's rant: I believe that the provisions for accounts receivable make it the single most misleading of all U.S. accounting standards, and one that's over-ripe for reform.)*

In the end, of the three main groupings of current assets—inventories, receivables, and cash—the Flow Ratio recognizes only cash as an asset. Unsold products and uncollected bills are weaknesses, not strengths. Understanding this gives you the numerator in our Flow Ratio, and already puts you ahead of many on Wall Street. To calculate the numerator, just subtract cash (including all short-term investments and marketable securities) from the total current assets. Here's the process, step by step.

Wonka Bars

	January 1998
Cash	$ 48 million
Marketable securities	$ 15 million
Accounts receivable	$ 40 million
Inventory	$ 71 million
Total current assets	$174 million

To calculate the numerator of the Foolish Flow Ratio, add together cash and marketable securities, then subtract that from total current assets. Simple stuff.

1. Total current assets ($174 million) – (cash [$48 million] + marketable securities [$15 million])
2. $174 million – $63 million
3. $111 million

The second half of the equation, our denominator, has us concentrating attention on the other side of the balance sheet, the current liabilities. Here, too, I Foolishly suggest that the forefathers of our accounting standards were taking nips from a bottle of Jägermeister as they worked through the labeling process. I believe that current liabilities are actually *assets* to the corporation.

Current liabilities reflect all bills that Wonka Bars will pay to its business partners over the next twelve months. Instinct thus suggests that we'd want current liabilities to be as *low* as possible, indicating that our company has no major outstanding bills. But be contrary: A company that can hold off paying its suppliers (Wonka Bars Inc.'s suppliers being the producers of cocoa butter, sugar, milk, salt, and such) is one that is enjoying a slow flow of expenses out of its business, one bill at a time. A few paragraphs above, I suggested that our ideal companies are those that "bring money into their business quickly, like the continuous rush of a waterfall, but pay it out slowly, like water drops from an old sink." In that context, rising current liabilities are actually good news, if a company has cash in the bank to cover them. Those climbing liabilities represent strong contracts with suppliers; they show us that a potential Rule Maker has the clout to slowly pay down its bills, with cash flowing out of its business like water drops from an old sink.

As we move toward the unveiling of the Flow Ratio, let's review the two key points. First, because two of the main groupings of current assets (inventories and receivables) are, in fact, liabilities, we'd like to see them held as low as possible. Second, among financially secure businesses, we hope to find those with the commercial authority in their markets to hold off the payment of short-term debits. Let's look at the ratio and see if we can't make sense of it:

$$\text{The Foolish Flow Ratio} = \frac{(\text{current assets} - \text{all cash})}{\text{current liabilities}}$$

You can probably guess whether we're rooting for a high or low Flow Ratio, just by folding closed the edges of this book, pressing your index fingers on either temple, and concentrating for a moment. Remember that the Flow Ratio hates noncash current assets (say, unsold Beanie Babies and uncollected bills from the retailer) and loves current liabilities (unpaid bills for the supply of Beanie Baby materials).

Because we'd like to see current assets minus cash to be minimal and current liabilities to be maximal, we want the Flow Ratio to sit low. We want the denominator (current liabilities) to be very high and the numerator (current assets minus cash) to sit as low as possible. In the best-case scenario, the businesses that we own have Foolish Flow Ratios below 1.0. In reasonably strong situations, they carry a Flow between 1.0 and 1.25. And, finally, we're anxious about the state of any company whose balance sheet shows a Flow Ratio sitting above 1.25.

Let's try out two examples:

Nike

	Fiscal 1998
Cash	$108 million
Current assets	$ 3.5 billion
Current liabilities	$ 1.7 billion
Flow Ratio	2.0

Dell Computer

	Fiscal 1998
Cash	$ 1.8 billion
Current assets	$ 3.9 billion
Current liabilities	$ 2.7 billion
Flow Ratio	0.78

As the results here would predict, rule-making investors were worried about Nike's prospects at the close of fiscal 1998, and in fact have been for the past three years. With its Flow Ratio above 2.0, the company was struggling with inventory controls and was padding its international sales. Those were both very bad signs, and the stock fell from $75 to $32. The second example, Dell Computer, is the charm. Dell has a Flow Ratio below 1.0, indicating that it carries very little inventory and isn't in the habit of preannouncing sales. Dell has been among a handful of the best-performing stocks of the past decade.

The Foolish Flow Ratio is an extremely powerful (though not all-powerful) calculation for determining the underlying financial strength of a public corporation. By running it, you'll be measuring how tightly a company manages the flow of its supplies and finished products, as well as how carefully it tends to the cash that moves into and through their business. The ratio can tell you a lot about, for instance, Wonka Bars Inc., forcing you to ask the right questions: Is the company being lazy in collecting its bills? Is Wonka being sloppy in managing its inventory? Is the business in such a weakened financial position that its partners demand cash payments from them up front? If so, look out: These chocolate bars may have gone sour and brittle; it's a company that is not yet ready for your investment.

The Flow Ratio is just one of many measures of quality, but for us it's a critical one. As an investor, I spend most of my time studying businesses with Flow Ratios under 1.0 (2 points)—companies like Coca-Cola, Microsoft, America Online, Schering Plough, and Intel. I'm interested in, but not overly enthused by, those with Flows between 1.0 and 1.25 (1 point). And any enterprise with a Flowie above 1.25 had better have unusually great excuses and unusually great business opportunities to win my attention (0 points).

A Two: America Online has one of the strongest Flow Ratios in the world, standing at 0.29. That's the consequence of carrying no inventory and receiving most of the payments for its service up front from consumers. In certain cases, customers pay two years in advance for AOL's access to the Internet. Off that model, it's no wonder that the stock has risen from $2 to $125 per share over the last four years. The market has rewarded America Online with a value of $25 billion, ten times its sales of $2.3 billion. The absence of inventory carrying costs and the fact that most payments come up front from customers put AOL in an extremely strong business position.

A Zero: Callaway Golf has a Flow Ratio of 2.14, the result of carrying too many unclaimed Big Berthas, as well as being forced to extend too favorable terms to its distributors. The retail outlets that sell Callaway's Big Berthas are able to withhold payment for the clubs until they're sold. In the best of all worlds, Callaway would either distribute directly to consumers, accepting payments up front, or the company would be in such a powerful position that it could tighten down on its retailing partners. With a Flow Ratio of 2.14, it's no surprise that even though the company has $830 million in sales, it's only valued at $723 million. The stock has fallen fast and far.

7. Your Familiarity and Interest

On the face of it, the seventh criterion for finding Rule Makers seems absurd. How does *your* interest and familiarity with a corporation improve *its* chances of excelling? It doesn't. This final requirement, rather than being applied to public companies, is applied to you, the investor. Even with the six previous criteria in place, absent an understanding of what your businesses really do, you open yourself up to subpar returns. The likelihood that you'll understand whether the bumps and bruises along the way are minor nicks or life-threatening injuries for your company is very high *if* you can understand and follow its progress.

Technology is making that easier; the advent of message boards like those at fool.com has helped individual investors stay on top of their portfolios. Still, all the technology and all the information in the world can't put everything into my circle or your circle of expertise. Reams of available information haven't helped me over the hurdle into an understanding of and an interest in industrial-equipment manufacture or aluminum mining. And the slew of free information at The Motley Fool Online might never be able to interest you in publicly owned sports teams, or the competitive world of shipbuilding, or the sale of titanium. This seventh criterion cheers your assessment of your natural limitations and encourages you to focus on what you understand, enjoy, and believe in.

Thus, the last criterion of the Rule Maker is that *you* find it easy to follow the operational direction of the business. It proposes that you'll dramatically improve your chances of scoring above-average investment returns if you weed out the unfamiliar and concentrate on companies whose products, marketing approach, management, and reputation with customers you'll enjoy following. Whether it's dedicated to the business of NASCAR racing, to selling sandwiches, or manufacturing personal computers, a company will more likely serve you well if you know it well.

Here's the scoring system for this last standard: If you personally use and enjoy the product, add 2 points to your company's score. If you're familiar with the company's products and believe in their value, but don't use them, score it as a 1-pointer. And if you've never heard of the product, don't know what it is, and don't give a hoot about it, that company gets 0 points.

A Two: Borders Books is just the sort of business that interests me; so is Barnes & Noble. And the same goes for Amazon.com—and not just because those three will act as the main distributors for this book. I can easily let an afternoon slip past in a bookstore. I'll even offer three of my favorite books from the past year: *The Diving Bell and the Butterfly, Titan: The Life of John D. Rockefeller,* and Philip Fisher's first-rate investment guide, *Common Stocks, Uncommon Profits* (a rereading). But you're not here for book reviews!

For me, the bookselling industry earns two points on familiarity and interest.

A Zero: If you're like me, you don't take much interest in learning more about a business that provides lead-wire assemblies to the disk-drive industry. That isn't to say that you have to be like me. You may be fascinated by the inner workings of a disk drive. You may work in the industry and be an expert on how they're constructed, how they're embedded in computers, and what distinguishes one product from the next. I don't have a clue about that—and I have even less interest in the business. Thus, for me, a company like Innovex, which manufactures said lead-wire assemblies, earns zero points on familiarity and interest.

Restatement of the Criteria

Because these seven criteria form the bedrock of rule-making investing, I'm presenting them in scorecard fashion below. Then I'll drive three public companies through a careful analysis using these criteria. Here they are again, with their accompanying point totals:

1. **Mass Market, Repeat Purchase**
   2 points: purchased more than once a month
   1 point: purchased from once a month to once a year
   0 points: purchased less than once a year

2. **Gross Margins**
   2 points: above 60%
   1 point: from 40–60%
   0 points: below 40%

3. **Net Margins**
   2 points: above 10%
   1 point: from 7–10%
   0 points: below 7%

4. **Sales Growth**
   2 points: above 10%
   1 point: from 5–10%
   0 points: below 5%

5. **Cash-to-Debt Ratio**
   2 points: 1.5 times more cash than long-term debt
   1 point: from 1 to 1.5 times more cash than debt
   0 points: less cash than long-term debt

6. **The Foolish Flow Ratio**
   2 points: below 1.00
   1 point: from 1.00 to 1.25
   0 points: above 1.25

7. **Your Familiarity and Interest**
   2 points: user of the products and interested
   1 point: familiar with the products and curious
   0 points: unfamiliar with the products and uninterested

Upon these seven standards will kings be made or legends shattered. Based on them, the public markets will either rise up to cheer the head of an approaching prince or stand on their toes to see it cleaved off. Companies which you know and respect that abide all seven—posting strong sales growth from automatic buying, carrying high margins and substantial cash reserves—are likely the market-beating giants of the future.

Let's apply these seven benchmarks to three public companies aspiring to the throne: Kmart, Disney, and Coca-Cola.

Model Business 1: Kmart Corporation

When speaking and writing about this investing approach, even after laying out the Rule Maker criteria, I'm sometimes asked, "Aren't you essentially suggesting that we buy big, familiar companies and hold them for the long haul?"

My answer is certainly No.

Over the past ten years, a great number of multi-billion-dollar public companies have underperformed the total market's return. In industries as disparate as metal, media, technology, and retailing, familiar names like Bethlehem Steel, Dow Jones, Apple, and Venator (a.k.a. Woolworth) have dramatically underperformed the market, earning their owners next to nothing during a period in which the general market has quadrupled. All of these corporations are familiar to us, each is large and apparently stable, and carries with it the *air* of dominance. But they've been laggards in their industries, falling down on their plastic crowns, either because management wasn't focused on creating enduring shareholder value or because management didn't understand how to direct a public company. Some of them may be rebounding today, struggling toward a regal perch, but thankfully, in all cases, the rule-making criteria kicked these businesses out of consideration before their decade of woe.

Of the three companies we'll take through the rule-making wringer, I'd like to start with Kmart (NYSE: KM), the nation's number-three retailer behind Wal-Mart and Sears. The company sells clothing, appliances, furniture, toys, and other knickknacks directly to consumers through 2,200 discount stores across the United States. Let's look at the company's financials, starting with its income statement. Through the nine months of fiscal 1998, Kmart's income statement reads:

Fiscal 1998 (Through Third Quarter)

Total sales	$22.4 billion
Gross profit	$ 4.9 billion
Gross margin	21.9%
Net income	$63 million
Net margin	2.8%

With those at the ready, let's consider the first four rule-making criteria.

1. MASS MARKET, REPEAT PURCHASE

At the starting line, Kmart breaks out into an early lead, as it meets our expectation of offering low-priced products that a mass market of consumers can repeatedly purchase. Whether it's the plastic plants, the baseball glove, the bedsheets, the kitchen utensils, or the ramen noodles,

Kmart has it all. And though the company's customer base has been eroding over the past decade, Kmart still scores the highest ranking for designing and implementing a business model that benefits from the repeated purchasing of low-priced products by people from all walks of life.

Score: 2 points

2. GROSS MARGINS

Unfortunately, Kmart is not running a light-enough business to adequately meet our second criterion. With gross margins of just 21.9 percent, the retailer well undershoots our ideal of 60 percent, and falls shy of the B-grade 40 to 60 percent gross margins. Though the business is expensive to run—stocking and maintaining superstores in neighborhoods across the country ain't cheap—the real check on Kmart's gross margins is the result of its lack of any real pricing power. The superstore retailing model is extremely competitive, and Kmart has failed to distinguish itself in ways that would allow it to ratchet up its prices.

Score: 0 points

3. NET MARGINS

Here as well, Kmart falls shy of our expectations on profitability. With net margins of 2.8 percent, earning just 2.8 cents on every dollar of sales, Kmart doesn't have the profit power to fund worldwide expansion while rewarding shareholders each step of the way. Forced into price wars by its competitors and trapped into an expensive and risky model for new-store development, when it comes to gross and net margins, Kmart has been knocked off its horse.

Score: 0 points

4. SALES GROWTH

Sadly, the superstore retailer hasn't been able to keep up here, either. Business has been a struggle over the past five years, during which the corporation has actually seen declining sales. Over the last twelve months, Kmart's top line has begun to expand again, but only at a rate of 2.4 percent. This falls at the bottom end of our expectations and earns Kmart 0 points.

Score: 0 points

On the income statement, Kmart has put in a thoroughly disappointing performance. The company is not reaching new customers, and has little to no pricing power when it does. The end result is a business that has little growth and low margins—a double-dip of disaster. Nipsey Russell and Charles Nelson Reilly are reaching to gong the golden platter and drive Kmart off the stage of consideration, but let's give it the full treatment, taking its balance sheet all the way through the process. Here are the key figures we'll need:

Fiscal 1998 (Through Third Quarter)

Cash and equivalents	$280 million
Current assets	$ 9.2 billion
Current liabilities	$ 4.3 billion
Long-term debt	$ 2.3 billion

5. CASH-TO-DEBT RATIO

Sadly, Kmart stumbles right off the bat, falling in an awkward heap of heavy steel as the audience gasps. On the balance sheet, we look for a company with cash and equivalents ringing in at more than 1.5 times long-term debt. Kmart's cash equals just 0.12 times its debt, representing 8 times more long-term debt than cash. This is a business that's exposed to heavy annual interest payments to its bankers and surrounded by threats of new competition. Kmart doesn't have the capital to much extend operations, defend itself against competition, or prepare for any dramatic changes in retailing. Over the next twelve months, the superstore retailer will be forced to pay out about as much in interest payments on that debt as it has cash in the bank today—much like the recent college graduate with substantially overdrawn credit cards.

Score: 0 points

6. THE FOOLISH FLOW RATIO

The Flow Ratio, perhaps our most important metric, again is used to measure how efficiently a company turns supplies into products, products into sales, sales into cash, cash into supplies, supplies into products, products into sales . . . and so on, and so on, and so on. Again, the simple calculation is current assets minus cash over current liabilities.

Here's how the numbers play out for Kmart:

1. $$\frac{(\text{current assets} - \text{cash})}{(\text{current liabilities})}$$
2. $$\frac{(\$9.2 \text{ billion} - \$280 \text{ million})}{\$4.3 \text{ billion}}$$
3. $$\frac{\$8.92 \text{ billion}}{\$4.3 \text{ billion}}$$
4. Flow Ratio: 2.07

Recall that we want the noncash current assets (inventory and receivables) to be low, and the current liabilities (unpaid bills and projected expenses) to be high, resulting in a Flow Ratio ideally below 1.0, but at least below 1.25.

Kmart's Flow Ratio of 2.07 is a fairly grave nonsuccess, but not unexpected. The problem for the retailer is the $7.8 billion in merchandise inventories that sit in its current "asset" group. Kmart is carrying a huge load of unsold products from one month to the next. For a company with $30 billion in annual sales, Kmart today is doing a poor job of understanding what its customers want and avoiding what they don't. The company must get its inventories under control, *soon*. Its Flow Ratio is unacceptable.
Score: 0 points

7. YOUR FAMILIARITY AND INTEREST

Because it's the most subjective of our rankings, I'll largely leave familiarity and interest rankings up to you, dear reader. Given its financial position and its inability thus far to distinguish itself in an overcrowded industry, Kmart is not the most interesting business to me. But it *is* a broad-based consumer brand with decades of history in America. So

I'm scoring 1 point for Kmart here, given my familiarity with its business and small curiosity about it.
Score: 1 point

Kmart's balance sheet, like the income statement, is a clanging tune or a torn canvas, anything but finished art. The company did not excel in any category of this round's rankings, and failed two of three. The balance sheet, offering the best representation of a business's underlying strength, is a financial statement that Kmart may have preferred not to release. It shows high debt, poor product and cash management, and vulnerability. Certainly the company's shortcomings aren't insurmountable. But they don't put out a welcoming mat for future investment, either.

KMART'S FINAL SCORE

On the five key financial points, Kmart came up with nothing but two empty hands and a sour look on its face. I wish it weren't so. But the business has low gross and net margins, little sales growth, a heavy load of debt, and exhibits poor management of cash and product flows. Carrying enormous amounts of inventory, unable to distinguish itself enough to gain pricing power, and now behind the eight ball with its banking "partners," Kmart rang up an unimpressive total score of three out of fourteen points.

Looking back at historical performance, Kmart's stock has reflected this financial deterioration. The stock has fallen from $27 in 1992 down to $13 in the summer of 1998. That's total growth of –52 percent for investors during a period in which the stock market's average return, as measured by the S&P 500, has risen more than 130 percent.

Kmart *is* now trying to turn itself around. Though still overweighted with debt, the retailer sold off its international stores to lighten the millstone tied chokingly 'round its purse. And the company within the last few years brought in a variety of promotional partners including Charlie's Angel Jaclyn Smith, *Sesame Street*'s Elmo (of "Tickle Me" fame), supermodel Kathy Ireland, and home magician Martha Stewart. The effort is underway at Kmart, and you can learn a lot about a struggling business by following its quarterly financial results in the years ahead. Kmart may even end up being a market-beating large company over the next ten years, if it can radically change directions—most notably by tightening inventory controls, paying down debt, and gaining some measure of authority over its suppliers. But it's in far too unstable a position today for Rule Maker investors to take note.

To return now from whence we came, I'll again answer this section's introductory question. "Aren't you essentially just suggesting that we buy big, familiar companies and hold them for the long haul?" No, I don't believe that all large consumer-franchise businesses should be bought and held. Kmart demonstrates the sort of mediocrity that today could not hold a kingdom for an hour.

That completed, let's take a look at our second model company, Disney, and its Mouse.

Model Business 2: Walt Disney Company

Each year, fewer and fewer people on the planet are unfamiliar with Disney, as the company puts a Mickey Mouse in every child's room around the globe. Based in Orlando, Florida, Disney is the most prominent and most valuable entertainment franchise in the world. The company owns theme parks, movie studios, radio stations, television stations, classic films, retail stores, cartoon productions, a hockey team, and a baseball team. In 1995, Disney bought Capital Cities/ABC, which carried with it ESPN and all of its various parts, which now include ESPN2, ESPNews, ESPN Classic, and *ESPN: The Magazine*.

Not surprisingly, Disney over the past fifteen years has been one of the truly great investments in America. As movies led to merchandise, merchandise to sequels, and sequels to profit, Disney worked its magic through each link in the chain. Today, you can buy dozens of different Buzz Lightyear products and watch your kids kick them around the living room during their fifty-seventh viewing of *Toy Story*. The reach and the reward of the tie-ins throughout Disney's business are astonishing.

But what about the company's status as a Rule Maker in the entertainment industry? How much financial authority does Disney really have? Can it control its own destiny? Or is it just another movie studio caught in the trap of trying to manufacture unrelated new hits each year? Here are the key figures on Disney's income statement. Let's put the Mouse to the test.

Fiscal 1998 (Through Third Quarter)

Trailing sales	$22.4 billion
Gross profit	$ 9.0 billion*
Gross margin	40.2%*
Net income	$ 2.0 billion
Net margin	8.9%

*Gross profit and gross margin figures are estimates.

1. MASS MARKET, REPEAT PURCHASE

There's no need for deep reflection on this point: Crowds of consumers return to Disney products, week after week. Of all ages, they come to buy stuffed dolls, rent Disney films, watch ABC television and ESPN, even to read books released by Hyperion, Disney's publishing house. And they take to Disney's products and properties each week with the gleaming eyes of children on holiday.
Score: 2 points

2. GROSS MARGINS

Unfortunately, Disney's accountants don't break out the company's gross margins for investors, instead lumping all costs together and leaving us with just an operating-income entry. So, I'm forced to make an estimate about their gross margins. Given that Disney's operating margins are 18 percent, and given its industry, I'm projecting that its gross margins are between 40 and 45 percent. That earns them one point.
Score: 1 point

3. NET MARGINS

Disney excels here, with net margins of 9 percent—the consequence of the pricing power and profit available to a leading brand. One reason that Disney is so profitable was covered in the previous section on branding. Because of its loyal and growing cadre of customers, Disney can gradually manage down its promotional costs. Repeat buyers don't

need to be reminded of products through constant advertisement. The consequence? Higher profit margins.
Score: 2 points

4. SALES GROWTH

The first sign of any distress at Disney shows up here. Through the first nine months of 1998, Disney has shown sales flagging from $17.0 billion in 1997 down to $16.8 billion this. Though only a 1 percent drop, the stalling demand represents a problem for Disney, because as we march down through the balance sheet, the matter of how they'll finance future sales growth becomes an issue. Disney's slowing demand today does not match up well with the company's decision to carry substantial amounts of debt so as to finance today's growth. That's certainly the central reason that, as of this writing, Disney's stock is 40 percent off its 1998 highs.
Score: 0 points

On the income statement, Disney has delivered a decent, though not outstanding, performance, scoring five out of a possible eight points. The company has been fighting to defend its high margins, but halfway through 1998, sales growth has flattened out. At the same time, the Mouse *is* sitting on an enviable repeat-purchase business model that has people around the world coming back for more.

We're only holding half the picture now, however. The income statement only provides us a snapshot of the company's short-term performance. Earnings are solid, and today Disney has loads of loyal customers. But what about the underlying strength of Disney's business—how much cash they have in the bank, how well they direct the circulation of products through their business, and how much authority they have in their industry? For that, my Fools, we must take to the balance sheet. First, here are the key figures:

Fiscal 1998 (Through Third Quarter)

Cash and equivalents	$ 850 million
Current assets	$ 4.6 billion
Current liabilities	$ 5.9 billion
Long-term debt	$11.9 billion

5. CASH-TO-DEBT RATIO

The first serious blemish has appeared: Disney carries a mountain of debt. With nearly $12 billion in borrowings and just $850 million in cash, the company's ratio of cash to debt is a mere 0.07, well below our ideal of 1.5 times more savings than long-term debt. Flipped over, the ratio shows that Disney has fourteen times more long-term debt than cash. The Mouse did borrow heavily to fund the purchase of Cap Cities/ABC in 1995, and debt from acquisition isn't as bad as operational debt. But debt still hurts. Through nine months of fiscal 1998, Disney has already made interest payments totaling a whopping $445 million. Even at low interest rates, these borrowings have forced Disney to play from a weak hand at a critical time—as it considers what role it will assume on the Internet. Thus far, the answer is a strikingly small and unimpressive one.
Score: 0 points

6. THE FOOLISH FLOW RATIO

Despite its debt, Disney has excelled at managing its Flow Ratio, holding it between 0.90 and 0.60 in recent years. Today, its Flow Ratio sits at 0.78, placing it in an elite group of public companies. Disney's financial managers have established a model that accelerates their products out of the door, opens their coffers for the cash, and forces their suppliers to wait on delayed payments. How does Disney pull it off? By distributing so much directly through to consumers. In doing so, the Mouse deals immediately with inventory matters as well as receives payments up front from customers. The resulting low Flow Ratio has been a strong contributor to Disney's durability and business success.
Score: 2 points

7. YOUR FAMILIARITY AND INTEREST

As an avid, though disheartened, fan of the Washington Redskins football team and the Georgetown Hoyas basketball team, I've spent plenty of time plinking between ESPN channels to watch the highlight reels featuring our opposing teams. I've also watched my share of Miramax films over the past few years. And I recently refereed a boxing match between Buzz Lightyear and Mickey Mouse, staged by a niece and nephew. Name me very familiar with and certainly interested by Disney's business.
Score: 2 points

DISNEY'S FINAL SCORE

With its leading brands, loyal customers, and terrific worldwide business opportunities, Disney is the world's premier entertainment company. The company has healthy margins, repeat buyers, tight management of inventory and receivables, and Mickey. The one red flag, and it does wave prominently in the midday sun, is the degree to which Disney has leveraged off its future to secure greater success today.

With nearly $12 billion in debt, Disney is partially behind the interest-payment eight ball. And despite its strong position in current media, the company will naturally react more slowly and less forcefully when media and entertainment hit a turn in the road, as it has with the Internet. Furthermore, were Disney's core business to suffer over an intermediate-term period, for any reason from international crises to a spate of bad films, the company could founder for a while. Costly interest payments matched up with a decrease in their margins could temporarily hamstring Mickey. We already got a taste of that in 1998, when Disney's stock fell from $42 to $25, or 40 percent, on news of poor results in Asia.

The Mouse has its problems, but I am nevertheless confident that a decade from now, in contrast to Kmart, Disney will be plodding ahead, trying to put Mickey on a wall, in a tree, under a pillow, on a computer screen, and in our heads (why doesn't Disney put out *Mickey Mouse: The Movie?*). I'm far less certain about Kmart's survival, even though it bears a name familiar to many of us. Kmart's financial standing is too insecure to guarantee it any measure of success, or even resiliency, over the next decade. Thus it's a business that rule-making investors have on their "avoid" list.

Disney earned a nine out of fourteen points on the seven criteria, putting it far ahead of Kmart, and ahead of most public companies in America. But that also leaves room for improvement, as it falls short of what I consider to be an outstanding ranking of twelve points or higher. Disney needs to get back to capturing the real profit centers of its business while methodically paying down its debt.

Now, what about our third aspirant to the throne, Coca-Cola—the big red can down in Atlanta, the brown bubbly flowing across the world? What do our Rule Maker criteria say about this business?

Model Business 3:
The Coca-Cola Company

The Coca-Cola Company today sells its products in over two hundred countries. In the United States, the average citizen drinks more than one Coke product every day—every single one of 272 million Americans tips back a Coke or Diet Coke or Sprite or Fanta or Surge or Minute Maid every day of their lives. Yet even so, Coca-Cola actually derives more than 65 percent of its sales from the international market. Mexicans and Chileans drink nearly seven eight-ounce servings of Coke beverages per week. The average Norwegian drinks five Coke products each week. The same is true in Israel and in Australia.

COKE IS IT, AND COKE IS EVERYWHERE

But is The Coca-Cola Company a pretender to the throne? Cast your eyes at the critical numbers on the income statement:

Fiscal 1998 (Through Second Quarter)

Total sales	$19.3 billion
Gross profit	$13.4 billion
Gross margin	69.4%
Net income	$ 4.4 billion
Net margin	19.7%

1. MASS MARKET, REPEAT PURCHASE

Coca-Cola is perhaps the world's best illustration of a repeated-purchasing business, with people across the planet buying its inexpensive products automatically, day after day. Each hour, 6.5 billion humans grow more familiar with the brand and the product, while at the same time, Big Red locks down even more tightly the *future* demand for its products. Wall Street, in its feverish search for next week's big winner, sometimes badly underrates the long-term value of repeatedly purchased convenience products. The Coca-Cola Company doesn't.
Score: 2 points

2. GROSS MARGINS

The manufacturing costs of Coca-Cola's business are low, and falling. Today, its gross-profit margins (gross profit divided by sales) are 69.4 percent, and rising. Again, that means that after subtracting out the manufacturing costs of mixing its syrups and concentrates, Coke retains 69 cents per dollar of sales to invest in its business. With $4.5 billion in sales in its most recent quarter, Coca-Cola has—after manufacturing—more than $3 billion to funnel toward the expansion of shareholder value.
Score: 2 points

3. NET MARGINS

One wonders what today's financial media would've said back in 1886, when Coca-Cola's founder, John Pemberton, announced sales of $50 for the year . . . alongside advertising costs of $76. For every dollar of sales, the company was losing $1.52 to advertising alone. In the minds of the financial media, that would make Coca-Cola just like so many of today's Internet companies—unable to turn a profit. But as much as Coke, in embryonic form, may have appeared to be spilling red ink, it was just making early investments in its long-term expansion.

Six years later, Coke was incorporated and capitalized at $100,000; twenty-seven years after that, it was sold for $25 million. Today, the company is valued at $192 billion. As the Coca-Cola Company moved from its brash rule-breaking ways toward a purple-robed life in the castle, it had to press through high promotional and distribution costs to find a world of wide and widening profits. And though Coca-Cola pours enormous investments into promoting its products across the globe today, because they're in a repeat-purchase business, the net cost of advertising can actually be reduced over time. When you walk into a restaurant, tuck a napkin into your shirt, and instinctively say to your waiter, "A glass of ice water and a Coke, please," you know just how strong this company's position is in the marketplace.

The reduction of the net cost of advertising helps Coca-Cola maintain net profit margins well above 7 percent. In fact, Coke's net margins over the past twelve months have been 19.2 percent.
Score: 2 points

4. SALES GROWTH

Sales growth has been the one income-statement item in which Coke does not excel. Over the past year, the soda maker has extended its top line by just 5.3 percent, earning it a middling score. As Coca-Cola has expanded into new international markets, they've chosen to drop prices on their products in order to create demand and cement their position: Coke, in effect, has been acting like a small start-up in markets like Russia and China, focusing less on profitability than on the acquisition of new customers. In time, the numbers will show whether this approach had merit or not. For now, Coca-Cola scores one point for posting only moderate sales growth over the past few years.
Score: 1 point

On the income statement, Coca-Cola has excelled in meeting nearly all of our Rule Maker criteria. The company's business is light on manufacturing and extremely profitable. Meanwhile, although sales growth has flagged a bit in recent years owing to its interest in gaining market share in new corners of the world, Coke's products *are* gaining acceptance globally—promising growth in the future. With seven out of eight points on the income statement, Coca-Cola is well ahead of both Kmart and Disney.

But now onward to the real strength (or lack thereof) of its business, as evidenced on the balance sheet. Spy the numbers:

Fiscal 1998 (Through Second Quarter)

Cash and equivalents	$ 2.2 billion
Current assets	$ 6.9 billion
Current liabilities	$ 8.0 billion
Long-term debt	$686 million

5. CASH-TO-DEBT RATIO

In Rule Makers, we look for companies maintaining cash levels equal to or greater than 1.5 times long-term debt. At various stages in a company's history, it'll make acquisitions with borrowed money, and that throws this ratio out of whack. But, in more cases than not, I've found that for larger companies the simple metric of cash to debt indicates a great deal about how the business is being run. When a retailer, for ex-

ample, borrows up to $2 billion to expand, is able to conserve very lit-
tle cash, and then blunders in predicting consumer activity for the
Christmas season, watch out. That's a difficult predicament to work out
of. Had that business more cash and lower or no interest payments, it
could easily have dug out of a bad season. In a king, we want that company which has the staying power associated with strong cash reserves.

In Coke's case, it does. The company has $686 million in long-term
debt and $2 billion in cash and marketable securities. That works out to
2.9 times more cash than debt.

Score: 2 points

6. THE FOOLISH FLOW RATIO

You may now have grown tired of my endlessly explaining the Flow
Ratio. But because it's a critical component to investing in Rule Makers,
and because it's the most complex of the criteria, permit me one last go.
The Foolish Flow Ratio depends on the following beliefs: (1) Cash savings are a good thing; (2) Unsold inventory is bad news; (3) Uncollected
bills are bad news; (4) Unpaid bills are good news. Thus, a company's
noncash current assets are a weakness, while its current liabilities are a
strength. By dividing noncash current assets by current liabilities, we'll
gain some insight into how well the company moves its product (inventory) out the door, collects payments for its sales (receivables), and delays settlement with its suppliers (payables). Ideally, we'd like to find
noncash current assets running lower than current liabilities.

Let's run the numbers for Coca-Cola.

1. $\dfrac{\text{(current assets [\$6.9 billion]} - \text{all cash [\$2.2 billion])}}{\text{current liabilities [\$8.0 billion]}}$

2. $\dfrac{\text{\$4.7 billion}}{\text{\$8.0 billion}}$

3. Coke's Flowie = 0.59

There are very few companies in the world that can boast a Flow
Ratio as low as Coke's. Microsoft, at 0.29, has the greatest Foolish Flow
I've ever come across. For this reason, as I've written in the past, I believe that two of the strongest companies on the planet, and two of the
most secure and rewarding Rule Makers in which we can invest, are
Coca-Cola and Microsoft. No two companies better display financial
might coupled with brand power than they. This is not the Conven-

tional Wisdom; I've also noted on many occasions that the rabble of media pundits and academics pronounce Microsoft and Coca-Cola ridiculously overpriced. I believe the people spouting this line have made one critical error in their analysis: They have focused on stock price and short-term valuation instead of trying to understand how a financial system is modeled to provide decades of earnings growth. They've played keno rather than played for keeps.

With a Flow Ratio of 0.59, Coca-Cola far surpasses our standards. Its product is getting out the door, payment is arriving up front, and Coke is an important enough piece of its suppliers' business that it can extend the length of its payment periods in contracts. Mark down another two-pointer.

Score: 2 points

7. YOUR FAMILIARITY AND INTEREST

The Coca-Cola Company is one of the easiest American businesses to follow. Its products are ubiquitous. In addition, its disclosure to shareholders is virtually unmatched: In each annual report, the company maps out its progress, country by country, for its owners—confronting mediocrity and highlighting success. Familiarity with this business is virtually automatic.

As for my interest level, two things strike my fancy. First, Coca-Cola is one of a handful of companies that can teach investors an enormous amount about how the world *works*, in even its most remote reaches. Second, as an investor, I take a natural interest in any company that has posted market-beating results for many years. Scoring familiarity and interest on a superior consumer-product company like this is simple.

Score: 2 points

COCA-COLA'S FINAL SCORE

The twentieth-century Coca-Cola shareholder, reinvesting dividends, has compounded 16.7 percent yearly growth on her investment. To restate from *The Motley Fool Investment Workbook*, that rate of return has turned a $4,000 investment at Coca-Cola's initial public offering in 1919 into more than $650 million after taxes today.

Lest you believe that the company saw all of its growth in the early days, that you've missed out on the fun, the value of Coca-Cola's business has actually been growing faster than ever lately, in total as well as percentage terms. Over the past ten years, Coke has gained twenty times in value, or grown at a rate of 35 percent per year. And had you purchased stock in the brown bubbly on the worst possible day to buy in the last quarter century—in the winter of 1972, right before Coke slid into a 75 percent decline—and then held on tight until today, you'd still have squashed the market's average performance. Not a single mutual fund in America has matched the performance of Coca-Cola over the past quarter century. Not one. Furthermore, the fact that investments in common stock don't carry along the annual expenses of mutual funds, or the often-substantial taxable distribution each year, makes investments in strong Rule Makers triply delightful.

But while long-term historical performance is an indicator of future success, it's no guarantee. A number of apparently great public businesses thrived for a decade or two, only to come tumbling down when their financial controls crumbled, when management ignored their shareholders, when creativity and discipline were split in two. That's why we do more than cheer yesterday's heroes, choosing to rigorously apply the rule-making criteria to any business with more than $1 billion in sales. We do so to get a very clear picture of a company's present standing and some clue about its future progress. Are profit margins healthy? Is management staying on top of the business? Does the company have the resources to expand operations across the world in an orderly fashion? Is it financially sturdy enough to support an improving performance in the future? Does it have a world-class brand?

In the case of Coca-Cola, which scores thirteen out of fourteen points on the financial statements, the answer today is clearly *yes*. As we progress toward the end of this book, tightening our filter even more narrowly around excellence, I believe you'll recognize Coca-Cola as one of the true business leaders of this century. Coke is king in her castle, making rules that drive out competition—rules that the people happily abide.

OK, So What Happened to Cybermedia?

Now, recall Cybermedia—the software developer that was announcing accelerated sales growth in the wake of its initial public offering. The investing community responded heartily, and the stock pushed over $30 per share. Then, without much warning, management broke ranks and the structure of the business collapsed. Within six months, the stock had traded all the way down to $3, and some technology investors wondered what had happened. Why had this stock so quickly fallen 90 percent from its highs, and how could they have seen it coming?

Without studying the company's financials, you can probably surmise that the warning bells sounded on the balance sheet, a document that too often gets lost in the shuffle of Wall Street earnings estimates and recommendations. When Cybermedia's stock began to fall, it was getting its comeuppance for having relied on accounts receivable to represent its real business growth. It's a temptation that many product companies succumb to—announcing sales for which they have no guaranteed receipt of payment. Throughout its public history, Cybermedia's uncollected sales were growing at a faster rate than those it collected (in other words, accounts receivable were outpacing sales growth). Think about that for a second: It's a grim portent of things to come. Within the latitude offered by our accounting standards, Cybermedia was announcing as sales monies that which it hadn't collected, for products that could be returned for a full refund. Hence our little two-line play:

COMPANY: Our sales are going through the roof!!
FOOL: *Uhh*, really?

Cybermedia was too small to be a Rule Maker, but following its IPO did take on some aspects of a Rule Breaker—it operated in a world-beating industry, displayed rapid sales growth, and owned strong brands. The investor who focused exclusively on Wall Street earnings estimates, blithely accepting the buy recommendations from the firms that had helped underwrite Cybermedia's IPO, were burned. Conversely, the investor Foolishly breaking down the balance sheet put this company on the red-flag list. Take a look at the direction of Cybermedia's Foolish Flow Ratio between 1995 and 1997:

1995: 0.51 *(excellent)*
1996: 1.27 *(poor)*
1997: 1.38 *(getting worse)*

Without knowing anything about the company, any Fool could see that as Cybermedia headed into the public markets in 1996, it was getting extremely sloppy about its capital and product management. The rapid disintegration of its Flow, from 0.51 to 1.27, was ominous, to say the least. Management was donning its short-term blinders and going for the gold. The stock rose; sales growth looked phenomenal. But the underlying business was weakening, and the upward direction of Cybermedia's Flow Ratio throughout 1997, even as the stock rose above $30, lit the night sky with warning flares from quarter to quarter. Announced sales, you see, were just a shadow of actual sales. And the Flow Ratio, a simple mathematic, communicated important information about Cybermedia's actual standing and future direction.

Until and unless our accounting standards change to address the misuse of receivables to misrepresent sales, rule-making investors will just have to exploit the inefficiencies of the system for their own profit. When a company like Cybermedia comes along, with announced sales racing higher, with accounts receivable rising faster, and with a Flow Ratio climbing up into the failure zone, think very seriously about crossing the company off your list, or shorting it. Chances are, its aims have grown impatient, and its vision has narrowed. Management's eyes are on their stockholdings, not yours.

Concluding Thoughts

Our search for businesses that make the rules in an attractive industry and serve their shareholders for years if not decades has taken us from Cybermedia to Kmart, through to Disney, and finally to the mountaintop, where Coca-Cola has staked its flag and pitched a royal camp. The use of the seven Rule Maker criteria, measures of fundamental business strength, has helped us narrow the field down from three companies here to one. The criteria—high gross and net margins, steady sales growth, more savings than debt, strict supervision of product and cash flows, and a focus on mass-market automatic buying—are designed to help you reduce the few thousand very large companies in America down to the few dozen superior ones. And though they're listed individually, the seven benchmarks are quite interrelated. Well-managed sales lead to increased cash flow, which leaves more cash on the balance sheet, which feeds back into expansion—twirling like a gyre, the cycle feeds real business momentum. Expert public managers know this; they know not to trade away the discipline that drives lasting operational momentum in exchange for short-term profits.

To master these seven measurements, we analyzed three different consumer franchises. Kmart approached the throne first and fell on the red carpet, a casualty of overexpansion, back-snapping loads of long-term debt, blitzing competition, and virtually no pricing power in its industry. It scored just three out of fourteen points. Disney then walked right to the royal chair, but knelt down before it, as debt coupled with stagnating sales kept it from assuming the throne. It scored an okay nine out of fourteen points.

Of the three companies reviewed, Coca-Cola was the only one deserving of a crown and our undivided affection, scoring an amazing thirteen out of fourteen. The company's addictive and conveniently placed products have translated into high and expanding margins, as well as an excess of cash. Coke's managers have also exercised a rare discipline in their product management and a comforting sobriety in their approach to accounting. Very few public companies demonstrate a real commitment to long-term value for their shareowners; Coca-Cola has. And those qualities are all evident in simple numbers for any investor who knows where, and cares, to look.

Like Binney & Smith, the soda maker has been around and thriving for the last eight decades, turning thousand-dollar investments into millions (or more) for those investors patient enough to evaluate the business rather than just value the stock, to invest like an owner rather than speculate like a Wall Street trader. Time has been Coca-Cola's friend, and the friend of Coke's owners, as the soda maker has for decades compounded familiarity among its customers while simultaneously opening up new markets around the world. Yet there are no guarantees that time will continue to be Coke's ally: Often enough, experience and age mask arrogance, which is nothing less than the primary failing of all greatness. Arrogance can cause a business to miss a critical change in the needs or interests of its customers. Coke's eighty years of public-market living thus may hinder more than help it. After all, the public markets make no promises to the heroes of yesteryear.

Time may indeed prove to be Coke's bogeyman. The numerics *do*, however, suggest that the Coca-Cola Company is extremely well positioned for more of the same—namely, an embarrassment of riches for long-term shareowners. But our analysis of Coke's present situation doesn't give us enough information about their future direction. We cannot yet tell if they're a Rule Maker. We have a few more tests to run. How can we tell if today's powerful commercial leader, a people's king, has the wherewithal and commercial vision to lead for another generation? The direction of dynasties is a subject for the very next chapter, and a pivotal one it is.

Chapter 13

Ascending
the Throne

The very life-blood of our enterprise.

—WILLIAM SHAKESPEARE,
HENRY IV, PART 1 (IV, i)

The Coca-Cola Company is indeed an extraordinary thing; a
king of commerce if ever there was one. Twentieth-century shareholders of this world-leading name, this obviously great investment, have
been thrown like roses into a life of prosperity, a life free from financial
concern. Just one $40 share of Coca-Cola stock in 1919 has multiplied
today into over 97,000 shares with a total value in excess of $7.5 mil-
lion. Two $40 shares? Fifteen million. Ten shares? Seventy-five million
today. A $4,000 position in Coca-Cola—100 shares—at its public offer-
ing in 1919 held through to today, with dividends reinvested, is worth
more than $650 million this morning.

Excellence and longevity make perfect bedfellows in the public
markets.

But so what? Who of us was around back in 1920, chomping nuts
through Chaplin films, dancing the shimmy, nipping a mint julep in a
dusty alleyway in New Orleans—and buying shares of The Coca-Cola
Company? Not me. Probably not you either. So my eighty-year compounding of stock growth here would seem a bit of madness and
masochism. Who could've landed those exact and incredible results?

Few living today. But that doesn't mean you couldn't have taken a small fortune away from investing in Coke. Even if you, like us, lacked a grandparent or great-aunt buying up shares back in 1920, you could've found, purchased, and held this rule-making brand to great success. In fact, the stock has been *accelerating* its rate of growth in recent years. Here's a glimpse of Coke's performance, looking back from mid-1998 to its birthing in 1919:

> 5-year rate of return: + 29.7% per year
> 10-year rate of return: + 31.8% per year
> 20-year rate of return: + 24.2% per year
> 50-year rate of return: + 15.8% per year
> 79-year rate of return: + 16.7% per year

Over the past decade, Coke has risen at an unthinkable annual rate of 31.8 percent, nearly double its average yearly performance this century. The worldwide soda-pop powerhouse has been growing faster over the last ten years—in total and percentage terms—than at any point in its history. Had you bought Coca-Cola even just five years ago, you'd be sitting on total returns of 265%, doubling the S&P 500's performance.

Sweetened, carbonated, caramelized water has rewarded twentieth-century investors, both early and late.

But let's stop tormenting ourselves with history and reflect instead on the future. The subject of *this* section of Rule Makers is expansion, the direction of a business, the numerics of tomorrow, the ascent to ruling authority. Because while Coca-Cola *has been* a phenomenal business, *has been* a superlative investment, *has been* one of the world's most familiar names, what protection for investors is there against it becoming a *has been*? What signed and framed certificate guarantees the soda maker another century of dominance? No certification. No guarantee. No protection. Even though the public-market machine does reward companies for histories of excellence, even though it also pushes stocks higher based on their present stature, still the core of all business value rests on some measure of future direction. What lies ahead is what matters most to investors, because a change in momentum can (and often will) steal the lead from leaders and crown an unknown prince. After all, what future awaited the typewriter at the dawn of computer word-processing? What future was there for slide rules when calculators arrived on the scene? What future existed for the Flat-Earth Club after Aristotle mathematically proved our world a sphere?

We Fools have to be careful not to just absorb the lessons of the past, but to keep our eyes on tomorrow and stay attuned to innovative thinking and change. We have to challenge the sort of conventional wisdom which assumes that life will always be as it is. That, say, the Commodore-64 will always rule the market for home computing, that Americans won't ever want more than three television networks, that the world's daily volume of e-mail will never exceed its volume of postal mailing, and other such misestimations.

Certainly, the opposite of that sort of intellectual slumber (to be distinguished from an honest mistake) is the path to truth. Life will *not* always be as it is; life will never again be as it is. The philosopher Bertrand Russell offers some pretty good advice on this issue. "In all affairs," he wrote, "it's a healthy thing now and then to hang a question mark on that which you've long taken for granted."

If we're to beat the stock market's average return, we have to hang question marks on the businesses that we own and muse a little about the slant of their commercial path. With the seven measures of excellence from the last chapter, you're actually a long way toward avoiding the stock market's also-rans. Our standards of healthy sales growth, high gross margins, high net margins, a low Flow Ratio, a mass-market convenience business, and substantial cash reserves serve not just as measures of how well the business is doing today, but also reflect how equipped it is for new growth and change in its markets. But we can do more.

Ali vs. Foreman

This third section on Rule Makers gauges a company's direction by measuring operational momentum on its financial statements. Heretofore, we've snapped photographs of public businesses, searching picture frames for the qualities of a king. We typed in some numbers, clicked a button, and an image appeared. Companies either came out looking like Meg Ryan or the Wicked Witch or something in between. But these photos all are flat, the images static, our analysis unacceptably lacking a real sense of movement. The forward direction of a business is every bit as important as its present location, and we need to measure that, too.

Think of Muhammad Ali's 1974 heavyweight-title bout with George

Foreman in Zaire—the Rumble in the Jungle. For a handful of rounds, the twenty-five-year-old Foreman mercilessly pounded Ali into the ropes. In business terms, Foreman was posting high profit margins and great product sales (overhand rights). He appeared to be making all of the rules in the early rounds of that fight.

But then the momentum turned. Muhammad—from whose playbook Microsoft has torn a page—had been sitting back, absorbing the harsh punishment. The younger, larger, and stronger Foreman hammered him with hooks, overhands, and uppercuts. But he was being tricked by Ali, Fooled into dealing away success in the fight's later rounds for smashing authority at the outset—you might say he used too much long-term debt to fuel growth in the moment. By the fifth and sixth rounds, Ali shuffled and moved, sticking Foreman with jabs, relentlessly banging at his crown. And by the eighth round, George Foreman was down, then out. It took more than twelve minutes of physical and psychological torment before Muhammad Ali could change the dynamics of the fight and forever alter boxing history. But his patience was rewarded, and a potential monopoly hit the canvas.

There are plenty more great examples of momentum turns in the late twentieth century, like the smashing popularity, then near-immediate demise, of Jordache jeans; or Gary Hart's front-running race for the White House ending in his lap aboard the *Monkey Business;* or the rise and fall, then resurrection of Apple Computer; or less prominent turns, like the first time I beat my brother in a best-of-seven series in Ping-Pong.

Momentum shifted.

The poet W. B. Yeats described this sort of dynamic change as a revolution in which everything falls apart, the center cannot hold. In business, that conversion can exact immeasurable pain on the ill-prepared. Andrew Grove, the chairman of Intel Corporation, has described the horrible sight of a business, even an entire industry. I see an image of a corporation barreling headlong into a hairpin turn with no brakes and no steering wheel to alter its course. Grove called that moment the *inflection point*, the point of no return, where the institutions that took the time to install brakes and a steering wheel in their car survived, but all others perished. Those companies who plow, unready, into the inevitable *inflection points* of commerce will bring their long-term owners misery.

That's why it's so critical for you to find these inflection points when they exist. If you can locate and properly classify turns in momentum, you'll radically improve your investment returns. You'll know to sell

Kmart instead of holding it forever into oblivion. Or, following the direction of things, you might add money to a position like General Electric, as its waves of operational success roll without impediment. And finally, if you learn to chart business momentum on the financial statements, you might be able to locate the Tweener company on course to lock down rule-making authority in its industry. In their corporate histories, every single Rule Maker made the transition from Breaker to Tweener, then from Tweener to Maker. If you can find the corporations that might be giants, without assuming unsettling levels of risk, your portfolio will be much the better for it. America Online and Dell Computer are excellent 1990s illustrations of Rule Makers in the making: Both companies have climbed more than 25 times in value over the past five years (Dell is up 110 times over that period), while the steady improvement of their business fundamentals was plainly evident to those who knew where to find it.

In trolling for Rule Makers, it's time now to elevate to this next level of analysis—to see through to where our companies are headed. Why this is so important can probably be best communicated by a simple and specific example. All other things being equal, which business is more attractive: (1) the corporation with net margins of 14 percent, up from 11 percent last year, or (2) the corporation with net margins of 14 percent, down from 18 percent last year? Both surpass our highest expectation of 10 percent net margins, but is not one preferable to the other?

The direction of an object tells us as much or more about the future than does its present location.

The Internet Hasn't Killed Windows

The beauty of moving beyond a flat screen or a still photograph, and integrating these two metrics (location and direction), is that we narrow even further our list of potential investments. We focus the looking glass on spectacular companies whose operational momentum is *improving.* That's doubly powerful. The history of our public markets has shown that even the unseen hand can't raze these kingdoms overnight. For example, it's common knowledge that Microsoft was a little slow in taking its business to the Internet. Yet even as Nielsen Media Research was reporting in the summer of 1998 that more than seventy million

American adults—four times more than in 1995—were regular users of the Internet, that mass movement had not slayed the Windows platform. Microsoft continued to sell extremely profitable upgrades to its operating systems and applications as it evolved onto, and gradually began to underlay, the Internet.

There's a similar story line for rule-making businesses whose operations have been improving from one year to the next. The transformation starts with a significant industry-wide transition forcing the dominant player to adjust. The markets test its ability to finance and intuitively find its way through to the other side. The leader's progress, or regress, in that journey can be measured each quarter, and thankfully, the truest Rule Makers continue making it across the gap, one transition at a time, one decade after another. They succeed in part because while they are all well capitalized and always full of pride, nevertheless they're so obsessed with their business and industry, and so thorough in their dealings, that they can comfortably survive the blows from any single massive momentum shift. They are largely immune from the death by immediate collision; the classic rule-making business model buys the company time to make the necessary adjustments. With a worldwide base of repeat customers and hundreds of millions or billions of dollars in cash to defend their positions, they resist panic and persist into the next phase of their corporate history.

Now, that doesn't mean that rule-making corporations are invincible, but it does suggest that they live in a world where the only revolution is evolution, a series of transitions. The challenge of the monster businesses that the rule-making criteria dig out—from Gap to Coca-Cola, from Microsoft to General Electric, from Pfizer to Schering Plough—is to stay awake at the wheel and to steer their operations to match the winding roads of commerce. And the challenge to you as an investor is to train your eye to the quarterly earnings reports and train your mind to sort through them efficiently. On your way, you'll need to dig out of the financial reports answers to questions like: Is this company pushing ahead into greater prosperity? What sort of business downturn would cause us not to add new savings to this position? What might force us to sell? And, more likely, what will encourage us to add to an individual holding?

Take a look at the branding champion of chapter 11—the Gap. America's casual clothier released 1998 second-quarter earnings on August 13. Here's what you'll find by comparing that quarter's performance to the same period in 1997:

Total sales	Up 42%
Net margins	Up 2 percentage points (from 5.2% to 7.2%)
Gross margins	Up 6 percentage points (from 34.4% to 40.4%)
Foolish Flow Ratio	A 16% improvement (from 1.21 down to 1.02)
Cash-to-debt ratio	Down markedly (from no long-term debt to a ratio of just 1.07 times)

Through these five simple metrics, you can get a pretty good sense of what's going on at Gap headquarters. Sales have blasted ahead, even as the company has significantly improved its gross and net margins and strengthened its power position in the industry. Now, it did achieve this by assuming $499 million in ten-year notes carrying an interest rate of 6.9 percent. The company used that debt to accelerate its advertising buys and to speed its store expansion.

The questions for investors are whether growth will carry Gap through to a repayment of those notes by 2007, and whether the borrowed money will put the company in the driver's seat for casual clothing over that period. The earliest indications, visible in Gap's improving margins and tight product management today, are that the debt is being used to powerful advantage. But keep the pencils and scorecards, or spreadsheets, at the ready for the next quarterly report, three months hence. When it lands, you can spend thirty minutes reviewing it, and settle on conclusions about Gap's commercial direction. Is the competition gaining ground and are shifts in consumer preference weakening the denim dealer—or not?

The direction of a business tells us as much as, or more than, its present location.

Robert Frost Wrote More Than One Poem

You may have noticed that none of this rule-making work yet considers the recent direction of the stock price or even a stock's price-to-earnings ratio. Meanwhile, financial television, newspapers, magazines, and Wall Street have committed themselves to keeping hourly watch of the zagging stock prices and their relationship back to the almighty P/E.

The two variables are easily the most watched in the financial world. And yet, indeed they are totally *inconsequential* to the Foolish Rule Maker investment approach.

Why? Because both today's stock price and today's P/E ratio are short-term devices, tools for those who focus on temporary things. The two statistics tell us nothing about the underlying strengths or weaknesses of a business, the very marrow to our approach. Investing in Rule Makers is all about finding superior corporations that will allow us to extend commission-free and tax-deferred growth for many years. It draws investors into using the stock market for its original intent—to provide both long-term capital financing and to enjoy opportunities for business ownership. And given the dazzling rewards of compounded growth, I think you should be considerably more interested—perhaps a hundred times more so, perhaps a thousand—in the long-term prospects of a business than in its short-term valuation by the investment community.

After all, at what point this century *should* the investor in a spectacular business like Coca-Cola or Schering Plough or Hershey's or Johnson & Johnson have worried about the immediate valuation of their stock stubs? Is Coke's 24 percent annual growth over the last two decades not sufficient? It would have turned a $20,000 investment with no new savings into $1.5 million. Was anyone—besides a broker and his firm— better off hopping into and out of Coca-Cola, trying to perfectly time entry and exit points while paying commissions at every leap?

Even if it were possible to time fleeting prices, it would be a costly endeavor. Costly, that is, for anyone but the army of technical analysts and market strategists on Wall Street, who are paid well to spend their days huddled over dozens of proprietary indicators burping out strong buy, strong hold, and sometimes even sell recommendations by the hour. And, in the short-term, they mostly get things wrong while nonetheless generating commissions. Coincidence? By studying the public markets as home to a collection of businesses, a Fool can instead eye the entire financial circus from a strange and enriching vantage point—on a dusty beam above the trading floor—and wonder if the mad shouting by professionals in the room below more represents client services or damages.

Among Rule Maker investments, I suggest that you ignore this huffing and wheezing of daily trading, committing instead to an analysis of the quarterly business reports of up to a dozen Rule Maker investments. In order to sort out the pretenders to every throne and discern enduring greatness, you will have to get beyond weekly speculation, beyond the numbers game played by the suits wagering other people's money—possibly *your* money. The prospects for individual investors who "play" the stock market like a ticket game generally match up perfectly with the prospects of playing the ticket games directly. If you absolutely must involve yourself in it, dear Fool, please *get a job* at your state lottery, *get paid* by an investment firm to sell and buy all those stocks on commission, *stand on the other side* of the blackjack table, *go to work* for The House. That's where the profits lie in gaming.

For the rest of us, who would instead prefer to *invest* for a lifetime, the benefits of upward compounding start slow, gather momentum, and then roll like a flood. Patience is the driver of that exponential growth. It takes patience to locate and fully capitalize on the companies demonstrating the sort of lasting momentum that drove Muhammad Ali to the throne for years, set Robert Frost at the pinnacle of American poets not for a single lyric but for five decades, placed Harrison Ford as the lead in 20 percent of the world's top thirty blockbuster films, and has helped the University of Tennessee's Lady Vols basketball team win six national championships over the last eleven years. Rather than obsessing over a single jump shot, just one poem, the most recent movie, or that first trade at market open, these leaders trained themselves to persevere and dominate.

As investors, we must do the same. We have to recognize the historical context of common-stock performance; we have to thoroughly understand the astonishing truths about compounding numbers; and we have to commit our eyes to a horizon line that extends farther than the nose on our face.

This mindset will force us to ask ourselves which way the world is headed and whether our businesses contribute to and benefit from that forward passage. As we track the course of our companies' financial statements, from one quarter to the next, we'll need to ask ourselves: Are they driving more profitable sales today than they did last year? Is management aggressively pursuing new opportunities while yet spending its money prudently? Is this company gaining in efficiency, moving into a more powerful operating position, or is the integrity of its position waning?

And in our examination of long-term commercial progress, I suggest that we concentrate on six simple measurements gleaned from financial statements, believing that in those waters sits the treasure. These calculations help me to determine whether or not to continue owning a company, consider selling my position, or decide to buy more.

Six Metrics of Business Momentum

1. RISING GROSS MARGINS

In expecting companies to extend their gross margins over time, we're counting on business leaders to match pricing power with manufacturing efficiency in order to extend the overall profitability of the institution. As an investor, you might ask, "Can Hasbro (1) charge more for that Yahtzee board than last year, (2) make it for less than it did last year, (3) both, while (4) attracting more new customers?" Again, rapidly rising gross margins indicate a company that is lightening up on the manufacturing burdens while raising prices into consumer demand. There are few better examples of this than Microsoft in the 1990s.

Tracking this quarter against the same period last year, the highest praise goes to companies with gross margins that have risen, earning them 3 points. Those with gross margins that have fallen less than one percentage point earn praise, or 2 points. Businesses whose gross margins fell from 1 to 3 percent are passable, for 1 point. And companies whose gross margins have fallen more than 3 percentage points over the previous year are in the doghouse, where they get zero points.

2. RISING NET MARGINS

Rising net margins provide an indication of how much cash a company is sending toward its balance sheet. That cash will help our corporation defend and extend its interests. The business that combines an increase in net margins with rising sales offers its investors a double dip of delight, because as more buyers return with greater frequency, the company is also growing more profitable.

Tracking one reporting period against the same quarter a year previous, I look for rising net margins, which earns a company 3 points. The runners-up show net margins that have fallen less than one percentage point, and earn 2 points. Third-place honors go to those whose net profit margins fell from one to three percentage points against the same period last year, for 1 point. And the last-place kewpie doll goes to those companies whose net margins have fallen more than 3 percentage points—0 points for them.

3. SHARE BUYBACKS

Few things are so sweet as the company that can afford to buy its stock on the open market and retire the shares. Stock repurchasing that is affordable for the company and that, in total, reduces the number of fully diluted shares of ownership from the one quarter to the next is a boon for shareholders. It signifies that from year to year the company is methodically buying itself out of the public markets, shrinking the size of its ownership pie, and effectively making the shares you own more valuable. While popular opinion has investors still celebrating stock splits, which fundamentally don't affect an owner's stake or value, rule-making investors cheer stock *buybacks*.

Tracking one quarter against the year previous, a standing ovation greets those businesses with fewer shares outstanding this year than last (3 points), while loud applause rains down on the ears of companies with from 0 to 4 percent more fully diluted shares (2 points). Half of the crowd politely claps for companies with 4 to 6 percent more shares of ownership (1 point), and silence, with zero points as well as one audible hiss, echoes for the business with more than 6 percent additional shares this year.

4. CASH OUTGROWING DEBT

There's nothing fundamentally wrong with debt financing. It can provide currency for our businesses to use in making attractive acquisitions; it can accelerate worldwide expansion; and, for Rule Makers, it almost always represents cheaper financing than the secondary sale of their stock does.

At the same time, internal financing (funding developments out of earnings growth) is considerably more attractive, as it brings with it no interest payments. Over time, long-term debt is a weakness, suggestive of operational impatience and taking a bite out of tomorrow's profit. Ideally, the companies that we own carry considerably more cash savings (including short-term investments and marketable securities) than long-term debt. Furthermore, their numbers improve with time.

In comparing the two, and looking for improvements from one year to the next, here's what I prize: The top dogs carry no debt. 'Nuff said (3 points). Second-place companies are those whose ratio of cash to debt has improved over the past year (2 points). Gliding into third place are those whose ratio of cash to debt has fallen less than 10 percent (1 point). And the losers are the businesses whose cash-to-debt relationship has fallen by 10 percent or more (0 points).

5. LOWERING FLOW RATIO

An extremely important metric for Cash-King stocks, the Foolish Flow Ratio tracks the power position that a company occupies in its markets. By stacking inventories and receivables up against current liabilities, Flowie tells us whether a company is beholden to its suppliers and weak with distributors—or precisely the opposite. In Foolishly contrary fashion, a falling Flow Ratio represents an increasingly authoritative position, as the business turns product into cash instantly but delays payment to its suppliers. A rising Flowie indicates a weakening position.

When comparing one quarter to the same period last year, blue-ribbon winners are those whose Flow has fallen more than 10 percent (3 points). Red ribbons go to those whose ratio has fallen from 5 to 10 percent (2 points). The white ribbon belongs to businesses whose Flow Ratio is between down 5 percent and flat over the previous year (1 point). And no ribbon goes to any company whose Flowie has risen over the past year (0 points).

6. EXPANDING POSSIBILITIES

This final metric is the most subjective. I like to lie out on my figurative hammock (if only I had a real one and two poplar trees to string it to!) and, with a glass of lemonade and a bag of oatmeal-raisin cookies, ruminate over whether a particular company has realistic expansion plans. Do my friends know about and love the company's products? Is worldwide expansion believable for their stuff? And is this company accurately reflecting its performance through conservative accounting? All strange musings, yes, but you don't typically have to think for more than ten minutes. But in those ten minutes, this is what I look for:

Companies for which I can clearly answer a "yes" to all of those questions sit at the top (3 points). If I catch myself saying, "Yeah, I pretty much agree," they get rewarded (2 points). If I'm scratching my head and confused, I place them in third (1 point). And if it's plain that, no, nobody knows about or understands their products, they have little chance for expansion, and they've been padding sales with receivables, then they get stuck in the cellar (0 points).

That's how I approach a quarterly financial statement in search of the forward, sideways, or backward momentum of a business. It may sound like an awful lot of work, tormentingly tedious, but it generally takes no more than fifteen minutes of calculation and reflection each year—and even less if it's a mere button click on a Foolish spreadsheet. Piece o' cake.

Model Company 1: Nine West Group

Whew! That was a lot of theory to throw at you, philosophy trickling down out of an ivory tower. A reflection here, a square root there, a smattering of symbols, and some broad theory about measuring the financial accomplishments (and shortcomings) of public companies. A few more pages like those, and I'll wipe out our entire readership. So, to hold your attention (and mine) for another hour, I'll actually apply that string of theoreticals to a popular consumer franchise, Nine West Group, the designer and retailer of women's leather shoes, purses, and bags. You've probably seen this company, or one of its labels, in malls across the country. Nine West sells its wares under multiple brands, among them Amalfi, Enzo Angiolini, 9 & Co., and Pappagallo. Nine West also has licensing agreements to sell shoes and handbags under the Calvin Klein and Evan Picone trademarks.

We're talking about a classic Peter Lynch company here, with bustling storefronts across the country and a known brand that draws repeat-purchasing customers. And that's just what we look for when we hunt down Rule Makers in important industries: a good name, healthy demand, and the habitual purchase of convenience merchandise. As for the stock, Nine West has been public since early 1993. Its share price ran from $20 in February 1993 to $58 by October 1996.

Those boots were made for walkin'.

But let's take a look at the development of its business over the past fiscal year, beginning in February 1997 and ending in February 1998. Is Nine West the sort of company we'd invest in? A fifteen-minute walking tour of its financial statements will confirm or deny it. We'll be using the rule-making criteria for commercial direction, searching for: (1) rising gross margins, (2) rising net margins, (3) share buybacks, (4) a rising cash-to-debt ratio, (5) a falling Flow Ratio, and (6) a believable plan for global expansion.

Onward.

1. RISING GROSS MARGINS

Nine West has battled to maintain its pricing power while also holding down its manufacturing and business costs. The company has done an adequate job of it in recent years, and suffered only a slight drop in margins in 1998, as we see:

1997	1998
43.1%	42.9%

From 1997 to 1998, gross margins fell 0.2 percentage points. Our rankings prize any rise in gross margins in excess of 3 percentage points, but still find commendable those whose gross margins fell less than 1 percentage point. That describes Nine West's performance in fiscal 1998, as its margins slipped less than 1 percent.
Score: 2 points

2. RISING NET MARGINS

Rising net margins signal a company that's becoming more profitable with each passing quarter, deriving more reward for each hour of labor. In Nine West's case, net margins have been on the rise; the company is turning more profit on the sale of a pair of leather pumps in 1998 than it did in 1997. Here are the company's net margins for the two years:

1997	1998
3.9%*	4.2%

*Excludes one-time gains.

A company earns an "ideal" ranking if it increases net margins year to year. Nine West increased margins 0.3 percentage points, earning them the first-place honors awarded to companies that press margins forward.
Score: 3 points

3. SHARE BUYBACKS

Every new ticket stub of ownership that a company releases—in the form of stock options, acquisitions, and secondary offerings—acts as a dilutant to your ownership position. If, for instance, one of your companies has 100 million shares of ownership and then releases 10 million new shares, management has diluted your position by 10 percent. Your hope is that they've increased the value of the total pie in excess of that dilution. But nine times out of ten, you'd prefer to see your companies containing the outflow of new shares, even buying back shares from the market. You'd prefer to invest in businesses that don't need to use the public markets as a financing tool for a second time.

Here are Nine West's fully diluted share figures over the past year (in millions):

1997	1998
38.9	39.4

The company did a fine job over the past year of keeping its total of fully diluted shares outstanding under wraps. From 1997 to 1998, total

shares outstanding rose 1.3 percent, earning Nine West a second-place ranking.
Score: 2 points

HALFTIME

Before cruising over to the balance sheet, let's celebrate together Nine West's strong income-statement performance over the past year. As the company's sales have risen to $1.9 billion, its gross margins are holding steady, while net margins are on the rise. Nine West has put the peanut butter in the chocolate and the chocolate in the peanut butter—rewarding shareholders with both growing and more profitable sales.

By halftime, this one has the look and feel of a real Rule Maker. Again, Nine West has a consumer brand name, a repeat-purchase business, rising sales, improving margins, and control over its total ownership pie. Out of a potential nine points, Nine West racked up seven points. You can almost just go out and buy this company at the open tomorrow—almost. But before anyone hurries over to their keyboard and punches up their online broker to buy, let's glance over the balance sheet.

4. CASH OUTGROWING DEBT

Uh-oh, somebody just threw a red flag in the air. Nine West's debt situation falls into the "bad news" category. Here's a look at its cash and long-term debt standing over the past year:

	1997	1998
Cash	$ 25 million	$ 24 million
Long-term debt	$600 million	$687 million

For starters, Nine West is well below our standard of 1.5 times more cash than long-term debt. Worse still, and most important to our coverage of *business direction*, the ratio has fallen consistently over the past twelve months, from cash equaling .042 times debt to .034.

Bad news. That marks a 19 percent drop-off from an already unat-

tractive position. In measuring momentum, that earns them a disinterested crowd and a last-place finish.
Score: 0 points

5. LOWERING FLOW RATIO

Was that the sound of raucous heckling from a stadium full of fans? Or am I just having a really, really bad nightmare?

The Flow Ratio—in my opinion the single most important rule-making criterion—measures the strength of a company's position in its markets. It tracks how efficiently the company turns product into cash and delays payments to its suppliers. A strong Flow Ratio derives from holding down inventories and accounts receivable, while forcing accounts payable (unpaid bills) higher.

We spend our time as investors looking for corporations with Flow Ratios somewhere in the ballpark of 1.0, and we strongly favor those that have a stable or falling Flowie.

Snap!

A shoe strap just broke.

Nine West's Flow Ratio is not only too high but it's been dramatically rising for the past few years. Between 1996 and 1998, the company has seen its inventories rise from $397 million to $544 million *(kapow!)*, while its current liabilities have fallen from $294 million to $209 million *(ooof!)*. A double dip of disaster.

Here's how that has played out in Nine West's Flow Ratio over the past year:

	1997	1998
Flow Ratio	3.03	3.70

This simply indicates that, over the past year, Nine West lost more of what had been the little authority it held in its markets. The rise in inventory is likely the result of Nine West tying its outlets to very aggressive sales targets, yet not rewarding those stores for keeping unsold inventory in check. In other words, the home office is encouraging stores to buy as much merchandise as possible, sell like mad, and then stack the storeroom with the load of unsold items. Those stacks have been growing higher.

That can work for a while, and generate the sort of alluring income statements that Nine West had been pumping out. But it's a very bad long-term model. And, now, weakening financially from its product binge, Nine West is having to pay its shoe, bag, and sunglasses suppliers in a very timely fashion, resulting in falling accounts payable—another sign of deterioration.

This is more bad news, worse than expected, and earns Nine West another last-place finish.

Score: 0 points

6. EXPANDING POSSIBILITIES

After celebrating Nine West's apparently healthy rise in sales and net margins, we've run into a series of bitter disappointments on the balance sheet. Can you see how the one can counteract the other? Over the past few years, Nine West has been so focused on growth that the extremely important management of that growth has weebled and wobbled, and now just about fallen down.

Inventories are out of control, which, again, is symptomatic of a retailer that has tied incentives to sales growth and ignored product management. Long-term debt is rising markedly, and suppliers are demanding more up-front payments. At the same time, the company's accounts-receivable entry has climbed at a rate of 29 percent per year since 1996; Nine West has been forced to cede a measure of power in any distributor partnerships that it has and accept payments for merchandise later and later. Nine West rung up a zero on the balance sheet, as ugly as it gets.

Fools, these aren't conditions bespeaking continued expansion throughout the nation, let alone the globe. Yes, many of our friends are familiar and happy with Nine West products. But no, the company is not well positioned today for anything more than accelerating its sales and earnings on fumes in the short term. Of course, Nine West can right its stumbling operations, but it'll take a meaningful restructuring, a write-off of inventory, a more sophisticated store-incentive plan, and a much more disciplined approach to retailing.

This is not the language of a business with expanding possibilities today.

Score: 0 points

NINE WEST'S FINAL SCORE

Not surprisingly, Nine West shares have been hammered over the past year. What's interesting, though, is that in February 1997, at the close of its fiscal year, Nine West was still enjoying the favor of the investment community. The stock was trading above $50 per share even though, at the time, the balance sheet betrayed the classic signs of business erosion: heavy, rising debt alongside a dangerously high and rising Flow Ratio. In fiscal 1998, the market woke up and the popular shoemaker went on a grim descent to $19 per share, off more than 60 percent.

As if that weren't too much bad news for a single page, the next chapter of the Nine West story was printed in early September, when the company announced that it would significantly underperform estimates in the coming year. By mid-September, Nine West's stock had traded down from $19 to $9 per share, a 53 percent drop to add to the already unfortunate decline. Now down more than 80 percent off its public-market highs, Nine West is still posting reasonable numbers on its income statement. Simultaneously, however, the company's also proving itself highly incapable of managing its product inventory and cash flow. The recent deterioration of Nine West's operations reaffirms that the foundation of sound business—the essence of rule-making authority—is in evidence on a company's balance sheet more than in the twirl of quarterly earnings-per-share figures and their comparisons to Wall Street estimates. Investors watching the balance sheet would have been out of Nine West at $50 per share, or earlier at a lower price, not crying in the dark for an explanation when the stock slid and the other shoe dropped.

Still, the game isn't over. The game is never over. Nine West scored just 7 points out of a possible 18 in business direction—well short of rule-making status. But the business *can* be righted. The question is, Will management pull back the reins on selling and focus now on efficiency? With a national brand name, the opportunities for growth and stability are there. In fact, I believe that, having read this chapter, *you* now have the framework to help lead Nine West out of the darkness. Just write down the inventory, rework the store-incentive plan, place a halt on new-store expansion, and strive toward stocking the highest-margin, most repeatedly purchased items that you can. It will take you an awfully long time to deliver this business into Rule Maker status, but it can be done.

If, however, you don't want to be on Nine West's executive team, you can still benefit from this section. Given its soaring levels of inventory, if you're a Nine West shopper, be sure to negotiate on price.

Model Company 2: Pfizer

To continue our investigation into the future momentum of public businesses, I'd like to hold the pfeet of one of the companies in our on-line portpfolio to the Pfoolish pfinancial pfire, just as we did to Nine West. Pfizer is the developer of such commonly known drugs as Viagra, Zoloft, and Norvasc, as well as consumer products including Ben Gay, Barbasol, Cortizone, and Visine.

The company has been in business since 1849; its biggest splash came with its mass production of penicillin a half century ago. Since then, Pfizer has been another one of those companies consistently churning out value for its shareholders, one decade after another. Pfizer's release of Viagra in 1998 brought it more fanfare than any drug maker in the world, earning it a slew of *Saturday Night Live* jokes as well as the adoration of millions of customers around the world.

Pfizer, too, is a repeat-purchase brand for millions of older Americans, who return to its cardiovascular and arthritis drugs over and again. Actually, the general business model for pharmaceuticals is an extremely attractive one; it includes heavy up-front investments in research and development, followed by the exceedingly profitable sale of repeatedly purchased and inexpensively manufactured product. The pattern has been duplicated, with small variations, by one drug-making stalwart after another, from Merck to Eli Lilly, Johnson & Johnson to Bristol Myers, Schering Plough to Warner Lambert. The pharmaceuticals industry overflows with both potential and existing Rule Makers.

Let's compare Pfizer's first two quarters of fiscal 1998 to the same two quarters of 1997. In making financial-statement comparisons, what matters is that we compare the same periods from year to year, whether this quarter versus the same period last year, the first three quarters of this year versus the same three last year, or this year versus a single year a decade back. You get the picture. Here's a look at Pfizer's first two quarters of 1998 versus the same period last year through the lens of our six measurements.

1. RISING GROSS MARGINS

Pfizer's gross margins are on the rise and have been for a number of years. The introduction of Viagra, priced aggressively yet in great demand, has improved Pfizer's net and gross margins alike. And the six-month comparisons are . . .

First Half 1997	First Half 1998
82.1%	83.8%

These figures show growth of 1.7 percentage points, which places Pfizer in the top group.
Score: 3 points

2. RISING NET MARGINS

Walking nearly in step with the rise in gross margins, Pfizer has pressed its bottom-line profitability higher over the past year as well. The six-month comparisons show that Pfizer's net margins have grown a full percentage point:

First Half 1997	First Half 1998
17.9%	18.9%

That places Pfizer in the top echelon again, among the elites.
Score: 3 points

3. SHARE BUYBACKS

Pfizer has been holding the line on its fully diluted shares, showing little creep over the past year. The company added just 7 million additional shares of ownership to its base of more than 1.3 billion shares outstanding. Shares (in millions):

First Half 1997	First Half 1998
1,310	1,317

That marks 0.5 percent growth from 1997 to 1998, which ranks Pfizer in second place on share buybacks, once more walking among the best. **Score: 2 points**

Tweeeeet!

HALFTIME

We just raced a lot of numbers by you, so let's trot out a report of the company's income-statement performance over the first six months of fiscal 1998. Pfizer has done a fine job of inching its business into greater profitability. The launch of Viagra helped fuel sales growth of 19 percent over the past year. This development, coupled with rising gross and net margins, illustrates that the business is on the rise. Pfizer scored eight out of nine points

But Nine West Group also excelled at the short-term performance measured on its income statement before hosing its shareholders on the balance sheet. The same could hold true of Pfizer. Let's look in.

4. CASH OUTGROWING DEBT

Pfizer's cash-to-debt comparisons have weakened over the past year. Six months ago, the company had $200 million more in cash than it does today, while long-term debt has essentially held steady over that time. Thus, the ratio has weakened. In 1997 it stood at 3.01, today long-term debt equals 2.76 times cash on hand.

This change marks an 8.3 percent decline in the relationship between cash and long-term debt. While not positive, these numbers aren't wildly negative, either. They place Pfizer in the category's third tier. **Score: 1 point**

5. LOWERING FLOW RATIO

The Flow Ratio measures the rapidity with which a company can on the one hand turn inventory into collected bills while on the other hold off payments to its suppliers. In essence, it's how quickly Hershey's can turn cocoa, milk, and sugar into a solid candy bar, then sell that bar for cash, then hold off payments for the cocoa, milk, and sugar.

Whooops, we're talking about Pfizer here, not Hershey's.

First half 1997 against first half 1998, here's the direction of Pfizer's Flow Ratio:

First Half 1997	First Half 1998
0.80	1.01

This is Pfizer's greatest shortcoming. The rising (and thus weakening) Flow Ratio is entirely the consequence of a 23 percent growth in accounts receivable. It's a bad sign when accounts receivable outgrow the rate of sales, which is the case here, because it's an indication that, to get product out to the public, Pfizer has lightened up on its collections from the doctors and hospitals distributing it. That behavior can fuel short-term sales growth and margin expansion, but compromise the real merits of the growth.

No, this is not a *serious* negative for Pfizer, as their Flow Ratio is still well below our 1.25 boundary line. That said, however, the direction is worrisome: Pfizer's Flow Ratio increased by 26 percent over the same period last year, dropping the company into the cellar in this ranking. **Score: 0 points**

6. EXPANDING POSSIBILITIES

Without a doubt, Pfizer has excellent worldwide expansion opportunities, what with its new drugs in the pipeline and promotable products today. As of September 1998, over 95 percent of Viagra's sales have been in the domestic markets. And Viagra has, in the U.S., proven to be the most successful drug launch in the history of the industry. So, with foreign markets just beginning to embrace Viagra, Pfizer has enormous opportunities for increasing customer loyalty while expanding its profits. Combined, that's an excellent one-two punch for any public company.

All of that said, with the recent rise in accounts receivable, I can't unhesitatingly drop the company into the top slot. Pfizer's Flow Ratio is on the move, and in the wrong direction. How the company manages its product and cash flow—strictly or lackadaisically—may be an early indicator of where the business is headed over the next two years, and I have some questions about Pfizer's direction over that time. But I have very few questions about the company's long-term direction. The financials, the product lines, and management are simply too strong for the market to keep this company down for any prolonged period.

In answer to the questions posed in the explanation of these criteria—the queries about customer loyalty, worldwide expansion, and conservative accounting—my response is, "Yeah, I pretty much agree." Which earns Pfizer second position here.
Score: 2 points

CONCLUSION

Pfizer's business is growing like a weed, all over the planet. The company has a brand, popular support, rising sales and margins, loads of cash, and it still exhibits a relatively tight management over its products and capital. Since its addition to the Rule Maker Portfolio online in February 1998, Pfizer has been our second-most-rewarding investment. Its business meets all of our baseline Rule Maker criteria, by wide margins. And its pipeline of new drugs is stuffed with possibility. This is one of the premier pharmaceutical companies in the world.

That said, there are some recent developments on the balance sheet that are worrisome. The pace of the growth in accounts receivable is something that Pfizer investors can't ignore, and the direction of its Flow Ratio as well as the relationship between cash and long-term debt should also be on any Pfizer shareholder's watch list.

All told, the drug maker scored 11 out of 18 points, meaning that the company is just okay, today. Our metrics for analyzing future direction are stringent; twelve is a good score for a mature company. Now, while Pfizer didn't excel in any single aspect of the rating system, it did post fine numbers on its income statement. At the end of our section on Rule Makers, at the close of this book, after working through all of our rankings, I'll provide the complete performance of a dozen different companies. There, you'll find certain businesses that are improving on their present conditions in a far more impressive fashion than Pfizer, but you won't find many companies that boast as robust a financial structure as Pfizer has. Pfizer has numerous opportunities in new markets. But we'll need to scrutinize the quarterly reports, as they come, to ensure that this stalwart clears the bumps, holding to the narrow road toward shareowner reward, and writing the Rules in its industry.

Model Company 3: Cisco Systems

According to our directional criteria, I'd like to review the Internet builder Cisco Systems. It is the leading manufacturer of networking products for local- and wide-area networks and computing systems. The company has been on an absolute roll during its eight and a half years in the public markets. It's hard to believe, but back in 1988, Cisco had less than $10 million in annual sales. Today, it's valued at $100 billion and is the runaway leader in building out and supporting the Internet. During its time in the public markets, the stock went up 400-fold, turning a $10,000 investment in early 1990 into more than $4 million today.

Let's take a trip down Financial Statement Lane, and study Cisco Systems' performance in fiscal 1998, with an eye toward our Rule Maker criteria. We'll start again with the income statement. Cisco certainly isn't experiencing a slowdown in demand for its networking products and services. Sales growth in 1998 rose more than 33 percent, from $6.4 billion to $8.5 billion. This places Cisco Systems in the ninety-ninth percentile of sales growth for companies with more than $5 billion in annual revenues. Now, on to our measures of profitability.

1. GROSS MARGINS

In fiscal 1998, Cisco Systems inched its gross margins higher by 0.3 percentage points, to 65.5 percent. The company is gaining ground in pricing power while marginally narrowing its manufacturing costs. This mark meets our baseline standards and pleasingly reflects upward momentum.
Score: 3 points

2. NET MARGINS

Cisco Systems' net margins for fiscal 1998 were 16.0 percent, down slightly from net margins in 1997 of 16.3 percent. The slight decline reflects higher marketing costs and a rise in research and development costs relative to sales. While not ideal, the decline is not significant enough to raise any red flags for rule-making investors. And net margins of 16 percent easily o'erleap our 7 percent standard bar.
Score: 2 points

3. SHARES OUTSTANDING

In fiscal 1998, Cisco Systems issued 3.7 percent more shares than in 1997, far within our acceptable range. The new issuances do mark a slowdown in the growth rate of fully diluted shares. Name this attractive as well.
Score: 2 points

Tweeeeeeeet!

HALFTIME

At the half, simply put, Cisco Systems has put up some fine numbers, scoring seven out of nine points. Gross and net margins far exceed our expectations and are either holding steady or on the rise. In the meantime, sales are soaring higher—confirming what many of us know to be true, that the Internet is in hot demand. Add to this that the company is not financing its future growth with the ever-dangerous secondary offering or heavy acquisitions, and you have an income statement on solid ground.

Looking toward the second half of this report, remember that both Nine West and, to a lesser extent, Pfizer had thrived on the income statement only to then post disappointing balance-sheet statistics. Nine West was suffering an inventory glut. Pfizer was lightly padding its performance with rising accounts receivable. The former was an absolute disaster. The latter, a mild disappointment. Given the context, Cisco Systems' short-term successes in evidence on the income statement may be crossed out by a fundamental weakening of their business, revealed on the balance sheet.

4. CASH-TO-DEBT RATIO

Cisco Systems closed out fiscal 1998 with $1.7 billion in cash and no long-term debt. The cash position represents an increase of more than $400 million over the previous year. And the relationship of cash to debt at Cisco obviously puts it in the upper echelons of Corporate America. Whereas we search for companies with 1.5 times more cash than long-term debt, Cisco has no debt and a growing pile of savings. Outstanding! First place.
Score: 3 points

5. THE FLOW RATIO

Cisco's Flow Ratio has improved dramatically over the past year, falling from 1.63 in 1997 to 1.17 in 1998. The stunning decline is the result of Cisco's slimming down inventory and fighting back the temptation to carry a load of uncollected sales. The nearly 30 percent decline in the Flow Ratio is a powerful positive for Cisco. And the company has also now ducked under our baseline expectation of no Flow Ratios over 1.25. First place.
Score: 3 points

6. EXPANDING POSSIBILITIES

It's hard to look at Cisco's business today, with a Foolishly trained eye, and not be very excited about their prospects for growth in the United States and around the world. The demand for that which speeds up the globe's communication network is dramatically on the rise, and unlikely to subside for many, many years to come.

Most important, Cisco Systems has modeled itself as a company with long-term interests and a legitimate claim to the throne of an extremely valuable industry. Even as Intel talks about moving toward embedding networking products into its overall business plan, even as Lucent Tech-

nologies sticks a toe or two in Cisco's swimming pool, I think it's going to be extremely difficult for anyone to supplant, or even slow down, this leader's progress. Thankfully, if there are serious obstacles along the way for Cisco, they'll show up in our simple analysis of the company's balance sheet.
Score: 3 points

CISCO'S FINAL SCORE

I'll put it simply: I believe Cisco Systems is one of a handful of the strongest technology companies in the world today. The company is the premier player in an industry exploding with demand: the construction of the Internet. And the operation is managed by executives that have remained focused on the long term. That's evident in Cisco's expanding cash reserves and its tightening-down on inventories and receivables.

Cisco scored 16 out of 18 points, ranking it among the top percentile of public companies in terms of the direction of their business. It's also worth noting here that when we run Cisco through each of the standard tests outlined in chapter 12, it meets or beats most of them. The network builder matches up a premier *location* with an impressive *direction* to its business; a mighty Rule Maker ascending a covetable throne.

Concluding Thoughts on Business Momentum

Our inquiry into the progress of public companies has taken us from a brief consideration of Coca-Cola to a more thorough analysis of the fashion retailer Nine West Group; the apothecary Pfizer; and the Internet architect Cisco Systems.

The results for the first, Nine West, were astonishing. The company's stock had been a strong performer since its IPO in 1993. The two primary tools that many investors still use to evaluate growth companies—the direction of earnings per share and the state of the P/E ratio—were compelling the markets to buy Nine West, and then buy more. After all, sales, earnings, and earnings per share were *all* on the rise. Unfortunately for investors, so too were the company's inventories, accounts receivable, and long-term debt, at a twice accelerated rate. This scenario of an improving income statement and a deteriorating balance sheet will always play out harmfully over time. When a company instead places constraints on inventories, receivables, and long-term debt, it demonstrates a truer long-term commitment to the market. When that company allows them to grow unchecked, it advertises short-term thinking and the possibility of long-term disaster.

Nine West was doing just that, managing its business for just this hour, generating little bursts of speed and revving its stock value. The shoe seller had obviously set high incentives for its stores to sell more stuff now, rather than to sell the right stuff in ways that would exactingly expand operations for a decade, and then two. Our work in this section was designed to help us, as investors, avoid the Nine Wests of this world by distinguishing one from the other: (1) the desire for immediate stock-market reward that erodes the balance sheet and (2) the commitment to durable operations that compounds enduring stock-market rewards (fulfilling what I consider to be the fiduciary obligation of a public company). Nine West was a disappointment.

We then turned to Pfizer, maker of Viagra, the wonder drug for male (and possibly female) sexual dysfunction. One of the finest businesses in the world, Pfizer underwent a tremendous expansion in 1998, leading to the flowering growth of sales and margins, but also bringing with it a mild erosion in the company's baseline financials. Accounts receivable crept higher, outpacing sales growth. And the relationship of Pfizer's cash reserves to its long-term debt took a very gentle turn for the worse. Within the full context of Pfizer's business, this latest softening of performance isn't enough to unnerve me. But it does warrant extra attention in the years ahead.

Our final stop was Cisco Systems, builder of the network for mass communications and the worldwide distribution of information. Cisco's margins were holding steady; it piled away as savings an additional $400 million over the past year; and the company was matching every inch of growth with more operational control. By holding inventories and receivables in check, Cisco was reporting pure earnings, untainted by debt, free of the shortsighted management that can only win the hour, and never the day. The networking company appears committed to shareholder value across all categories, rather than for a small team of executives and investment bankers. It deserves serious consideration as one of the few worldwide leaders in technology, as we plow into another century that will be marked by innovation.

If investors are to find these Rule Makers, to see their way through the narrow corridors of today and follow the directions into tomorrow's world of commerce, they must learn to track the intentions of a business; they must learn to read the balance sheet of companies like Nine West, Pfizer, and Cisco Systems. Despite their being three separate industries, the charter of expanding into the consumer marketplace with greater force and sustainable speed is common to all.

What isn't common to all is the degree to which they've been successful. Nine West stumbled and plunged into the moat, up to its neck in muddy water; Pfizer performed like a prince; and Cisco Systems showed all the signs of rule-making authority in a critically important industry. By putting our ears to the ground, right down on top of the financial statements, we have listened for something wonderful or something wicked this way coming. And we've heard a little bit of the future, seen the motion of things, calculated the probabilities of their success.

This mode of adjudging the direction of a business focuses us more on where an individual company's world is headed than just where it was and is today. To rule the public markets, Fools must measure both the present location and the future direction of corporations, because a great thing weakening is not so attractive for investors as a good one strengthening. Sometimes it's not even as rewarding as a dead thing rising.

If we abide that thinking, we might anticipate the long-term downslide that seems to travel with impatience. The undefeated boxer who refused to train. The high school beauty who forsook charity for pride. Actions without faith, ambition without service. Greed in place of stamina. Only by following the positive direction of a business, measured below the surface and fueled by perseverance, can we locate the public company that will gradually ascend the fray and dominate its markets. In its commitment to the service of a wide range of customers, to high-margin product lines, to tight controls over inventory, and to vigilance toward the cash that flows through operations, our protagonist can rise to a station of financial authority. Only then will it become the Maker of Rules, a natural monopoly, and the subject of the next page.

Chapter 14

The Monopoly Board

What infinite heart's ease
Must kings neglect that private men enjoy!
And what have kings that privates have not too,
Save ceremony, save general ceremony?

—WILLIAM SHAKESPEARE, *HENRY V* (IV,i)

You actually started learning about rule-making businesses many years ago when you played Monopoly for the first and second time. Seated around a card table nibbling on Triscuits and gritting your teeth, you tried to eat through the competition. You might've been the top hat or the terrier, or been stuck with the thimble. Starting with $1,500, you collected a $200 salary each time you steered your piece past Go. Maybe, eighteen turns in, you traded your Reading and B&O Railroads to the owner of Pennsylvania Avenue, to complete a railroad monopoly for her and a property monopoly for you. Then, alas, two hours later, besieged on all sides, your game ended with a luckless roll that ran you into someone else's hotel on Marvin Gardens. Smiling, but flustered, you counted away all of your cash, sold properties for more, and still ended up $250 short. Your quest to run the board, building out commercial properties, assessing fines, and seizing the assets of your bankrupt competitors had come to a chaotic and unhappy end.

Silver terrier meltdown.

This final section of our book deals expressly with the Monopoly board of public business, the elbowing battle for dominance in consumer-driven industries. Every single company that is ascending toward Rule Maker status is trying to build an ongoing series of natural or patent-based monopolies. The Gap would love to control casual clothing stores along the sidewalks of the planet. Coca-Cola intends to deliver all forty-eight billion ounces of liquid that the world consumes each day. Intel wants to own the chip that runs technology devices. And Microsoft has designs to quilt every data and communications platform with its operating systems.

These franchises (and their competitors) want consumers to pony up a small toll every time they buy a pair of khakis, pour a glass of lemonade, or switch on their personal computers. Our system of commerce actually directs them to strive toward this monopolistic control of an industry, under which the people choose to pay them steady rent, hour after hour, with every rotation of the planet. *Cha-ching.* As a public company's cash flow increases from collecting such tolls, so does its overall value and wealth for its shareholders—and then the globe begins its next rotation. After three months, the accountants deliver their record of financial performance to the public, and investors either reward the *constant* and *predictable* expansion of earnings, or punish the lack of it. Then the world turns again. Every four quarters, the business closes out its fiscal year with a financial report, and the earth continues to spin around. Just like silver pieces on a Monopoly board, one round after another, wending from property to property, once past Go and then again, with cash squandered or gained, control being won or lost. So goes real-life business.

Turn after turn, year after year.

I'm not proposing that we live in a frigid and gray automated world, where machines clang and buzz, humans methodically tap on keys or hammer the anvil, numbers are toted and filed away, and our planet revolves around the sun in a most predictable fashion. No, the world and its people are vast, various, and undivinable. Tomorrow, you might wake up and take a different road to work, or take the day off, or decide to take a different job. Or take to the hills. You could end up in Appledoorn by midnight, huddled in a dark alehouse, nipping from a bottle of cognac and learning your first few Dutch words. Constant choice wound up in pure chance renders our lives a mystery, and the same is true for every institution. Each business takes its own daily route toward success, failure, or some point in between.

Yet even as our commercial democracy promotes choice, there *is* nevertheless a general pattern to all public business enterprise, a common goal sought through common plans. A company fights for its life after its initial public offering (IPO), struggles for stability in its key markets, strives to march its core business into a position of thorough dominance, and then, in select cases, hires a few hundred lawyers to battle the Department of Justice for latitude and liberty. Since I'm not trained legally, I won't fake a mastery of the ins and outs of antitrust law (if I were, I would). I'm not going to pretend to know where the boundary line falls between fair competition and inappropriate business practice. But we all know that literally thousands of public companies envy those few that are served notice of a trust-busting investigation into their control of an industry. Even though the federal scrutiny will create an awesome legal task, heavy with expense, it's also a badge of success. It's the ultimate legitimizer in the consumer markets, a nod to a company's bulldozing triumph—the aim of every public business. It's what our marketplace demands.

Just play Monopoly again and, as one turn leads into another, watch as monopolistic thinking escalates around the table. Watch as your brother-in-law plots, out of necessity, to undermine and overthrow your every success. With each roll, his aim to dominate the board, absolutely, actually becomes less a combative maneuver than a survival tactic. Because the game of Monopoly—like public-market business—relies on the timeless concept of limited opportunities and limited space, like a glass filling up with water. A roll of the dice leads to the purchase of land, land ownership generates rent monies, rent revenues lead to property development, which leads to an increase in rent and the buildup of cash necessary for future expansion. With every round of rolling, the board crowds up with buildings, like that jar filling up with water. And the squares that your terrier doesn't own are only so many money pits and pratfalls in the way of your success. As a monopolist, you must own to survive. You must come to possess that jar of water.

No matter how unique the personalities of Monopoly players are, they eventually realize that what isn't theirs is yours, and what is yours is their demise. Thus, each player searches for the same outcome: to increase profit through methodical expansion, until one day, her houses and hotels cover the entire board, from Indiana Avenue to St. James Place, from Boardwalk around the bend to Baltic Avenue. So too in business (thankfully, not all of life): To survive and to fulfill its charter as a public company, one day the corporation will need to own the jar of water, the whole of its industry, the entire game board.

EVEN BEN & JERRY'S
TRIES TO BASH THE COMPETITION

Believe it or not, the directive of a *public company* is far more aggressive and demanding than your cutthroat approach to the game of Monopoly. Unlike the silver terrier that only you control, a public company is owned by thousands of individuals and institutions who count on it to extend its interests, increase profits, and actually risk less over time. Shareholders have sunk their money into the support of this company; they've banked their futures on it. One owner hopes to put her kids through college with the investment, while another wants to fund an early retirement with his shares. Charities hold their shares in a trust. Banks carry their pieces on the books. And even our institutions of higher learning, at every level, are owners of businesses ascending from Rule Breaker to Tweener into Rule Maker, making the climb toward monopoly. Our collective reliance on commercial growth runs equally from small, private share owners to mammoth and plodding institutions. To serve each, a publicly held business has to be pushing forward on a path to greater authority.

The investor who gets smart to this truth will treat the stock market as a long-term savings vehicle, the purpose for which it was originally designed. He'll probably enjoy rooting for the underdogs—most of us do—but will gradually place larger and larger investments on the overdogs. Think how much commercial rubble General Electric, Microsoft, Intel, and Wal-Mart have left in their collective wake over the past fifteen years. Many lower-grade operations, once richly valued, were demolished, or worse, under the toes of these giants as they pounded ahead like NFL linemen, and drove consistent rewards with increasingly *less* operational risk. The investors that took to them, ignoring the market pundits and the short-term bears, accumulated wealth through years and decades of compounded growth—14 percent more this year, then 14 percent more of that more next, then 14 percent more of that *mored* more, and so on—all the way until an average of $200 in new wealth rolled into their accounts each month, then $2,000 per month, maybe even, someday, $10,000 per month on average.

This is wealth being created through investment, not labor. Through pause, not haste. It is wealth that's most available to those who search for emerging and existing consumer-name-brand monopolies—to those who follow the ascent of Rule Breakers into Rule Makers. These investors buy companies whose flow of earnings grows more predictable, more defensible, and more sizable with every year, companies that religiously serve their customers and end up Makers of Rules in their industries. Companies that bark like a monopoly and bite like an overdog. No matter the business, whether it's Pfizer or Federal Express, Ben & Jerry's or Boeing, they all have a primary responsibility to represent the greatest commercial interests of their long-term owners, and, by extension, to drive their competition off the field.

In this and every other way, the public corporation shouldn't be confused with the private company, nor with other institutions which naturally hold other aims and actions dear. The charter of a public company is to create long-term shareholder value. Roberto Goizueta, chief executive of Coca-Cola before his death in 1997, wrote about the mission of a publicly held business:

> In a world of democratic capitalism, people create specific institutions to help meet specific needs. Governments are created to meet civil needs. Philanthropies are created to help meet social needs. Churches are created to help meet spiritual needs. Businesses are created to help meet economic needs.
>
> When institutions try to broaden their scope beyond their natural realms, when they try to become all things to all people, they fail.

Those are the basic guidelines of the game, offered up by one of the great business leaders of the century. A church is not a government, a philanthropic endeavor is not a business, a business is not a church. Public companies, the subject of this book, face a unique set of circumstances, confront uncommon obstacles, serve a select purpose, and fail when they fail to recognize this.

Of course, simply understanding the rules of the market doesn't mean winning the game. The most common form of corporate failure comes through short-term thinking—yielding to the temptation to rush in for monopolistic success. You've seen it before: Someone starts a business today, raises venture-capital money tomorrow morning, uses that cash to buy powerful distribution on Thursday, then aims to explode into the public markets before the weekend.

The strategy is to win—*now.*

It's the same as trying to proudly (and often sloppily) dominate the first few turns of Monopoly. Huzzah! Unfortunately, winning early, by any means necessary, usually does not result in a controlling position in the thirtieth or fiftieth turns of the game. Hurriedly buying Park Place and Illinois Avenue and Water Works and North Carolina Avenue and the Short-Line Railroad after eight turns may be tempting, but it could just translate into mortgaging them after twenty-five dice rolls, then selling them for half their worth on the fortieth turn. On the flip side, stockpiling cash and slumming it into the middle rounds with a beggar's monopoly on Connecticut, Vermont, and Oriental Avenues *might* position your little terrier for a long-term win.

While there is no single route to commercial success, if we can agree that public companies compete in an endless race to serve their shareholders, then endurance is *at least* half the challenge.

THE DRAGON AND THE CARDBOARD SWORD

Which isn't to say that speed doesn't matter.

There you are pushing your silver terrier around the Monopoly board, extending your portfolio of properties, deciding where to place new houses, paying rental fees to your competitors, and always feeling a sense that time is getting away from you. Public companies proceed with a magnified sense of that urgency, too, always anxious to accelerate their performance, always feeling the pressure to spend money now in order to extend their operations. But, to survive, they do need to couple sustainability with that need for speed. Think of Netscape, which owned more than 90 percent of the Internet browser market when it filed for its IPO in 1995. After a raucous offering, Netscape was valued in excess of $7 billion. But two years later, the company was worth just $2.1 billion. And when Netscape was bought out by America Online, it was still 45 percent off its IPO highs—putting the hurt on public-market investors. As we apply a few Monopoly metrics to Microsoft, our model company this chapter, I think you'll conclude that Netscape's decision to go public as a trash-talking direct competitor to Microsoft was a very ill-advised one. It was like choosing to fight the dragon with a cardboard sword, and shouting upon entering its lair to boot.

By the end of this chapter, you may even wonder why Netscape ever sold a browser, since for public-market success both speed and sustainability of speed are critical. The only time that endurance isn't critical for a public company is when that company's executive team is intently concentrated on the shutting and opening of its stock-option window. Here again think of K-Tel's executives, opportunistically associating their business with the Internet—then selling $60 million in stock before their mighty tumble. Or think of Nine West, rallying its stores to sell more shoes *now,* even as it jeopardized long-term product management. Or think of the accounts receivable creep at any number of companies that announce sales today but are forced to delay collection of those bills for months. Such actions all represent a rush for the rich valuations now in exchange for miserable migraine headaches later.

It's an approach that would still work swimmingly well for long-term shareholders if the game of Monopoly were just about one duel, a single swing of the bat, the first throw of the dice—a game where immediate, albeit thoughtless, aggression won every time. You opened the board, set up the pieces, divided out the cash, poured four cups of tea, then rolled *once* to determine the winner. If the dynamics of our public markets worked like that, then corporate America would be swarming with thugs and speculators. They'd lead with a fist, win with a blow, and level all comers. They'd bet all their wealth on a hedge fund selling loans into Russia in pursuit of quick profit. And they'd win.

But Monopoly cannot be won in a turn, and corporate America isn't a crowd of goons. The typical winners in the business world walk softly and slowly, carry a pen that is mightier than the sword, and are no more threatening in appearance than a fly or a field mouse. And though it may be tempting for a public company to furiously rush for victory, to aim to vanquish its competition by noon, *that* approach usually proves self-destructive over the long term. Its opposite—calmly standing and delivering for years and decades—is the route down the winding path to goldenrod, a greener patch, and the broadening of shareholder value.

THE MAKERS OF RULES

With the table thus set for estimating monopoly power, I'd like to walk through five variables to measure how well a company is doing at gaining and maintaining monopoly status. In this, the last set of our ranking criteria, score four points when a company meets the standard; two points if it is outperforming its competition, but by a measure shy of the standard; and zero points if it trails the competition. Let's look at the five metrics.

1. Gross margins 5 percentage points ahead of its foremost competitor.
A company that has a significant gross-margin advantage in its industry is in position to knock back its competition over time. Intel can under-

mine Advanced Micro Devices on pricing at every turn; Coca-Cola can convert some of Pepsi's bottlers overnight. The manufacturing efficiencies and pricing authority that light-product consumer monopolies deliver provide them an extraordinary competitive advantage.

Score four points if your company has gross margins 5 percentage points ahead of the competition; two points if its gross margins are better than the competition but by less than 5 percentage points; and zero points if its competition has higher gross margins.

2. Net margins 5 percentage points ahead of its foremost competitor. Down on the bottom line, a 5 percentage–point lead translates into a whole lot more cash flowing into a company's coffers than toward its competitors. It also signifies that a company is gaining more reward than its competitors for the same amount of work. And the reward, cash, is nothing more nor less than pure oxygen to a corporation. We'd prefer that our investments have more air to breathe than not.

Score four points for companies with a 5 percentage–point lead or greater in net margins; two points for those outrunning the lead competition but falling short of the standard; and zero points for losing out on profit margins.

3. A 25 percent better cash-to-debt position than the competition, or five times more cash. As a business creates its industry and climbs to its peak, it relies throughout on capital to finance its next stage of growth. Rather than prattle on, I'll turn to a quotation from Ron Chernow's excellent recent book, *Titan*, on John D. Rockefeller's monopolist approach to business:

> It is impossible to comprehend Rockefeller's breathtaking ascent without realizing that he always moved into battle backed by abundant cash. Whether riding out downturns or coasting on booms, he kept plentiful reserves and won many bidding contests simply because his war chest was deeper.

Poker players know this as well, recognizing that among four perfectly equal competitors, the one starting with the most cash will always win.

Score four points for the business with a ratio of cash to long-term debt that is 25 percent better than the competition; two points if its ratio is better than competitors but by less than 25 percent, and zero points if it's in a worse cash position than the competition. And because the ratio can be thrown out of whack when companies have no debt, set the score at four points for any company that has five times more cash than its lead competition. Also, remember to always include short-term investments and marketable securities in calculating cash savings.

4. A Foolish Flow Ratio 25 percent below that of its foremost competitor. The three key variables in the Flow Ratio—inventories, accounts receivable, and accounts payable—are critical drivers to market dominance. The company that grows greedy for sales and sloppy with its inventories is in trouble. The company that so covets a rich valuation that it excuses wildly rising levels of receivables is in trouble. The company that is forced to pay down its payables instantly is in a weakened position in its industry. Invert all three, and you have a business that is more methodical than maniacal, concerned more with creating enduring value than immediate valuation—one that can play more offense than defense over time.

To score four points, companies need to keep their Flow Ratio 25 percent lower than the competition. Mark two points down for a company with a better Flow than its competition but short of our standard. Zero points go to the business with a worse Flow than its lead competition.

5. Name-brand victory through convenience. The final characteristic relies on your ability to make a judgment call about the company's product delivery and brand. To establish Rule Maker authority, a business must position its products as the most accessible and convenient in its industry. History shows that in virtually every consumer sector, there are few ways to underrate the value of being the leader in convenience for customers. Whether it's buying midlevel shelf space in a supermarket, placing the gas station fifty yards closer to the exit ramp, delivering books right to the doorstep, selling coffee on the corner, or preloading software on a computer, convenience for the customer is crucial to long-term success.

In measuring monopoly status, try to determine if a given company provides the most accessible products or services in its industry. If so, award them four more points. If there's no advantage nor disadvantage in convenience, mark two points for the company. If, however, its products or services are less convenient than those of the lead competition, reward them with a goose egg.

CONCLUSION

This handful of measurements provides clues to how powerful a business is in its industry, whether it is sustaining that authority, and what we might expect from it as investors in the years ahead. Consumer companies with superior gross and net margins, swollen cash levels, a heightened sense of the need to manage products and cash through the business, and a commitment to providing the greatest convenience in their categories are businesses on the verge of monopoly success. They can be expected to generate market-beating returns for investors, for stretches of five years and more.

There is, however, one difficulty in applying these metrics: identifying just who constitutes potential Rule Makers' direct competition. Given their size and scope, most giant corporations are engaged in a number of loosely related businesses. How can we account for this? I typically start by picking the biggest single competitor in a company's core business. But even that can be difficult—is Microsoft's competition IBM, or Sun Microsystems, or Oracle? Or is it America Online or Netscape? What about Disney or Time Warner—they're big competitors of Microsoft's now too, right? Or how about Intuit or even Merrill Lynch?

Depending on how much time you have, you might run these five simple numbers against all of a company's competitors, and take the average of the entire group. In this case, however, due to space limitations and my interest in securing a little bit of time outside before this summer ends, I'll just run Microsoft's numbers against its core software competitors: IBM, Oracle, and Sun Microsystems.

Model Company: Microsoft

Technology, change, and the potential for great reward—they have traveled together in open markets for centuries. And, yes, the world has been changing dramatically over the past two decades. Since the first delivery of a personal computer into the home, five major computing companies—Microsoft, Intel, Dell, Cisco, and Compaq—have created over $600 billion in wealth where no value existed previously. I don't have to drone on endlessly, spitting out statistics like a solar-powered calculator or a baseball manager, to illustrate our nation's transformation from a heavily industrial economy into a world of light technology and communications. All I really have to do is ask you, "Which do you spend more time looking into?"

a. A television set
b. The morning newspaper
c. The windshield of your automobile
d. Your desktop and laptop computers
e. Your refrigerator door

Now, consider what your answer would have been ten, twenty-five, fifty, and one hundred years ago. You may still watch more television today, or spend more time over a newspaper; you may even pass more hours behind a steering wheel. But the world is gradually heading in a very different direction: Children are being schooled on computers, our major corporations rely on e-mail every day, and the total number of digital commercial transactions has exploded over the past three years. Cars are being researched, priced, and purchased through computers, as are books, software, clothing, music, concert tickets, travel packages, and much more. And networked computing has been chewing up classified ad sales, the profit center of every local newspaper in the country. In the meantime, an increasing number of financial transactions are taking place online, including buying and selling stocks and mutual funds, tracking and paying bills, and organizing the family budget.

I won't bore you with a pile of statistics, but just one: In the summer of 1998, the Internet was being used regularly by more than 75 million American adults. The rest of the world lags behind, but is headed that way, too. And Microsoft, the focus of our attention in this, the monopoly chapter, today operates in and leads this extraordinary industry. Think of the role that software and the Internet will play in the future of communications, the collection and display of information, the global sale and distribution of products, the flow of money, even in improvements in transportation over the next century. The immediate demand for these services is staggering. The yet unseen opportunities will, of course, prove far more astounding.

MICROSOFT VS. OUR STANDARDS

1. Gross margins 5 percentage points ahead of its foremost competitor.
Much of our search for enduringly great businesses drives us toward in-

dustries in great demand, whose leaders are experiencing a blistering rise in revenues. But one of our many other challenges as buyers of the Makers of Rules is to track down "light" products or "very soft" goods being sold into that buzzing demand across the globe. The mass production and delivery of small things, at inexpensive and inflatable prices, have proven an extraordinary model for successful business in the twentieth century.

Let's see how well Microsoft fits the mold:

1998 GROSS MARGINS   Microsoft: 92%
     Oracle: 68%
     Sun Microsystems: 52%
     IBM: 38%
     Microsoft: 4 points

2. Net margins 5 percentage points ahead of its foremost competitor. In addition to wide gross margins, we look for broad *profit* margins, too. Microsoft has $3.5 billion in trailing profits today, and to justify its valuation, it will have to double those earnings in the next three to five years. To double its profits five years from now, Microsoft will need to generate the equivalent of $13 more in earnings per U.S. citizen than it does today. Each citizen of thirteen different Americas will have to hand over a dollar of new profit if Microsoft is to pull it off.

The task is enormous, but the opportunity to play the role of distributor or enabler to so many different industries at such little manufacturing expense makes it quite possible. Microsoft's managers won't succeed at this unless they can couple sales growth with a continuing rise in net margins. But look at their lead over the competition!

1998 NET MARGINS   Microsoft: 31%
     Oracle: 13%
     IBM: 8%
     Sun Microsystems: 8%
     Microsoft: 4 points

3. A 25 percent better cash-to-debt ratio than the competition, or five times more cash. As it racks up these profits, Microsoft is directing an enormous flow of savings into its coffers. That's cash that they can use for both defense and offense. The company's $400 million purchase of WebTV in 1997 is a perfect example of this. With it, Microsoft is aggressively pursuing new markets while also defending its business on the personal computer. The overdog can literally buy its way onto new technology platforms—the buildup of savings allows for it.

Microsoft has $13.9 billion in cash savings and not a dollar of long-term debt.

Sun Microsystems has cash of $1.3 billion and debt of $0.

Oracle has savings of $2.2 billion, debt of $300 million, and a ratio of 7.3.

IBM has savings of $5.5 billion, $14.6 billion in debt, and a ratio of 0.38.

Because Microsoft has five times more cash than Sun Microsystems, it gains the highest rank.
Microsoft score: 4 points

4. A Foolish Flow Ratio 25 percent below that of the foremost competition. Microsoft is among the most tightly managed companies in the world, with little inventory to carry and a rigorous accounting standard that defers uncollected sales. The company carries a Flow Ratio of just 0.29, the lowest I've ever found. That marks a 54 percent better score than the runner-up in the category, IBM. Mark down another four points for the technology leader.

FLOW RATIO   Microsoft: 0.35
                IBM: 0.54
                Oracle: 0.82
                Sun Microsystems: 1.33
                Microsoft score: 4 points

5. Name-brand victory through convenience. Though the most subjective of all of this chapter's rankings, convenience in the software industry begins with the letter *M* and ends with *T*. Microsoft certainly provides the most conveniently placed software for individuals and corporations. Flip on any computer, a Dell or Gateway, a Compaq or Apple, and preloaded Microsoft icons will peek out at you. Redmond, Washington's software giant committed early on to trying to provide the most accessible and most visible applications for desktop computing.
Microsoft score: 4 points

PUTTING IT ALL TOGETHER

The disclaimer up front is that Microsoft has grown to be the largest position in our Rule Maker Portfolio online. We purchased the stock in February 1998, and since then the shares are up more than 60 percent. When we bought a piece of this business, the market had never valued the company so dearly. And we took our ownership position with the understanding that Microsoft stock might fall 50 percent at any given time. Perhaps the U.S. stock market would get hammered after further banking corruption was exposed in Asia, or a currency crisis spreading through Latin America might stall commercial activity around the planet. Or it might just be that our software giant would flail about atop its empire building, like King Kong, surrounded on all sides by smaller, whizzing competitors. Ultimately, we could indeed lose money on this holding.

But that's generally how we approach each investment that we make: It *could* lose us money. For that reason, we always diversify into between six and twenty different stock investments. That being the case, Microsoft looked and looks extremely promising to me. With gross margins above 90 percent, pumping more research and development money into the Internet than its largest online competitors combined, and armed with a truly world-class brand name as well as a clear lead in an industry for which demand will double and then double again and again in the years ahead, Microsoft really is the classic Rule Maker. In its Monopoly Ranking, Microsoft scores an even 20 out of a possible 20 points. In fact, as you'll find at the back of this book, Microsoft has the highest total score of any public company in America.

The question then, is this: Is Microsoft now such a monopoly that the Department of Justice will regulate or split it into pieces? And how will that affect it as an investment?

John D. Rockefeller Incarnate. Over the past few years, arguments about Microsoft (Nasdaq: MSFT) have broken out across the technology industry. Does its dominant position in providing the PC operating system give it an unfair advantage in the sale of the high-margin applications that neatly integrate back into that operating system? The debate has spread through the halls of our nation's capital, as Janet Reno and the Department of Justice (DOJ) have embarked on a grueling search for more information about Microsoft's business practices.

Unfortunately, I can offer few guarantees about the future direction of the DOJ's case, a subject that falls far outside of my tiny area of expertise. The only thing I can offer with any certainty is that interaction with the Justice Department will be a permanent feature of Microsoft's development over the next decade. Beyond that, the numbers suggest to me that over the next ten to fifteen years, Microsoft will have to be heavily regulated or broken out into smaller entities, in much the same way that Standard Oil was back in 1911. The mathematics of the company's growth rate, even as it slows, indicates that Microsoft will eventually assume a position that destroys the economics of competition in its industry. And the Department of Justice and our antitrust laws won't permit that, aiming to protect the consumer.

You say, "What? You're comparing Microsoft to an oil company at the turn of the century?"

Consider this. In very general terms, Microsoft is blessed with a number of Standard Oil-ish qualities: (1) extraordinary demand for its merchandise; (2) a product that fuels a new economic age; (3) spectacularly high profit margins; and (4) superior, farsighted financial management. In these ways, Microsoft is much more analogous to Standard Oil than it is to IBM, which suffered its own arduous antitrust investigation into its business practices in the 1980s. IBM was seeking a market-control monopoly, in which it would vertically dominate the world of technology. Big Blue hoped to lord over everything from hardware to software, data retrieval, and connectivity.

That's not true of the oil and software titans, who focused narrowly on becoming high-profit monopolies integrated into their industries. Standard Oil didn't make automobiles or trains. Microsoft, likewise, doesn't sell computers or microchips. The company focuses instead on where the profits are while even helping to drive the forceful expansion of its lower-margin machine makers—Compaq, Dell, Gateway, and, now, Apple. Neither John D. Rockefeller nor Bill Gates had pretensions to manufacture the machinery of a new age; they just wanted to deliver the high-margin accelerant for those machines. Both men found the cookie jar of profit in their sectors, spent their early days expanding it by putting their "fuel" into every machine (and helping to sell the machines), then dedicated the next stage of their careers to defending their profit jar. The commercial pictures of these two so resemble each other, and the basic mathematics of their games are so alike, that speculating similar ends for both isn't so farfetched.

And, believe it or not, that wouldn't be a bad thing for Microsoft investors.

For Standard Oil owners, the end of Rockefeller's reign meant a new beginning. Broken out into thirty-four separate companies, whose shares were distributed in representative allotments to every prior shareholder, the Standard Oil entities kept churning out extraordinary investment returns for decades, right up until today. Exxon, Mobil, Chevron, Arco, Amoco, and Pennzoil—these are some of the children of Standard Oil. With a very light business model, product to integrate into a wide range of machines, and financial managers committed to a rigorously honest depiction of their progress, Standard Oil as a whole and in parts survived as a market-beating entity for a century.

In the decades ahead, I suspect that the same will hold true for Microsoft. The company will continue integrating its applications into automobiles, onto interactive television, across the Web, into home appliances, as well as trying to lay these same applications down like a jacket over every trading desk on Wall Street. Software is Microsoft's petroleum product, and it's clear that the world will not run out of room for new applications any time soon.

And the real enduring value that the software industry offers investors is that its products are not limited by space, but only by our imagination. When we own seven personal computers (yikes), we'll still be purchasing new software applications for them. And there's still plenty of room for improvement in those applications, too. Signing onto the Internet has to be made much like picking up a telephone or flipping on a television set; landing at www.fool.com to track your investments each day should not require a whirring and hiss, a slowly framed unfolding of screens, and limits on our ability to sort and arrange features and data. The Internet can't continue to be so slow and expect to attract daily visitors in the hundreds of millions. Moving around the network will have to require no more time or effort than the clicking of channels on a remote control—even when sound and moving pictures have been integrated into the experience.

Better machines will make this possible, yes. But software will make it happen.

Concluding Thoughts

Our search for companies with monopolistic authority in the very best consumer industries has made us revisit many of the qualities and calculations covered in previous chapters; the only alteration we made here was to turn this into a comparative game. The truest Makers of Rules have heightened gross and net margins that outpace those of competitors. And they have more cash, tighter product controls, higher accounting standards, and easier access to the world of consumers than do their competitors. They win at what matters most. They play for keeps, and are more than willing to wait if it improves their chance of winning.

But though these qualities are simple enough to identify, for a company to achieve them it actually has to live them each day, for years. Coca-Cola was private for more than two decades; Microsoft waited eleven years before going public. The superior performance at public companies that leads to Rule Maker status and market-beating rewards compounded for years takes *time* and a *financial discipline.* The end result is a blessing of the highest order for executives, managers, employees, customers, and shareholders alike. But it is misery for the competition. If you think that a Rule Maker's competitors consider it a hard-hitting linebacker with an attitude, an avalanche that never slows, forever rustling like an icy wind in their ears, the despoiler of every countermeasure—you're right. The goal of every publicly traded company, like the goal of every Monopoly player, is to gradually assume the position of highest authority, to dominate the board. To become king.

Unlike the game of Monopoly, though, this game never ends.

In our public markets, there has never been, nor ever will be, a true monopoly. Because the company that comes to accept its power and lays laws as it chooses, acting like a fatuous king all day—this company dies a slow, torturous death. In Greek mythology, it was arrogance that ruined the great leaders. In America, the cable companies, the telephone industry, and portions of the traditional media have all had their comeuppance. That which can so frustrate the individual (to be distinguished from the business competitor) will be thrown out of doors, beheaded in the town square, and left for squirrels and flies to feed on.

Because in the end, the only Rule Maker in an open economy with freely flowing products and ideas is *the customer.* The company that acts like a king will crumble. There is no true Rule Maker but the customer, no one but you.

Chapter 15

The Last Word on Rule Makers (For Now)

A Look at All the Rankings

What follows is a brief review of all the qualities used to analyze potential Rule Makers in consumer-driven industries. The expectations we've set out over the past few chapters include, among others, superior mass-market branding, peak profitability, strong consumer demand, tight controls over inventory, and an operational direction that looks far beyond the company's present location.

You'll notice that a new ranking, "Pure Enjoyment," has been added. This last item requires you to vote on whether you believe that you'll enjoy following this business over the years. Ironically, it also acts as the final one point that neatly fills out a total possible score of sixty points per Rule Maker candidate. Obviously, any company that racks up sixty points under this model is considered an extreme powerhouse and, in my estimation, one of the best companies in the world with which to stabilize your investment portfolio. I don't, however, expect that any company can score a clean sixty out of sixty.

Here's how the points play out: A business can earn seven total points on its branding and message, fourteen on its operational location, eighteen for its business momentum, twenty on its leadership authority, and one for *your* enjoyment. Toted up, that equals a potential sixty points per company. Here are the individual entries by category:

A. Rule-Making Message (0–1 point per item)
1. Familiarity
2. Openness
3. Optimism
4. Legitimacy
5. Inevitability
6. Solitariness
7. Humor

B. Rule-Making Location (0–2 points per item)
1. Mass-market repeated purchasing
2. Gross margins
3. Net margins
4. Sales growth
5. Cash-to-debt ratio
6. Foolish Flow Ratio
7. Your familiarity and interest

C. Rule-Making Direction (0–3 points per item)
1. Rising gross margins
2. Rising net margins
3. Share buybacks
4. Cash outgrowing debt
5. Lowering Foolish Flow Ratio
6. Expanding possibilities

D. Rule-Making Authority (0–4 points per item)
1. Gross-margin lead
2. Net-margin lead
3. Cash-to-debt lead
4. Foolish Flow Ratio superiority
5. Name-brand through convenience

E. Your Pure Enjoyment (0–1 point)
1. Yes or no

To organize the scoring of companies, you can scratch out these categories on a pad of paper or set it all up in Microsoft Excel. The Motley Fool also offers a Rule Making spreadsheet—to get information or to order the spreadsheet, e-mail us at

RuleBook@fool.com

or call 1-888-665-FOOL.

Also, I've run the rankings on a dozen public companies for your perusal in the appendix.

Once you have a system in place for tracking the performance of the public companies that you own or that interest you, you'll notice that applying these measurements won't take more than a half hour per quarter, tops. The sweat of your brief labor can be what turns you away from Kmart and toward Johnson & Johnson, away from General Motors and toward General Electric—decisions that could prove the difference between your financial insecurity and security over the long run. Though our high schools, colleges, and even a few business schools neglected to help us make the simple connection between savings, business ownership, and financial security, even a Fool now can carry out this research, and earn rewards from it. I hope that you'll agree, after carrying out a few of these reviews, that they are simple, logical, and effective.

But even with a spreadsheet in place, it's not entirely clear what you're supposed to do with these numbers. Is a company with a score of 48 points a buy, a hold, or a sell? The answers follow in the Total Score Analysis . . .

Total Score Analysis

I've broken the rankings out into four tiers, which I use in determining whether to buy, hold, or sell positions in my portfolio.

Before diving into this simple scoring system, remember that these rule-making criteria should be applied only to businesses with *more* than $1 billion in annual sales. The business models and the financing strategies of smaller companies often directly contrast those of larger companies. Ranked according to our rule-making principles, America Online five years ago would've looked, sounded, and smelled like a junkyard dog—which would have led to the sort of ghastly misreads that came from the old-line financial media. The mistake they made was analyzing a Rule *Breaker* as if it were a Rule *Maker.* By doing so, they steered their readers away from America Online, a now-classic consumer brand that has proven to be one of the best-performing stocks in the world this decade. Our Foolish suggestion is to use this billion-dollar benchmark to help you confine rule-breaking analyses to smaller companies and rule-making analyses to the giants.

Finally, because this rule-making analysis relies on a fundamental assessment of the merits of each business, I do use these scores to pick and choose monopoly investments for my portfolio. The numbers, after all, result from reasoning based on the guts of business development, and they've given me a clear perspective into the present merits of corporations banging their way toward the crown. That said, each score does represent a unique situation at a unique business. So, rather than blindly selling a position that has descended to a lower tier, I first try to understand what's been hampering the company. And, similarly, rather than blindly buying a top-tier business, I reason through from whence it came and whither it's headed. These rule-making scores focus my attention and heavily influence my thinking, but they don't phone up a discount broker and place the order for me.

OK, here's how I break out the tiers.

1. TOP TIER (50–60 POINTS)

These are the cream of the crop, the businesses to own for a decade. They represent pure monopolies, churning out predictable earnings as they expand operations around the globe. With ample savings, name brands that the world is embracing, and the discipline to account for performance in the most conservative fashion, these companies earn the Fool's throne, the crown, the robe, and two golden slippers. Arrogance now is their greatest threat.

2. SECOND TIER (40–49 POINTS)

These runner-up businesses also typically make for solid investments. The key here is to determine whether a company is moving up toward the top tier or falling down toward tier three. Second-tier businesses on an operational path toward the throne will be some of your greatest investments.

3. THIRD TIER (30–39 POINTS)

When building an investment stable of Rule Makers, I almost totally ignore third-tier businesses, leaving them for investors who prefer to find companies in need of a major momentum shift. With debt, low margins, and little cash, most of these businesses are doomed for enduring mediocrity, or worse. When I already own a company that has fallen to the third rung, I think very carefully about liquidating my position.

4. FOURTH TIER (BELOW 30 POINTS)

Sell.

Conclusion:
The Truth Was Found in the Numbers

You may have completed this section on Rule Makers and not yet felt the great urgency to dial up your discount or full-service broker and order the sale of every actively managed mutual fund in your account in exchange for common stock. No, not yet.

But at least consider it.

Because if, after these sections, you still believe that the safest place to have your money is with a big fund family teeming with financial analysts, I've failed to really clarify one of the most attractive elements of this investment approach. Even if these rule-making companies are *just average* in the future, no better nor worse than mediocre, their owners will thrash the performance of the great majority of managed mutual funds. Over 80 percent of all stock funds over the past twenty years have failed to even match the market average. And during the boom market of the 1990s, that figure has increased to over 90 percent of all professionally managed stock funds.

Submediocrity, thy name is mutual fund.

But rates of return are only half the story. Because even if a collection of ten Rule-Making investments did just as poorly as the average mutual fund and finished below the returns of an S&P 500 index fund, they would still substantially outperform those funds over time. How so? Consider the investor who buys and holds businesses through a discount broker. With discount brokers today charging from $5 to $15 per trade, that investor can build an entire portfolio for $50 to $200. Given that low, one-time expense, this investor will create (or preserve) tens or hundreds of thousands in wealth, even if he only keeps pace with the poorly performing fund.

Half of the mutual-fund tragedy is about subpar performance. The other half of the haunting tale is about overly high annual fees.

If it seems an outrageous claim that, over time, you could save tens or hundreds of thousands of dollars by doing it yourself, consider two portfolios that each grow at a rate of 9 percent per year for fifty years. The first portfolio is run by a team of hired guns at the Wisenheimer Fund Group, which boasts the motto "Long-term capital management with prudent hedging in foreign loans is our favorite dish. . . ." And they charge a 1.75 percent expense fee each year (the industry's average). The second portfolio is managed by you, the individual investor, using an on-line discount broker that charges $5 per trade. Both portfolios begin with $75,000. Here's how the numbers play out from one decade to the next:

	Growth Rate	Annual Expense
The Wisenheimer Fund	9%	1.75%
Your Rule Maker Portfolio	9%	0.00%*

* Includes $50 up-front cost (ten investments at $5 per trade, via an online discount broker).

Long-Term Returns on a $75,000 Portfolio

	Tenth Year	Twentieth Year	Thirtieth Year	Fortieth Year	Fiftieth Year
Wisenheimer	$150,000	$300,000	$590,000	$1.2 million	$2.3 million
Rule Maker	$180,000	$420,000	$1.0 million	$2.4 million	$5.6 million

The difference is shocking. Within ten years, even though both portfolios are earning the same annual rate of return, the Rule Maker Portfolio has generated $30,000 more than the Wisenheimer Fund. By the thirtieth year, the gap between the two has grown to $410,000, illustrating how important it is for families to take control of their money. By the fiftieth year, the difference is a mind-boggling $3.3 million, emphasizing the need to teach kids the basics of investing in order to free them from the interruption of professional money management in their adult years. Mutual-fund fees and trading activity are indeed an *interruption* to the success of the individual investor today. The average annual expense ratio of 1.75 percent eats into compounded growth. In the fiftieth year of the above scenario, the Wisenheimer expense ratio will claim over $40,000 in fees.

Remember that this scenario compares two investment portfolios that start with the *same* amount of money and grow at the *same* rate. The one difference is in the fees. The Rule Maker Portfolio chalks up $50 to get started; the Wisenheimer Fund demands repeated (and increasingly painful) annual expense-ratio payments. Whether you can hold your original ten positions for fifty years in a Rule Maker Portfolio is in question, but with these fundamental metrics you can follow their trials and tribulations without much effort each year. And any transactions that you make, for $5 or $10 through the discount broker, will certainly never add up to the $40,000 you'd pony up to the Wise in year fifty.

THE BIRTH OF THE PEOPLE'S MARKETS

That mutual-fund business model, which has resulted in the management of over 5 trillion American dollars today, will wither over the long haul. The combination of historically subpar returns, elevated fees, and the development of a global network that enables mass communication about those truths will draw individuals away from managed funds and toward index funds, common stock, and five-dollar transaction fees. With more information and opportunities to talk to veteran investors around the world, people are already beginning to shop for investments with an eye toward the fee-adjusted performance. This persistent interactivity online is today undermining the financial industry's power brokers: people are starting to ask the intelligent questions. Here's one I came across at www.fool.com that's worth repeating:

Tom, if the *fiduciary obligation* of financial advisors, consultants, and money managers is to provide their clients with the lowest-priced investment vehicle offering the highest and most secure investment returns, doesn't that mean that the professional who recommends managed funds today is likely in violation of that oath? With the crummy performance, the high fees, and the high turnover ratios of managed funds—what am I missing?

My answer? I don't think you're missing anything. Either many professionals today are neglecting to do the proper research when they recommend managed funds that have consistently lost to the market, or they're knowingly ignoring their fiduciary obligation to clients. Either way, it isn't pretty.

I think what we'll see over the next few years is the demise of a bloated Wall Street business model that put corporate profit ahead of corporate service. In the decade ahead, those priorities will be reversed as our entire financial system is turned into the mainstream *service* business that it was always meant to be. With this mass conversation on the Internet, I think that the turn of this century will mark the unwinding of Wall Street as it ushers in a return to the original intent of our public markets—a way for companies to raise capital and a way for investors to profit from commercial expansion. We're standing on the precipice, staring at the death of Wall Street's arrogant authority, and gliding toward the birth of the people's markets.

The Final Qualities of a Rule Maker

For posterity's sake, I'll restate some of the primary qualities of a rule-making consumer business. Focused on mass markets, these corporations lock out the competition by selling to the world's daily habits, generating enormous cash flows, believing that their dominance will only come over the long haul, and fairly representing their progress to shareholders. The reason for all the discussion of companies like Microsoft and Coca-Cola in these chapters is that they better reflect the rule-making model than any corporations I've studied. My emphasis on them has been to encourage you to study the greatest businesses of this century, and to largely disregard short-term stock valuation. The long-term compounded rewards that America's greatest companies can deliver to investors boggle the mind.

None of that means that the Rule Maker model is complete, though. I encourage you to join us online at www.fool.com/rulemaker, where you'll find an active conversation brewing among thousands of investors about new ways to look at this analytical model. In the months ahead, you can bet that we'll add new criteria and tinker with the total scoring system. The single reason for holding the highest potential score of a Rule Maker down to sixty points was to leave room for forty more points of new criteria generated by the collective efforts of Fools around the globe. See you online!

Chapter 16

Drink Me

Let me see some more. "The purpose you undertake is
dangerous;" —why, that's certain. 'Tis dangerous to take a
cold, to sleep, to drink; but I tell you, my lord fool, out of this
nettle, danger, we pluck this flower, safety.

—WILLIAM SHAKESPEARE,
HENRY IV, PART 1 (II, iii)

Come, I'll drink no proofs nor no bullets. I'll drink no more
than will do me good.

—WILLIAM SHAKESPEARE,
HENRY IV, PART 2 (II, iv)

You have now traveled with us along the path of The Great
Business: from Rule Breaker to Rule Maker. What remains is just to
start investing.

Consider first this directive lifted from the pages of *The Motley Fool
UK Investment Guide* (p. 212), the outstanding work of our very talented lead British Fool writer, David Berger:

> When you've decided what strategy you might like to follow, then
> immediately do nothing.

It seems appropriate to begin our ending of *The Motley Fool's Rule
Breakers, Rule Makers*—with its decidedly Shakespearean undercur-
rents—by trotting out a dictum that is so very Hamlet. One school of

literary thought holds that for most of the play that bears his name, Hamlet personifies Do Nothing. He has the right ideas about things, but he acts on them a wee bit too late and winds up getting himself killed. We'd like to suggest here that you try to avoid the opposite mistake: Don't get killed by acting on things too *early* or too *quickly.* We're suggesting that when you think you're ready to begin investing, you should swipe a clef out of Hamlet's songbook and, immediately, *do nothing.*

In our previous two books, *You Have More Than You Think* and *The Motley Fool Investment Guide,* we emphasized the importance of two things: (1) not investing any money in any particular way until you feel comfortable doing so, and (2) as a way of becoming more comfortable, "doing it on paper" first. Doing it on paper simply involves playing the game of I Would Do This Now (buy or sell such-and-such), and then following on paper how you are doing. This is the best possible (and cheapest) way to learn about yourself as an investor and to see how well you understand what you're trying to do.

Don't be persuaded *forever* by that advice, of course. We love investing! We think you should, too, and we think that the sooner people begin investing their long-term savings in the stock market, the better off they'll be heading into retirement. And, indeed, twentieth-century history has proven this point over and over again. So, starting too early with reckless abandon is far worse than starting too late with some caution. But *never starting* is its own disaster.

After turning the last page of this book, you don't *have* to invest all of your money in Rule Makers—which are far more suitable investments for newcomers than Rule Breakers—by Thursday of next week. And you certainly needn't instantly hitch your Emersonian wagon to some rule-breaking star just because your reading of this Foolish book suggests that the thing might double. Take your time to flesh out a portfolio of the ten to twenty best investments you can find. Be prepared to learn from your mistakes and stick tight to your successes. And remain always ready to adapt, in the same way that Darwin and Gould teach us that adaptation is survival, and survival, adaptation.

Be fully prepared to screw up—we've been wrong before on many an investment. And you know what? You will too. *Anyone* who spends much time at this investment stuff will enjoy his share of losers. Comes with the territory. The trick is not to take your losers too seriously (we mean that about "enjoying" your share of losers), while still learning lessons from them.

Investing Foolishly means investing with an open mind and with logic, backed by simple mathematics. If you're doing this correctly, you'll still often find that for every one of your true-blue winners, you may have anywhere from one to three (or more) stocks that are mediocre to worse. But that winner itself, when bought and held through its Breaker status, or when bought and held as a Maker, or (best of all) when bought practically at the IPO and perhaps never sold—that winner itself can make you rich. A single stock held to long-term gains of 500 percent, 1,000 percent, or more will earn you far more than you'll lose on your three worst stocks combined.

These principles (and a few others littered throughout our works) together constitute the elixir that Foolish investors must imbibe before stepping into the wonderland of the investment world. DRINK ME reads the label. Of course, once *this* is done, you're Hamlet no longer. You are Henry the Fifth, ascendant.

Afterword:
We Few, We Happy Few

The words that Shakespeare provides Henry in his speech to his men before the battle at Agincourt rank among the greatest exhortations of all time. Among them:

> By Jove, I am not covetous for gold,
> Nor care I who doth feed upon my cost;
> It yearns me not if men my garments wear;
> Such outward things dwell not in my desires.

It may strike the reader as strange that Henry would be talking of gold—in fact, his lack of interest in it—prior to a bloody life-and-death struggle. Why not stick with what would best appeal to the rabble, and talk of the approaching wealth and power afforded the victor? One would expect many military leaders to rouse their commoner troops with thoughts of the plunder that awaited them should they overcome great odds and beat France on its own turf. And yet Henry explains that he does not covet gold. (What he does covet we shall see shortly.)

It also might strike the reader as strange that at the end of an investment book, the authors would now hold up Henry's passage as a model for conduct, an ideal to be shooting for, spoken by a figure to be emulated. Why not instead conclude by attempting to *rouse* our readers at the thought of the fantastic riches that await those who understand and capitalize upon the breaking and making of rules?

Ah, but we ourselves wish to break the rules of money books, and in their place make new ones, as Henry yearns to do:

But if it be a sin to covet honour
I am the most offending soul alive.

These lines immediately follow those quoted earlier, and, as you can see, Henry recognizes something worth far more than its weight in gold, far more than gold itself: a good name. The esteem of others. Respect. A keen sense of integrity. Taken together these count for far more than the total at the bottom of your ATM stub, or the returns of Nasdaq's top-performing stock last year. Taken together, they are honor.

Honor does not come about by happenstance; it doesn't pop up like balls in a lotto machine, nor is it handed out to the highest bidder at a country auction. *A good name. The esteem of others. Respect. A keen sense of integrity.* Honor is not something conferred, but earned. Not passive, but active. Anyone who upholds honor has made a personal decision to blaze a path that will light the way for all around him. In an age that seems more interested in tearing apart heroes than finding them, it's refreshing to encounter heroes like Henry who serve us all as avatars.

Such heroes make what seems a rather dark period for our financial markets—we write in October 1998, with stocks having surrendered 30 percent of their value in just a few months—rather light. And we may fairly ask whether the Chicken Littles have not lost perspective, as they predict a global meltdown brought on by the Year 2000 bug, deflation, and mass recession. Let's remember that a lot of people have already made a lot of money on our stock market over the past decade or three, even though we've watched nearly a third of that value get chopped out very recently. Anyway, The Motley Fool continues to believe that longer-term investors in common stock will be rewarded handsomely over the next few decades.

So, what will you do when you have your money?

What are you already doing with what you have?

Do you covet honor?

The form taken by that honor need not be anything grand. What unites world beaters like Henry V with anyone reading this sentence right now—anyone in any place in any position anywhere—is that we are all individuals with the capacity to extend ourselves for others' benefit, to break out of our selfish here-and-now and lose ourselves in something far greater. Henry was an incredible individualist who at the same time managed to sublimate his individualism into communal effort that created benefit for many. His was a can-do optimism that created results, results made so much more significant through cooperative endeavor. The lesson right here, right now, is that anyone can do it at any time.

But money makes it easier. What a great reason to invest.

You see, money isn't really green or gold. Money is just *opportunity:* It's the opportunity to retire early and manage the local Little League team, to put your children and theirs through school, to start your own business or foundation, or to take a trip around the world with your three best friends. And it's the opportunity to extend ourselves on others' behalf. When you give some money away, you are really just sharing a portion of your opportunity with someone else—a joyous act. And an incredibly honorable one.

Just a few years after his most glorious victory, Henry V died of camp fever as a young man—he was thirty-five. It happened while campaigning; Henry was away all the time at war. Using hindsight, historians consider it a failure of his reign that he spent too much of his energies in foreign conquest and not enough helping his subjects at home. Fair enough. Consider the fatal typhus he contracted as his comeuppance, with the insult to his injury being that he never got to meet the one-year-old son he had by his French queen.

Nevertheless, William Shakespeare has immortalized Henry for his honor . . . and the extent to which he shared it with others, creating and giving *opportunity*. The words given him by Shakespeare in *Henry V's* fourth act will ring forever:

> We few, we happy few, we band of brothers.
> For he to-day that sheds his blood with me
> Shall be my brother; be he ne'er so vile,
> This day shall gentle his condition;
> And gentlemen in England now a-bed
> Shall think themselves accurs'd they were not here,
> And hold their manhoods cheap whiles any speaks
> That fought with us upon Saint Crispin's day.

Let us then quest together to beat the market, redistribute riches away from the wasteful Wise, and take our newfound opportunity out to the world around us. In so doing, we shall be breaking the rules of the old world, and together making rules for a new and better one.

Folly forever!

Appendix: Ranking Rule Makers

What follows are the numbers run for twelve large public companies in America. In each, I walk the company through the standards set in the book and then rate their monopoly standing by ranking them alongside their lead competition.

The end result is a total score, comment, and—as always—the recognition that the market changes from quarter to quarter, that kingdoms can lose their shine in a year. For that reason, and because some of the rankings are subjective (Does the company interest you?), I recommend that you drop by www.fool.com/rulemaker and work on the numbers with our staff and collection of Fool members there. You'll find worlds of additional information on the Rule Maker approach there.

AMERICA ONLINE

Brand (0–1 point)
Familiarity	1 point
Openness	1 point
Optimism	1 point
Legitimacy	1 point
Inevitability	1 point
Solitariness	1 point
Humor	1 point
Subtotal	7 points

Financial Direction (0–3 points)
Gross Margins	2 points
Net Margins	3 points
Shares Outstanding	0 points
Cash-to-Debt	2 points
Fool Flow Ratio	0 points
Expansion Potential	3 points
Subtotal	10 points

Financial Location (0–2 points)
Mass Market Habit	2 points
Gross Margins	0 points
Net Margins	2 points
Sales Growth	2 points
Cash-to-Debt	2 points
Fool Flow Ratio	2 points
Your Interest	2 points
Subtotal	12 points

Monopoly Status (0–4 points), no clear competition
Gross Margins	4 points
Net Margins	4 points
Cash-to-Debt	4 points
Fool Flow Ratio	4 points
Convenience	4 points
Subtotal	20 points

Recent Financials

	Quarter ended Sept. 30, 1998	Sept. 30, 1997
Sales	$858 million	$522 million
Gross Margins	36.4%	37.4%
Net Margins	12.6%	6.1%
Shares Outstanding	275 million	252 million
Cash & Equiv.	$1.3 billion	$631 million
Long-Term Debt	$375 million	$372 million
Current Assets	$1.6 billion	$930 million
Current Liabilities	$929 million	$894 million

Enjoyment: 1 point
SCORE: **50 points**

Comment: The runaway leader in the lucrative business of providing online access and services.

CISCO SYSTEMS

Brand (0–1 point)
Familiarity . . . . 0 points
Openness. . . . . 1 point
Optimism . . . . 1 point
Legitimacy. . . . . 1 point
Inevitability . . . . 1 point
Solitariness . . . . 1 point
Humor. . . . . 1 point
Subtotal. . . . . 6 points

Financial Direction (0–3 points)
Gross Margins . . . . 3 points
Net Margins. . . . . 2 points
Shares Outstanding . . . . 2 points
Cash-to-Debt. . . . . 3 points
Fool Flow Ratio . . . . 3 points
Expansion Potential . . . . 3 points
Subtotal. . . . . 16 points

Financial Location (0–2 points)
Mass Market Habit . . . . 1 point
Gross Margins . . . . 2 points
Net Margins. . . . . 2 points
Sales Growth. . . . . 2 points
Cash-to-Debt. . . . . 2 points
Fool Flow Ratio . . . . 1 point
Your Interest . . . . 2 points
Subtotal. . . . . 12 points

Monopoly Status (0–4 points), compared to 3Com
Gross Margins . . . . 4 points
Net Margins. . . . . 4 points
Cash-to-Debt. . . . . 4 points
Fool Flow Ratio . . . . 4 points
Convenience . . . . 4 points
Subtotal. . . . . 20 points

Recent Financials

	Year ended July 25, 1998	July 26, 1997
Sales	$8.5 billion	$6.4 billion
Gross Margins	65.5%	65.2%
Net Margins	16.0%	16.3%
Shares Outstanding	1.6 billion	1.55 billion
Cash & Equiv.	$1.7 billion	$1.3 billion
Long-Term Debt	$0	$0
Current Assets	$5.1 billion	$3.1 billion
Current Liabilities	$1.8 billion	$1.1 billion

Enjoyment: 1 point
SCORE: **55 points**

Comment: Among the top five technology companies in the world, and climbing.

COCA-COLA

Brand (0–1 point)

Familiarity . . . . 1 point
Openness . . . . 1 point
Optimism . . . . 1 point
Legitimacy . . . . 1 point
Inevitability . . . . 1 point
Solitariness . . . . 1 point
Humor . . . . 1 point
Subtotal . . . . 7 points

Financial Direction (0–3 points)

Gross Margins . . . . 3 points
Net Margins . . . . 1 point
Shares Outstanding . . . . 3 points
Cash-to-Debt . . . . 2 points
Fool Flow Ratio . . . . 2 points
Expansion Potential . . . . 3 points
Subtotal . . . . 14 points

Financial Location (0–2 points)

Mass Market Habit . . . . 2 points
Gross Margins . . . . 2 points
Net Margins . . . . 2 points
Sales Growth . . . . 0 points
Cash-to-Debt . . . . 2 points
Fool Flow Ratio . . . . 2 points
Your Interest . . . . 2 points
Subtotal . . . . 12 points

Monopoly Status (0–4 points),
compared to Pepsi

Gross Margins . . . . 4 points
Net Margins . . . . 4 points
Cash-to-Debt . . . . 4 points
Fool Flow Ratio . . . . 4 points
Convenience . . . . 4 points
Subtotal . . . . 20 points

Recent Financials

	Quarter ended Sept. 30, 1998	Sept. 30, 1997
Sales	$4.7 billion	$5.0 billion
Gross Margins	69.5%	66.5%
Net Margins	18.7%	20.4%
Shares Outstanding	2.49 billion	2.51 billion
Cash & Equiv.	$1.8 billion	$1.8 billion
Long-Term Debt	$688 million	$801 million
Current Assets	$6.0 billion	$6.0 billion
Current Liabilities	$7.8 billion	$7.4 billion

Enjoyment: 1 point
SCORE: **54 points**

Comment: The beverage monopoly with emerging markets to conquer.

DELL COMPUTER

Brand (0–1 point)
Familiarity	1 point
Openness	1 point
Optimism	1 point
Legitimacy	1 point
Inevitability	0 points
Solitariness	0 points
Humor	1 point
Subtotal	5 points

Financial Direction (0–3 points)
Gross Margins	3 points
Net Margins	3 points
Shares Outstanding	3 points
Cash-to-Debt	0 points
Fool Flow Ratio	0 points
Expansion Potential	3 points
Subtotal	12 points

Financial Location (0–2 points)
Mass Market Habit	1 point
Gross Margins	0 points
Net Margins	1 point
Sales Growth	2 points
Cash-to-Debt	2 points
Fool Flow Ratio	2 points
Your Interest	2 points
Subtotal	10 points

Monopoly Status (0–4 points), compared to Compaq
Gross Margins	2 points
Net Margins	4 points
Cash-to-Debt	0 points
Fool Flow Ratio	4 points
Convenience	2 points
Subtotal	12 points

Recent Financials

	Quarter ended August 2, 1998	August 3, 1997
Sales	$4.3 billion	$2.8 billion
Gross Margins	22.7%	22.2%
Net Margins	8.0%	7.6%
Shares Outstanding	1.4 billion	1.5 billion
Cash & Equiv.	$2.6 billion	$1.8 billion
Long-Term Debt	$512 million	$17 million
Current Assets	$5.1 billion	$3.9 billion
Current Liabilities	$3.1 billion	$2.7 billion

Enjoyment: 1 point
SCORE: **40 points**

Comment: A strong company in what may well prove an increasingly difficult industry.

DISNEY

Brand (0–1 point)

Familiarity . . . . 1 point
Openness. . . . . 1 point
Optimism . . . . 1 point
Legitimacy. . . . . 1 point
Inevitability . . . . 1 point
Solitariness . . . . 1 point
Humor. . . . . 1 point
Subtotal. . . . . 7 points

Financial Location (0–2 points)

Mass Market Habit . . . . 2 points
Gross Margins . . . . 1 point
Net Margins. . . . . 1 point
Sales Growth. . . . . 0 points
Cash-to-Debt. . . . . 0 points
Fool Flow Ratio . . . . 2 points
Your Interest . . . . 2 points
Subtotal. . . . . 8 points

Financial Direction (0–3 points)

Gross Margins . . . . 1 point
Net Margins. . . . . 1 point
Shares Outstanding . . . . 2 points
Cash-to-Debt. . . . . 2 points
Fool Flow Ratio . . . . 1 point
Expansion Potential . . . . 2 points
Subtotal. . . . . 9 points

Monopoly Status (0–4 points), compared to Time Warner

Gross Margins . . . . 2 points
Net Margins. . . . . 4 points
Cash-to-Debt. . . . . 4 points
Fool Flow Ratio . . . . 4 points
Convenience . . . . 2 points
Subtotal. . . . . 16 points

Recent Financials

	Quarter ended June 30, 1998	June 30, 1997
Sales	$5.2 billion	$5.2 billion
Gross Margins	40.0%*	42.0%*
Net Margins	7.9%	9.1%
Shares Outstanding	2.085 billion	2.064 billion

* Estimated

Cash & Equiv.	$853 million	$317 million
Long-Term Debt	$12.0 billion	$11.1 billion
Current Assets	$4.6 billion	$4.6 billion
Current Liabilities	$5.9 billion	$6.6 billion

Enjoyment: 1 point
SCORE: 41 points

Comment: A leader in entertainment but thus far unable to capitalize on the Internet.

GAP

Brand (0–1 point)

Familiarity	1 point
Openness	1 point
Optimism	1 point
Legitimacy	1 point
Inevitability	1 point
Solitariness	0 points
Humor	1 point
Subtotal	6 points

Financial Direction (0–3 points)

Gross Margins	3 points
Net Margins	3 points
Shares Outstanding	3 points
Cash-to-Debt	0 points
Fool Flow Ratio	0 points
Expansion Potential	3 points
Subtotal	12 points

Financial Location (0–2 points)

Mass Market Habit	2 points
Gross Margins	1 point
Net Margins	1 point
Sales Growth	2 points
Cash-to-Debt	1 point
Fool Flow Ratio	1 point
Your Interest	2 points
Subtotal	10 points

Monopoly Status (0–4 points), compared to Limited

Gross Margins	4 points
Net Margins	4 points
Cash-to-Debt	4 points
Fool Flow Ratio	4 points
Convenience	4 points
Subtotal	20 points

Recent Financials

	Quarter ended August 1, 1998	August 2, 1997
Sales	$1.9 billion	$1.3 billion
Gross Margins	40.4%	34.4%
Net Margins	7.2%	5.2%
Shares Outstanding	406 million	410 million
Cash & Equiv.	$545 million	$913 million
Long-Term Debt	$496 million	$496 million
Current Assets	$1.8 billion	$1.8 billion
Current Liabilities	$1.3 billion	$991 million

Enjoyment: 1 point
SCORE: **49 points**

Comment: A dominant retailer with a world of opportunities.

INTEL

General Brand (0–1 point)
Familiarity	1 point
Openness	1 point
Optimism	1 point
Legitimacy	1 point
Inevitability	0 points
Solitariness	1 point
Humor	1 point
Subtotal	6 points

Financial Location (0–2 points)
Mass Market Habit	1 point
Gross Margins	2 points
Net Margins	2 points
Sales Growth	2 points
Cash-to-Debt	2 points
Fool Flow Ratio	1 point
Your Interest	2 points
Subtotal	12 points

Financial Direction (0–3 points)
Gross Margins	0 points
Net Margins	1 point
Shares Outstanding	3 points
Cash-to-Debt	0 points
Fool Flow Ratio	0 points
Expansion Potential	2 points
Subtotal	6 points

Monopoly Status (0–4 points), compared to Advanced Micro Devices
Gross Margins	4 points
Net Margins	4 points
Cash-to-Debt	4 points
Fool Flow Ratio	4 points
Convenience	4 points
Subtotal	20 points

Recent Financials

	Quarter ended Sept. 26, 1998	Sept. 27, 1997
Sales	$6.7 billion	$6.2 billion
Gross Margins	52.2%	58.1%
Net Margins	23.2%	25.6%
Shares Outstanding	1.75 billion	1.8 billion
Cash & Equiv.	$8.4 billion	$9.7 billion
Long-Term Debt	$583 million	$448 million
Current Assets	$14.7 billion	$15.9 billion
Current Liabilities	$5.3 billion	$6.0 billion

Enjoyment: 1 point
SCORE: **45 points**

Comment: Monopolistic power in a slightly eroding technology niche.

KMART

Brand (0–1 point)
Familiarity	1 point
Openness	1 point
Optimism	1 point
Legitimacy	1 point
Inevitability	1 point
Solitariness	0 points
Humor	0 points
Subtotal	5 points

Financial Direction (0–3 points)
Gross Margins	3 points
Net Margins	3 points
Shares Outstanding	2 points
Cash-to-Debt	2 points
Fool Flow Ratio	2 points
Expansion Potential	0 points
Subtotal	12 points

Financial Location (0–2 points)
Mass Market Habit	2 points
Gross Margins	0 points
Net Margins	0 points
Sales Growth	0 points
Cash-to-Debt	0 points
Fool Flow Ratio	0 points
Your Interest	1 point
Subtotal	3 points

Monopoly Status (0–4 points), compared to Wal-Mart
Gross Margins	2 points
Net Margins	1 point
Cash-to-Debt	4 points
Fool Flow Ratio	0 points
Convenience	0 points
Subtotal	7 points

Recent Financials

	Quarter ended July 29, 1998	July 30, 1997
Sales	$8.1 billion	$7.8 billion
Gross Margins	21.9%	21.0%
Net Margins	1.0%	0.4%
Shares Outstanding	493 million	487 million
Cash & Equiv.	$556 million	$253 million
Long-Term Debt	$1.6 billion	$2.2 billion
Current Assets	$8.0 billion	$8.0 billion
Current Liabilities	$3.8 billion	$3.6 billion

Enjoyment: 0 points
SCORE: **27 points**

Comment: Restructuring with serious competition.

MICROSOFT

Brand (0–1 point)
Familiarity . . . . 1 point
Openness. . . . . 1 point
Optimism . . . . 1 point
Legitimacy. . . . . 1 point
Inevitability . . . . 1 point
Solitariness . . . . 1 point
Humor. . . . . 1 point
Subtotal. . . . . 7 points

Financial Location (0–2 points)
Mass Market Habit . . . . 2 points
Gross Margins . . . . 2 points
Net Margins. . . . . 2 points
Sales Growth. . . . . 2 points
Cash-to-Debt. . . . . 2 points
Fool Flow Ratio . . . . 2 points
Your Interest . . . . 2 points
Subtotal. . . . . 14 points

Financial Direction (0–3 points)
Gross Margins . . . . 3 points
Net Margins. . . . . 3 points
Shares Outstanding . . . . 2 points
Cash-to-Debt. . . . . 3 points
Fool Flow Ratio . . . . 3 points
Expansion Potential. . . . . 3 points
Subtotal. . . . . 17 points

Monopoly Status (0–4 points), compared to IBM
Gross Margins . . . . 4 points
Net Margins. . . . . 4 points
Cash-to-Debt. . . . . 4 points
Fool Flow Ratio . . . . 4 points
Convenience . . . . 4 points
Subtotal. . . . . 20 points

Recent Financials

	Quarter ended Sept. 30, 1998	Sept. 30, 1997
Sales	$4.0 billion	$3.1 billion
Gross Margins	92.2%	92.0%
Net Margins	38.5%	30.6%
Shares Outstanding	2.72 billion	2.66 billion
Cash & Equiv.	$17.2 billion	$13.9 billion
Long-Term Debt	$0	$0
Current Assets	$19.0 billion	$15.9 billion
Current Liabilities	$6.4 billion	$5.7 billion

Enjoyment: 1 point
SCORE: **59 points**

Comment: The strongest company in America, thriving in a burgeoning industry.

NIKE

Brand (0–1 point)
Familiarity	1 point
Openness	1 point
Optimism	1 point
Legitimacy	1 point
Inevitability	1 point
Solitariness	1 point
Humor	1 point
Subtotal	7 points

Financial Direction (0–3 points)
Gross Margins	1 point
Net Margins	1 point
Shares Outstanding	3 points
Cash-to-Debt	2 points
Fool Flow Ratio	0 points
Expansion Potential	1 point
Subtotal	8 points

Financial Location (0–2 points)
Mass Market Habit	1 point
Gross Margins	0 points
Net Margins	0 points
Sales Growth	0 points
Cash-to-Debt	0 points
Fool Flow Ratio	0 points
Your Interest	2 points
Subtotal	3 points

Monopoly Status (0–4 points), compared to Reebok
Gross Margins	2 points
Net Margins	4 points
Cash-to-Debt	4 points
Fool Flow Ratio	2 points
Convenience	4 points
Subtotal	16 points

Recent Financials

	Quarter ended August 31, 1998	August 31, 1997
Sales	$2.5 billion	$2.8 billion
Gross Margins	37.6%	40.0%
Net Margins	6.5%	9.2%
Shares Outstanding	292 million	298 million
Cash & Equiv.	$168 million	$109 million
Long-Term Debt	$376 million	$379 million
Current Assets	$3.4 billion	$3.5 billion
Current Liabilities	$1.5 billion	$1.7 billion

Enjoyment: 1 point
SCORE: **35 points**

Comment: Dominates its niche, but not a very attractive niche.

PFIZER

Brand (0–1 point)

Familiarity	1 point
Openness	1 point
Optimism	1 point
Legitimacy	1 point
Inevitability	1 point
Solitariness	0 points
Humor	1 point
Subtotal	6 points

Financial Location (0–2 points)

Mass Market Habit	2 points
Gross Margins	2 points
Net Margins	2 points
Sales Growth	2 points
Cash-to-Debt	2 points
Fool Flow Ratio	2 points
Your Interest	2 points
Subtotal	14 points

Financial Direction (0–3 points)

Gross Margins	3 points
Net Margins	1 point
Shares Outstanding	2 points
Cash-to-Debt	3 points
Fool Flow Ratio	3 points
Expansion Potential	3 points
Subtotal	15 points

Monopoly Status (0–4 points), compared to Merck

Gross Margins	4 points
Net Margins	2 points
Cash-to-Debt	4 points
Fool Flow Ratio	2 points
Convenience	2 points
Subtotal	14 points

Recent Financials

	Quarter ended Sept. 27, 1998	Sept. 28, 1997
Sales	$3.3 billion	$2.7 billion
Gross Margins	85.8%	84.6%
Net Margins	17.0%	20.0%
Shares Outstanding	1.32 billion	1.3 billion
Cash & Equiv.	$3.7 billion	$1.6 billion
Long-Term Debt	$528 million	$725 million
Current Assets	$9.9 billion	$7.4 billion
Current Liabilities	$7.3 billion	$5.0 billion

Enjoyment: 1 point
SCORE: 50 points

Comment: All around the strongest pharmaceutical company in the world.

SCHERING PLOUGH

Brand (0–1 point)
Familiarity . . . . 1 point
Openness. . . . . 1 point
Optimism . . . . 1 point
Legitimacy. . . . . 1 point
Inevitability . . . . 1 point
Solitariness . . . . 0 points
Humor. . . . . 1 point
Subtotal. . . . . 6 points

Financial Direction (0–3 points)
Gross Margins . . . . 2 points
Net Margins. . . . . 3 points
Shares Outstanding . . . . 2 points
Cash-to-Debt. . . . . 3 points
Fool Flow Ratio . . . . 0 points
Expansion Potential . . . . 3 points
Subtotal. . . . . 13 points

Financial Location (0–2 points)
Mass Market Habit . . . . 2 points
Gross Margins . . . . 2 points
Net Margins. . . . . 2 points
Sales Growth . . . . 2 points
Cash-to-Debt. . . . . 2 points
Fool Flow Ratio . . . . 2 points
Your Interest . . . . 2 points
Subtotal. . . . . 14 points

Monopoly Status (0–4 points), compared to Merck
Gross Margins . . . . 4 points
Net Margins. . . . . 2 points
Cash-to-Debt. . . . . 4 points
Fool Flow Ratio . . . . 2 points
Convenience . . . . 2 points
Subtotal. . . . . 14 points

Recent Financials

	Quarter ended Sept. 30, 1998	Sept. 30, 1997
Sales	$2.0 billion	$1.7 billion
Gross Margins	80.2%	80.9%
Net Margins	21.8%	20.7%
Shares Outstanding	745 million	741 million
Cash & Equiv.	$937 million	$714 million
Long-Term Debt	$46 million	$46 million
Current Assets	$3.4 billion	$2.9 billion
Current Liabilities	$2.7 billion	$2.9 billion

Enjoyment: 1 point
SCORE: **48 points**

Comment: The most financially disciplined of all the large pharmaceutical companies.

Rankings of the 12 Companies in Order of Rule Maker Status

Tier One
Microsoft: 59 points
Cisco: 55 points
Coca-Cola: 54 points
Pfizer: 50 points
America Online: 50 points

Tier Two
Gap: 49 points
Schering Plough: 48 points
Intel: 45 points
Disney: 41 points
Dell Computer: 40 points

Tier Three
Nike: 35 points

Tier Four
Kmart: 27 points

Acknowledgments

Our first thanks go out directly to all of our employees at The Motley Fool, who day in and day out do some of the most genuinely good work we have ever had the pleasure of witnessing. Go, Fools.

In particular, we would like to thank Gabrielle Loperfido for her help in compiling this book, enabling us to meet (OK, OK, almost) our deadlines. Any actual failure to make our deadlines is, as usual, Tom's fault—um, our fault. Thank you for your tireless good cheer and hard work as project manager, Gabrielle.

Our extreme gratitude goes to Mona Sharma, our superb Fool HQ research assistant for this book. We particularly appreciated Mona sacrificing some of her precious weekend time to cull for us the various articles, items, and info that we then cherry-picked to justify our foregone conclusions. Hey listen, Mona can find texts in libraries that the librarians weren't aware of. Thank you so much, Mona.

We would also like to recognize the efforts of the Fool editorial department, including (but not at all limited to) helpful comments from Jeff Fischer, Louis Corrigan, Dale Wettlaufer, Alex Schay, and Paul Larson.

We must acknowledge as well the tireless support of The Motley Fool during all his waking hours provided by Jay Stocki. Jay is not only a true Fool but an amazing human being, and this book would probably not have seen the light of day if it weren't for his karma and his rumored telekinetic abilities.

At Simon & Schuster, we have our editor Bob Mecoy to thank for his efforts on behalf of the book. Though Bob has since moved on to another publishing firm, let it always be remembered that years ago, he was the first person in the publishing world ever to e-mail us his interest in doing a Fool book. We've done a few since, eh, Mecoy? There will be many more. Thanks, Bob.

Also at Simon & Schuster, Isolde C. Sauer demonstrated once again that she is the most pedantic person we have ever met. And you have to realize that "pedantic" has wildly good connotations in this context. Isolde, gee whiz, you are splendiferous.

Also to be thanked at Simon & Schuster are the eminently Foolish vice president and associate publisher, Annik LaFarge, and, for an unexpected pinch-hit appearance, Geoff Kloske (who doubled off the wall).

Suzanne Gluck has done a fine job representing us via our agency, International Creative Management. She is every bit as impressive and fun to work with as we have let on in previous acknowledgments of previous books. So, ditto all that.

Love and gratitude to our parents, as well, now and always.

David wishes to acknowledge the unstinting loving support from his copacetic wife, Margaret, and from his two children, Katherine and Gabe, as well as the yet-unmet third one on the way! All four had to put up with lots while this book was getting done. Thank you so much, Margaret. Also, my assistant Melissa Flaim is a constant, friendly source of aid and is directly responsible for the ghost of Andy Warhol finding its way into these pages. Thank you for all of that and more, Melissa. Thanks as well to Joy Frelinghuysen for her good straight read of the ending, and her friendship and insights into the way the world works. And heck, thanks to my brother Tom too, for his late-night edits of my section, communicated even later at night—and no more lying about your ping-pong ability, Tom. Finally, last but most, I would be extremely remiss if I did not thank God, who surely exists and must therefore surely be thanked for such gifts and bountiful blessings.

Tom would like to thank the following Fools for their contributions to his study of corporations and the public markets as well as for teaching him how to get beyond just Breaking Rules all the time into an appreciation for Making a few as well:

Thank you to my full-time sister and assistant, Mackie, for maintaining order and restoring humor throughout the writing process. Thank you to my friends and colleagues, Gary and Erik—you helped me to graduate from college, to drink less beer, and to make the corporate world a little more Foolish. Thank you to my pal, Karin, for the Stanley Cup seats and the invaluable punched-up editing of my prose. Thank you to Jake Congleton, John Conner, and Margaret Edwards for throwing life into classrooms and schoolyards; you've helped me make a playful study of the world. Thank you to Lou, for running all the numbers and for speaking her libertarian mind. And thanks to my brother and his wife for supplying food as needed.

Finally, I owe a debt of gratitude to Groton School, for introducing a little design and discipline into my working life; to Brown University, for blasting it with freedom and disorder; and to Beauvoir, for teaching me how to peddle a tricycle.

Index